Hiram Iddings Bearss, U.S. Marine Corps

Hiram Iddings Bearss, U.S. Marine Corps

Biography of a World War I Hero

GEORGE B. CLARK

McFarland & Company, Inc., Publishers
Jefferson, North Carolina, and London

LIBRARY OF CONGRESS CATALOGUING-IN-PUBLICATION DATA

Clark, George B., 1926–
    Hiram Iddings Bearss, U.S. Marine Corps : biography of a World War I hero / George B. Clark.
    p.   cm.
    Includes bibliographical references and index.

    ISBN 0-7864-2111-8 (softcover : 50# alkaline paper) ∞

    1. Bearss, Hiram Iddings.   2. United States. Marine Corps— Officers—Biography.   I. Title.
VE25.B33C53   2005
359.9'6'092—dc22   2005004742

British Library cataloguing data are available

©2005 George B. Clark. All rights reserved

No part of this book may be reproduced or transmitted in any form or by any means, electronic or mechanical, including photocopying or recording, or by any information storage and retrieval system, without permission in writing from the publisher.

On the cover: Hiram Iddings Bearss (courtesy Library of Congress); ©2005 clipart.com

Manufactured in the United States of America

McFarland & Company, Inc., Publishers
  Box 611, Jefferson, North Carolina 28640
  www.mcfarlandpub.com

For my dear wife Jeanne,
who for more than 50 years has helped me
immeasurably in this and every other accomplishment
that I have been involved with

Contents

Preface	1
1. The Ancestry and Youth of Hiram Iddings Bearss	7
2. Remember the *Maine* and to Hell with Spain: Mike Becomes a Marine	13
3. Life Begins Anew	22
4. The Philippines: Operations on Luzon	35
5. Recruiting, Panama, Marriage and Back to the Philippines	81
6. Guantánamo and Vera Cruz	106
7. Santo Domingo	124
8. The Great War with the Marines	150
9. Paris and Home	200
10. Retirement Years	216
11. Conclusions	226
Appendix A Officers Assigned to the Samar Battalion	233
Appendix B Enlisted Marines Assigned to Company D	234
Appendix C Major L.W.T. Waller's Report on the Sohotón Cliffs Operation, 17 November 1901	235
Appendix D Comments on Bill H.R. 12916	236
Appendix E Decorations of Hiram Iddings Bearss	237
Notes	241
Bibliography	259
Index	263

Preface

This is a biography of Hiram Iddings Bearss, a very complex character and an outstanding Marine even during a period when there were many others. His comrades and contemporaries included Smedley Butler, Frederick "Fritz" Wise, and David Porter along with others like them including the many enlisted "stars" such as Dan Daly and John Quick. This placed him in a very select group of fighting Marines. His awards were legendary, being the highest the United States and friendly nations could offer its champions. He is now also one of the least known heroes of the U.S. Marine Corps. I hope this modest effort will correct this slight.

I became interested in Bearss many years ago but found little material through which to develop a comprehension and appreciation of the whole man. A friend with a like interest, Norm "Vern" McLean, developed some biographical material that he kindly shared with me. I found that Bearss' brief professional USMC biographical sketch barely scratches the surface and barely acknowledges his contributions to the Corps and our country. Therefore, I decided to attempt a serious but nonacademic biography utilizing the slight material available. Nothing written by anyone else was taken at face value. Everything of importance was checked against other sources if possible. If questionable, the material has been so identified or left out. This is not an academic exercise, but simply a "popular" biography. Perhaps, for others so inclined, just a place from which to begin.

Hiram I. Bearss had a few serious personal defects. He was often petty and performed obnoxious deeds that earned him many enemies, several of whom were highly placed at a period when Hiram instead needed powerful patrons. He was often nearly his own worst enemy, but there were many others who gladly occupied that place. The friends he had, while important and numerous, were also often in need of friends. This will become much clearer in the pages ahead. I have not tried to whitewash him or his memory but only to tell as much about him as possible. It is essential that his full personality be brought forward, so the reader can develop his or her own opinion about the man himself.

Bearss as a colonel, commanding the 102d Infantry, 1918.

Hiram I. Bearss was a man of average size, but physically he was the smallest in a family of large men. I strongly believe that this contributed mightily to making him a combative and aggressive child and man. His antecedents were all aggressive, no-nonsense Hoosiers, but none are known that were as ready for a scrap as was Hiram. Incidentally, in his youth he was known by one and all as "Mike," a nickname the doctor gave him at birth. It was an established fact that Hiram hated his given name, to such an extent that he would fight any male, of any size, at the drop of "Hiram" from the tongue. His youthful tormentors tried that several times but no one individual more than once. Though he was often beaten by larger, and usually older youths, he stayed the route until they gave up — either because he had given as much as he took or they tired themselves out.

From the brief section about his childhood it should become extremely clear that he was a handful for his parents right from the beginning. It appears that they tried their best to keep him on the straight and narrow — especially his father, who seems to have been his primary supervisor. My analysis is that he was treated with kid gloves much of the time. He was, even into middle age, his father's "baby." That is not to attempt to certify a moral weakness, but simply to declare that, as a child, he was spoiled rotten. The horse race when he was only six years of age, and his frequent wanderings as a young boy, seem to justify this conjecture. There were many other indications of his obstinacy, but lack of space precludes bringing more of his youthful indiscretions forward. How he managed to succeed to his majority without serious mishap is hard to envision. But he did, with the good offices of his family and some fine teachers. Several of the latter obviously impressed him, sufficiently so for him to visit one of them many years later while he served in the Philippines and she was there teaching Filipino children.

Preface

Bearss' home state of Indiana was settled by a diverse group, some from the northeast, others from various southern states. Those that came west from a protected and settled eastern community were tough. They had to be. The weak would have never made the grade. When his ancestors came west, the country was still wild and inhabited by, among others, warlike Miami and Shawnee Indian tribes. Life was brutal and ofttimes short for the unprepared. Those who came were like their forebears; they were looking for freedom — freedom to worship, freedom from the shackles of servitude or from political tyranny, or the freedom to be haves rather than have-nots. Most were have-nots. Bearss' grandparents and parents were strong individuals whose heritage helped propel him forward on the path that he chose. They appear to have all been rock-solid and loyal to their state and country. One thing is very obvious: Bearss was and remained a Hoosier his entire life. Though he traveled a great deal, and settled in diverse places, that was his real home.

Hiram I. Bearss was an outstanding combat soldier. His biographical sketch in *The National Cyclopædia of American Biography* provides us with a splendid overall description of the man as a leader: "He believed that the secret of handling soldiers was 'to feed them, see that no other officer bothered them, and never ask a man to go where the commander himself would not go.'"

That seems to fit Bearss to a T. He became a severe but fair disciplinarian, though you may wonder, from his youthful pranks which continued into his adult life, where he learned it. It appears that he could discipline others but not himself. That was a nearly fatal weakness, which he somehow survived.

He was awarded every medal of consequence that the United States had during his tour of duty in the U.S. Marine Corps—and also a host of important foreign decorations as well. In those times, medals were awarded only to men who proved themselves in combat-related exercises. They were few and far between and not awarded lightly, especially to officers. Bearss earned many decorations while in service and only his contemporary and friend Smedley D. Butler managed to exceed him on that score. The most prominent award was the Medal of Honor, which was finally presented to him by President Franklin Delano Roosevelt in 1934. The award was more than 30 years overdue. It was for something that he and Dave Porter did in 1901 at the Sohotón cliffs in the Philippines. He was also the recipient of a Distinguished Service Cross for his successful command of the 102 Infantry, 26th "Yankee" Division at Marcheville on 26 September 1918. He certainly should have been awarded another for his aggressive behavior at St. Mihiel. That and all his other decorations and citations will be covered in appendix E.

Bearss was in physical agony for most of the period he was in France. Following the end of the war the American Expeditionary Forces (AEF) managed, at his request, to rapidly dispose of him. Later so did the Marine Corps, presumably both for the same or similar reasons. There were probably other reasons, but his health was the basis advertised. The lack of a war didn't slow him down any. Bearss was busy following his retirement. He was doing things that mattered.

For many reasons "Hiking Hiram" Bearss was famous both within his corps and without during his tenure. Most of his 20-year career as a Marine was spent in various campaigns in which the Marine Corps was involved. And, as usual, the Corps was heavily involved in many large and small wars, all over the globe. Bearss' earliest service included some hectic moments, especially in the Philippines. Later he spent much of his service time in the Caribbean helping to settle the hash of many Cuban, Mexican, and Dominican "rebels" and, afterward, providing excellent administrative services. First you beat them and then you govern them — and Marines have been superb proconsuls in "every clime and place." But he didn't miss the real big one either — that which is now known as World War One. He spent many active months overseas during the period. Between July 1917 and December 1918 he served overseas in the 5th Marines and later the 6th Marines, both part of the famous 4th Marine Brigade. Additionally, he commanded two battalions in the 9th Infantry, which was also a part of the 2nd Division. Eventually he commanded the 102d Infantry of the 26th "Yankee" Division and later the 51st Brigade, of which the 102nd was part. He was commended by many senior U.S. Army officers, most especially by General Pershing, who tried several times to promote him to brigadier general in the AEF.

For much of this biography, especially the early years in Indiana, I must thank Asa J. Smith, Esquire. Mr. Smith was a private in the 74th Company, 1st Battalion, 6th Regiment of the U.S. Marines in France during the Great War. During June 1918 he was wounded in action at the battle for Belleau Wood. In World War II he reenlisted, ultimately became a lieutenant colonel of Marines and was commander of the Marine Barracks at Auckland, New Zealand. He was said to be a personal friend of both Gerald C. Thomas and his assistant Merrill B. Twining, both of whom would later become generals of Marines. Smith was for many years an attorney of esteem in Indianapolis— sometimes a prosecutor, who engaged in many noted and controversial trials. One of the most famous was the conviction of the Grand Dragon of the Ku Klux Klan, D.C. Stephenson, for second degree murder of Ms. Madge Oberholtzer in 1925.

When, how, and why Smith became interested in Hiram Bearss is not known. It could have happened because he was a member of the 6th Regiment of Marines in France while Bearss was assistant commander. Or it is possible that the relationship began because of Bearss' famous scrap with the KKK in Peru, in the early 1920s. Whatever the time and reason, Smith did much groundwork. Most of what he collected seems to have been gathered sometime after the Second World War and Korean War ended. Smith may even have interviewed Bearss in the 1920s or '30s, and perhaps also some of his many relatives. We have one recorded instance of a personal interview while Bearss commanded the guard at the New York Federal Bank. It is difficult to be sure, but it appears as though Bearss gave Smith some information that no one else would have been privy to. Much of that has to be used very cautiously. Either Bearss was getting "forgetful" and passing on a modified version of events, or Mr. Smith misunderstood. The former seems more likely. In light of some of the problems that Hiram got himself into, it wouldn't have been unlikely for him to disguise his part in the events.

There were some errors of a personal nature, possibly because of misinformation provided by Bearss. In one or two places Smith was off quite widely in details concerning Bearss' WWI service. Otherwise, it is information that made it much easier to comprehend the adult Hiram Bearss, though I'm not convinced that anyone could ever get to the root of his complex personality.

I have utilized many sources. Some barely mention Hiram Bearss; others give him his due. Sources about most heroes are frequently at a bare minimum. Those about Hiram I. Bearss are scarcer than that. Smith's rough draft of a biography was deposited with the Indiana State Library in Indianapolis. Edwin Cole Bearss, noted Civil War historian and a distant cousin of our hero, directed me to it. A copy was kindly provided, upon proper recompense, by Ms. Andrea Bean Hough of the library, and has been the prop upon which this biography has been built. Because of Mr. Smith, the library and Ms. Hough, this book is much better than it had any right to be.

Mr. Trevor Plante, reference archivist at the National Archives, was a great help. He pointed me in the proper direction to obtain important archival material, as did Lt. Col. Merrill "Skip" Bartlett, USMC (ret.), noted and well-regarded Marine Corps historian, who satisfactorily answered several pertinent questions. James Hallas, another highly regarded military historian and well-known author of books about Marines, made a very substantial contribution by advising me where to curtail my verbosity, which I believe I did. Ms. Regine Brindle, of the Family History Center in Peru, Indiana, assisted me in obtaining several cogent points of information regarding the Bearss family in Peru. Any faults, however, are entirely of my own execution.

Notes come from many sources. Most are from the appropriate federal records. All unidentified or listed as "Smith" are from the Asa Smith biography.

George B. Clark
Pike, New Hampshire

1

The Ancestry and Youth of Hiram Iddings Bearss

Our subject's American ancestry was long and notable. The earliest ancestor arrived at Barnstable in the Massachusetts Bay Colony in the 1630s, from either Scotland or England. There are still descendants of that name in the Barnstable area, as well as roads bearing the Bearss name. According to legend, the Bearss family was of Flemish origin, and had been but a short period in Britain before crossing the Atlantic Ocean. Over the years members of that same line managed to relocate themselves to various parts of the frontier, and almost always westward to the farthest and most dangerous part.[1]

Hiram's paternal grandfather, Daniel Robert Bearss, after a circuitous route, landed in Peru, Indiana. Here he and his descendants established themselves as a leading family of the new district. Grandfather Bearss and Hiram's maternal Grandfather Iddings were deeply immersed in politics—Republican politics. Later, Hiram's father, Franklin Wallace Bearss, who continued to be a farmer, was also in politics. Therefore it is understandable that Hiram, after his Marine service, also delved into local politics. The family did well in the marketplace, always maintaining a comfortable existence, and, as the saying goes, most members of the next few generations "married well." Daniel Bearss went into partnership with his father-in-law, Judge Albert Cole, in general merchandising. Daniel also owned numerous Peru city blocks and built what became known as the Broadway Hotel, now the Peru Motor Lodge.

In 1875 there was a new addition to the Frank and Desdemona Iddings Bearss family. On 13 April of that year the doctor informed Frank, when he arrived at the railroad station, that his wife had delivered a "Mike" while he had been absent on a business trip. For some unfathomable reason that nickname stuck to the newborn and held well into his early adulthood.

For this part of his life we will continue to identify him as "Mike" Bearss. His many boyhood friends and enemies, more of the latter than the former, only called him by his baptismal name upon pain of physical abuse.

The Franklin W. Bearss family had another son, Braxton, and three daughters. First was Emma, then Desdemona, and finally Lucy. The first married well, to Oscar George Mulfeld; Lucy remained unmarried and resided in the 14-room family home until it was razed in the late 1960s for a new high school. What happened to Desdemona is not known.

Mike was a rascal. No, he was more than that: He was an exceptionally difficult child. Even as an infant, he was difficult for his parents to train and control. Mike was prone to do only what he wanted to do, nothing more, and that was always contrary to whatever his parents or teachers wanted. As he grew in size and age, he got progressively more contrary. It appears that his parents didn't often physically chastise him and when they did, it curtailed his exuberance for only minutes rather than days. Mike didn't do well with authoritative teachers, then or later. An encounter in the local school, with his teacher, the principal and even the school board, is an excellent example. And this was when he was but a ten-year-old-student. It was only when he took on his father, Frank, that the latter pointed out the various interesting aspects of the family woodshed.

Mike's primary education was a hit or miss process, spread around to various locales. During his early years of schooling, Mike was shipped around to his relatives, mostly his Iddings grandparents in Fulton County. No clue exists for why Frank and Desdemona shipped a six-year-old off so many miles, to be away four months from his home. After the first several years he mainly went to local schools, but was generally in trouble with his teachers and administrators. His later grades were somewhat worse, but somehow he managed to gain enough credits to enable him to continue his education. He did get along with certain of his teachers, several in particular with whom he maintained a fine relationship for many years. Mostly he learned by absorption rather than by rote.

Meanwhile, Mike learned to handle horses, and he became a considerable horseman early on. When he was only six years he was entered into a horse race and won it. Frank learned that Mike was going to race on Frank's favorite horse just minutes before the race began. He could do nothing to stop it and could only cheer his baby on to victory. Winning the race brought Mike glory, nothing more. The prize of $25 went to the old man, who had entered him in the race. But the money wasn't the important factor; he was but six years—it was the thrill of doing something that he normally wouldn't have been allowed to do by his parents.

Mike ran away at least once when he was a teenage rebel, and it took

Frank several weeks to locate him and bring him back home. He was found in a town many miles distant, caring for some prize horses that were being displayed around the countryside. He loved them so much that he was pleased to be able to sleep in their stalls. Mike refused to return home unless Frank allowed him to continue caring for their horses back home. That grew to be less and less interesting as the odor intensified and weeks went by. By fall he was willing to sleep in his bed once again. Mike loved horses and sports. Nothing else seemed as gratifying. Only when he became a Marine would his penchants for some of these distractions, and his behavior, modify somewhat.

Subsequently he proved to be a splendid semiprofessional baseball player, and loved the game ever after. Still later, he proved to be a superb football player, even though he was of very modest physical proportions.[2] Sports, especially those two, were his main interests for many years, and learning was in a very bad last place. But Frank, his father, was persistent. Somehow or other when Mike was in his teens, his father managed to get him into several first-class preparatory schools.

First was the University of Notre Dame prep school, and Mike lasted there the entire first year. Frank had learned that the school was famous for its discipline and though the Bearss family was not Roman Catholic, Frank was willing to try anything at that point. Mike even went so far as to get on the honor roll beginning in February. Regardless, it seems that he was doing much as he had prior to his arrival — getting into fights and playing pranks on the teaching Brothers and students. He managed to play several sports and participated in field events, earning something of a reputation while doing so. The reason he wasn't allowed to return is not known, but it is fair to assume it was Notre Dame's decision, and probably based upon disciplinary problems.

He spent that summer at home and immediately engaged in baseball for the local nine. In those times every community had a baseball team that played all the teams in the surrounding areas. They were very touchy events, and no matter which team won, the other community started a brawl to prove itself. Mike was, to say the least, as aggressive as any other player on any team and was always in the thick of the fracases.

Mike was next sent to the prep school at Purdue University, even then developing a reputation as a top school. Essentially the same thing happened as at Notre Dame. Fights, pranks, trouble with the faculty and several incidents well remembered within the town of Lafayette, which caused several ladies of quality to remonstrate with the school officials. Generally, all hell was raised. Mike was always in the middle of any situation, such as an outhouse removed from its proper location and parked on trolley lines; and worse, with the name of the head of a local sanatorium plastered on a sign across the front door. Mike lasted only one semester at Purdue. Home he went to Peru where he laid low until the baseball season began. That summer he joined the local nine and had more fun and fights. We can well imagine that Frank must have been quite upset.

Frank then made a substantial donation to DePauw University, and that fall it, too, accepted Frank's erring son, Mike. Mainly we know of his attempts to make the football team, which initially was a tragedy for Mike, who was 120 pounds, soaking wet. The coach did everything in his power to dissuade this slight creature, but every day at practice Mike was there waiting for the call. Finally, Coach Sagar could not stand looking at the woebegone childlike gnome in his battered baseball uniform and put him on the field to scare him out of harm's way. Mike said he played halfback and Coach Sagar tried him out in that position. Mike did his thing and when the ball was passed to him ran down the field like a gazelle, straight-arming several opponents (it was legal in those days) and finally dropping the ball over the goal line. He got to play and was the hero several times that season, even though Sagar infrequently put him in. Mike saved the game on one auspicious occasion and then Sagar immediately pulled him out again. Nearly in tears, Mike asked, "Why?" The answer: "Because I was afraid if I left you in, you'd have gotten killed." Mike played occasionally and earned an enviable reputation as a football player. His scholastic record isn't known, but he somehow managed to remain the entire year—for him a kind of victory. The next summer, back he went to the local nine.

From this point onward, Mike was not to have it quite so easy, although in the long run the next move was all for the better. At DePauw something, to which we are not privy, happened. Certainly Mike was thrilled playing football and somehow seemed to manage to produce acceptable grades. He had to, otherwise football wouldn't have been allowed. However, for some reason, of which no record seems to exist, either Mike wanted out or DePauw wanted him out, or both.[3] So far Frank had invested in three of the best schools in the area and Mike had not managed to survive one of them intact. The next fall, Frank tried something entirely different. He not only found a school much farther away from Indiana but he decided to send Mike's younger brother Braxton along as a sort of chaperone.

In the fall of 1894 Brack and Mike arrived in Northfield, Vermont, to begin their association with Norwich University, a first-class military school. The school's first charter, in New York State, began in 1819 when it was known as the American Literary, Scientific and Military College. Var-

1. The Ancestry and Youth of Hiram Iddings Bearss

ious moves about northern New England finally located the school where the Bearss brothers found it. Norwich was a small, beautifully placed institution, in a nice, quiet little town in northern Vermont — quiet, at least until the Bearss lads arrived.

This was the final educational resting place for Mike. Here he would remain for two whole years — and in trouble right from the start. But the military discipline took hold, and Mike could no longer get away with the childish games he'd been playing for so many years. A few occasions spent in the brig cooled his heels rapidly enough.

The first semester was the hardest. Mike planned to desert but Brack had a clearer mind and stopped him before he got too far. Football came roaring into view and Mike managed to get carried along with the team. He was accepted soon enough, and it was here that he expended so much of his boundless energy. He rapidly gained a reputation as a maverick but also as essentially a fine player. Norwich soon enough directed him toward helping to win most of its contests.

He loved his uniform: brass buttons on a dark blue coat and trousers, with a red stripe. His U.S. Army regulation helmet was just the cat's pajamas, as far as Mike was concerned. He liked his weapon, too, but preferred to drop it while in formation when he became angry with the sergeant for telling him to "press down on that rifle." That helped put him into confinement, as did another incident when he threw a potato at a waiter in the mess hall. When Frank learned of Mike's arrest, he was elated. Finally, here was a place that put his son where he belonged, when he deserved it. His incarceration never lasted more than a few hours or days, but it helped to properly mold his attitude. Mike learned quickly enough that Norwich was a bona fide Vermont state military organization whose regulations were to be obeyed. To be at variance subjected one to military punishment.

The first winter the weather was deplorable, as winters usually are in Vermont. But neither of the Bearss boys could settle down, and they continued their well-practiced pranks even in the bitterest weather. One morning an important piece of "bedroom furniture" was found atop the flagpole, upside down but fortunately with its contents removed. For some reason Mike was considered as a possible participant in the placement of said furniture. At this point in time both lads were close to the dead-line insofar as demerits were concerned, Mike closer than Brack. But somehow he always managed to avoid that final thrust that would have presented him with the opportunity of traveling home to Indiana for all time. Sometimes the administrators had to give Mike good merits so as to reduce the demerits. Both lads survived, somehow, and were going to be allowed to return the following year. This was a first and surely there were parties to celebrate the occasion.

By fall they were again both back in Vermont. It was the football season again and of course both were heavily engaged in that most important endeavor. On October 21 the St. Johnsbury Academy kicked off and H.I. Bearss was the receiver. He "made a long and difficult run for fifty yards. Next play carried it through for a touchdown." In the second half, "Bearss made a touchdown and kicked the goal. Score 18–0." Further on in, the Norwich Annual for that year added, "Bearss made 20 yards around end. From this point Bearss made touchdown and kicked goal. Score 24–0." He was playing right half and he was the captain, and he was good.[4]

In Reveille a short story appeared that has been credited to him even though it was anonymous. It told of a handsome young cadet who managed to win the affections of a "lady fair" only to have her mother throw water on the relationship. Mike wasn't the handsome hero but rather took the girl's place, wearing a veil, and fooled the swain at a clandestine meeting. When the young cadet lifted the veil to kiss his sweetie he shouted, "Damn you, Mike." Who the actual participants were can't be proved, but it certainly sounds like what Bearss would have done had the occasion presented itself.[5]

In the spring of 1896 Mike was elected captain of his baseball team. By this time his academic standing was somewhat better than it had been previously, and so was his lack of demerits. In other words, he was starting to shape up. When the school year ended he was 21 years of age, five feet seven inches tall, and weighed in at 155 pounds, all muscle.[3]

This was the end for Norwich. It isn't clear why Mike didn't return or even if Brack did. The reason is obscure but Mike was in good academic shape and seems not to have been forced out. That must have been pleasant for everyone, including Frank, the bill payer.

2

Remember the Maine *and to Hell with Spain: Mike Becomes a Marine*

Mike was back home again in Indiana, which all his life he considered paradise, but, as always, was betwixt and between. At 21 he was no longer a boy, or even a youth. Norwich had done a lot to make some changes and he was much the better for it. His mind was keen and he had finally learned to learn, but only what he wanted to learn. His learning was still mainly by absorption rather than through concentration.

The one thing that Mike had absorbed was a modest amount of military discipline. It was structured and everyone around was forced to participate. It was definitely a man's world, and he felt somewhat comfortable as part of it. But he wasn't even thinking along those lines at first. His father wanted him to study law, which wasn't the formalized study that we know today. If you were to become a lawyer, you studied under someone who was a lawyer. Back in Peru he found himself reading law in the dusty old offices of his father's friend, Judge Bailey.[1]

This was not satisfactory for a man who craved physical activity of any kind, and all the time. He tried but failed to acquire anything useful studying law, although apparently the judge was satisfied with his work. Other than the drudgery of writing abstracts he also gained a modest income from playing baseball with the local team. However, after spending a dilatory 18 months in the law office, he was admitted to the bar in Indiana; obviously it was a simpler matter then than today.

At about this time, in the spring of 1898, at age 23 Mike considered running away from home. He felt stifled and longed to do something adventurous, perhaps to become an explorer. In the late nineteenth century there were still places to explore, so why shouldn't he go off to the wilds? Africa was just the place, or perhaps the South American jungles. Any place other than Ridgeview or Peru. He loved his home and always would, and when he was done with the outside world that was where he returned. But now he wanted to leave. He was in luck—as always, something unforeseen managed to provide him with an out. This time it was the sinking of the USS *Maine* in the foreign port of Havana in Cuba, a Spanish possession.

Difficulties between the United States and Spain, relating to Cuba, had been brewing for many years. Many Cubans had been in a state of revolt for a number of years. In the past, Spain had stopped the revolutionaries before they had managed to gain any appreciable control over the island. But each time the defeated Cubans learned a lesson or two and came back stronger than ever. During this decade they would gain much more success than ever before, so much so that the United States began interfering loudly and openly. It was not in the best interests of the United States to have constant fighting going on just 90 miles south of its borders. So the U.S. government made several efforts to mediate and when that failed, sent a modern warship to Havana "to protect U.S. citizens."

As we know, while anchored in the harbor, the USS *Maine* was blown up. No one today is absolutely sure what or who caused the explosion, but at the time Spain was the easily selected "guilty party."[2] The newspapers, especially those published by William Randolph Hearst, insisted they were guilty. Consequently, the easily misled American public went right along with the specious charges. No proof was necessary, nor any available, but it wouldn't have mattered anyway. The citizens of the United States were feeling their oats—they desperately needed a war to feel superior to someone else (this was of course assuming that the United States would win the war).[3] So the war came and many young men rushed off to participate. Eventually, so did our hero.

You can well imagine how this excitement affected the poor withering soul in Ridgeview. Like most of the young American men, Mike wanted desperately to get to Cuba and kill any Spaniards he could get his hands on. Or, if he couldn't do that perhaps he instead could "deliver a message to Garcia" or to someone else on the island. Anything would suit, as long as it was adventurous.[4]

Mike even went so far as to enlist a company of volunteers in Peru. Led by Mike, this group marched away with flags flying and a local band to provide music for them on their road to glory. The road ended at Indianapolis where the local military authorities, entirely unimpressed, refused the whole group. The company disbanded but then Mike tried to enlist as a private and was refused. Frank stepped in and asked a former major,

2. Remember the Maine and to Hell with Spain

George Steele, a congressman friend of his, to do something for his lad. Frank begged for "anything, otherwise he'd be going to Cuba all by himself." Mike was offered an appointment at the Naval Academy, which he promptly refused. He wasn't about to waste four years of his life in another institution of learning when there was a war on.

Steele promptly replied that he was doing whatever he could so that Mike "would be as speedily as possible placed where he would certainly be shot, killed and buried, to end his agony." If the sarcastic message was seen by Mike, most probably it would not have been appreciated. Meanwhile, Admiral Dewey[5] entertained the Spanish fleet at Manila Bay and ruined their entire day. The war was going by and Mike wasn't any nearer to being in it; this caused him great pain and anguish. News provided to the American public showed clearly that the war would soon be over and of course, the Americans would win it.

It was about then that a telegram from Steele was received. It informed Frank that he had managed to obtain an appointment for Mike as a temporary second lieutenant in the U.S. Marine Corps. Mike said, "What is the Marine Corps?" Like many of his fellow citizens he'd never heard of the Corps. Steele added that "this was as close to committing suicide as Mike would ever have." Mike decided that the Corps' name meant that it had something to do with the navy. That made him feel better about the whole situation. The navy was a service that he could recognize and was by all accounts heavily engaged in the war, so he accepted the offer and in due course found himself on his way to Washington, D.C.

Upon arrival he made his way to the home of Congressman Steele, where he had been invited to stay. Both Major and Mrs. Steele treated him as a long lost son. He was made to feel completely at home and that took a load of potential distress off his shoulders. Mike soon made his way to the Marine Barracks at the old navy yard on the Potomac River where his preliminary examinations were to take place. Since first hearing its name, Mike had learned something about the Marine Corps. Mike learned that it had a proud and noble history. Since 1775, when it was first organized, until 1898, 123 years later, it had always been on call and ready for any duty for which it would be called upon. And, it seems, the Corps had always performed its responsibilities in the most estimable manner. It had already become the darling of the media, primarily because when news copy was necessary it always provided a "good show." Some members of the press had already provided it with utterances that would stand the Corps in good stead in the many dark days ahead. "Tell it to the Marines" was one that was used regularly, signifying that the Marines already knew everything worth knowing. The best, though, was coined by a famous correspondent who always seemed to be where the action was. Richard Harding Davis sent in an account, probably from the Caribbean, that simply stated, "The Marines have landed and the situation is well in hand." The Corps didn't need much better than that to gain the public's attention.[6]

Col. George C. Reid was in charge of examinations.[7] Mike was stiff, erect and reasonably prepared for what he was about to receive from the colonel. Fear and trembling may not have afflicted him but he wasn't all that far away from getting the heebie-jeebies while the exam was going on. Regardless, he did all right — his Norwich training had served him well. It was both verbal and written and consisted of questions relating to lore and other not-so-stringent queries. He wasn't alone. We know that other young men also underwent just about the same experiences. One candidate, a 16-year-old bearing the unfortunate moniker of Smedley Darlington Butler, was suffering the same as was Bearss, and he, too, was accepted into the brotherhood. Butler had even less education than Bearss and would wind up as another devil-may-care hero of the Marine Corps. Their paths would cross many times.[8]

Mike and the others who were interrogated had to wait until 26 May 1898 to learn their fate. Mike was accepted and commissioned as a second lieutenant of Marines. He alternately shed tears and danced a jig when he received word of his acceptance. So did the elderly Mrs. Steele. It appears that Mike had already made a conquest. On his acceptance he flew to the military tailor Heiberger on Northwest Street, to order a set of "Seagoin' Blues." It was a magnificent uniform, with beautiful buttons that shone brightly, and it was something of which he was personally extremely proud. He carried his prize package back to the temporary home he would soon leave. The Steeles were as proud of him in uniform as any parents would have been.

It wasn't long after that Major Steele brought his young charge to visit his new boss, Col. Charles Heywood, the commandant of the Marine Corps. Mike was now addressed as either Mr. Bearss or as Lieutenant Bearss. His name was now formally Hiram I. Bearss. Mike, the name of his childhood was out. He accepted the fact that at age 23 he was no longer a boy.[9]

After being sworn in he was advised to take a short leave and to familiarize himself with the history and legends of his Corps. He duly set about learning every detail so he could be ready should anyone, officer or enlisted man, ask him any question. He probably bought a history of the Corps written by a Marine officer, Richard S. Collum.[10] If he did so he would have learned a great deal about the Marine Corps. In addition, there were lectures to attend, some given by long-service noncommissioned officers and others by even older men, some of whom had served as officers during the Civil War. There were other young men in his class. The School of Application had been cancelled in April 1898 and wouldn't resume until 1903, but still there was a modicum of schooling for new officers.[11]

In their classes they learned that Marines had served on ships of war since the time of the ancient Phoenicians and their Greek opponents—and it was the same between the Carthaginians and the Romans. The Spaniards were first to utilize "soldiers of the sea" but later the English found that their new navy also needed fighting soldiers aboard their ships, as did the French and the Dutch. Each group was separate and distinguishable from the sailors who manned the oars or sails. They could fight their opposites in any encounter, as archers, with pikes and swords or

Second Lieutenant Hiram I. Bearss, 1899. He had just accepted his commission as a second lieutenant. Courtesy Special Collections, Norwich University, Northfield, Vermont.

later with muskets. In more recent times Marines manned the smaller batteries aboard navy ships or landed on hostile shores to project the will of the United States anywhere, at any time. Marine officers also learned something about their trade: How to lead a small formation of Marines on a parade ground or on foreign soil; how their weapons worked; and knowledge of the rules of war. They learned to command their followers and how to follow commands. Bearss had no difficulty with the former but, as we shall witness, on infrequent occasions he did with the latter.

Bearss listened intently. This was learning that he could accept, because he found it interesting. He had finally found his niche in life. This was what he had always been preparing to do, but he hadn't known it. Like almost all Marines he fell in love—not yet with a woman but with his Corps. It is a phenomenon that still exists today. In fact, Hiram would have been considered strange, even in those days, if he hadn't felt that way. The reasons why this should be are not commonly known. There is a load of conjecture about it, but no really satisfactory answer. The French words *esprit de corps* come closest to describing the feeling. For the very first time in his life his cup was full, right up to the brim and overflowing.

During this period he went out and bought his first dress sword and scabbard and then paraded up to the Steeles' home for their approval and his self appraisal before their long mirror. He liked what he saw, and so did they. Bearss recited many of the history lessons he'd learned and ended by singing the Marines' Hymn, at which, it has been said, Mrs. Steele could no longer contain her own emotions. Tears flowed at this display of extreme emotion by this young lad who had finally found his niche in life. Shortly afterward, he purchased his other uniforms including those for dress and service. Barely two weeks after being commissioned, Bearss was ordered to report to Maj. William S. Muse at the Marine Barracks in Norfolk, Virginia.[12] He thought this was splendid because Norfolk was closer to Cuba than Washington. Perhaps his chance had finally come.

In those days, Norfolk was the largest naval station in the United States. The navy yard was actually in Portsmouth but was and is commonly called Norfolk. Since the Spanish war was primarily a naval war there was much activity at Norfolk. But some of it was old hat to Bearss. He found that Muse was giving the new bunch of second lieutenants close-order drill in the manual of arms. That didn't sit too well with this alumnus of Norwich University Military School. He already knew everything there was to know — except he found that he too was occasionally able to learn something new.

Almost daily, young officers were dispatched to different posts and duties; some to the scene of war but most to other stateside naval posts for the protection thereof. It wasn't too long before Bearss found himself the only officer remaining at Norfolk. In fact, for a short period he was in command of these formidable barracks. But although this made him seem important he found that he really had nothing of importance to do. His responsibilities included supervising the Marine guards and their Spanish prisoners of war, and routine drill and inspections. What was really troubling was that the war was going on without him.

As the lone Marine officer it was his duty to attend the local functions and festivities and to be in attendance on the local, and usually lovely, Southern belles. The soirees and dances and charming girls were almost his alone, but he still wasn't satisfied. One positive thing did happen to him while there. It was his opportunity to meet two of the Marine Corps' most distinguished senior officers, Littleton W.L. Waller and John A. Lejeune, both of whom would later be comrades in arms and teach him valuable lessons.[13]

In addition to the abuse he suffered, which mainly included not being in Cuba where the action was, he soon found out that the island of Guam in the Pacific had also fallen to American naval forces. Was there no end to his shame and pain? The taking of Guam was possibly the easiest conquest of American arms. One of the U.S. Navy's newest metal warships, the USS *Charleston*, under the command of Capt. Henry Glass, pulled up into the harbor at Apia on 20 June 1898 with full expectations of a fierce fight from the Spanish forces on the island. Little was known about Guam except that the Spaniards had built three forts there and Glass was expecting a full-blown brawl while trying to take it.

The *Charleston* immediately approached Fort Santa Cruz, which was situated on a small island in the harbor, and let go with its main battery. Nothing happened — there was no return fire. Shortly thereafter a small boat with a group of Spanish officers aboard pulled out and up to the *Charleston*. They issued an apology because they weren't able to respond to the "courtesy." They had assumed that the gunfire was the natural and usual salute from one nation to another. The Spaniards were unaware that war existed between Spain and the United States. Glass was advised that the three forts each had guns that were not operable because they were not considered safe. A grand total of 56 Spanish marines, with a sprinkling of Chomorro natives, were the only armed force on the island. With that information 1st Lt. John "Handsome Jack" T. Myers and the Marine detachment aboard ship were dispatched ashore to secure Guam for the United States, which they did without difficulty or consequence.[14]

The war was soon over and the Spaniards lost. Applause from the citizenry toward the victors was deafening. Bearss was at the very center of the ovation, he being one of the lucky few still on duty on the mainland. He was very embarrassed and went out of his way to avoid the plaudits of the crowds. On November 11, just one day after the birthday of his Corps, he received orders to report to the USS *Prairie* to relieve 1st Lt. Eli K. Cole.[15] Three days later he joined his ship, a transport that had most recently plied its trade to Cuba and Puerto Rico and back, after dropping off its valuable cargo. At the moment the ship was in dry dock and was not about to be sent anyplace so Bearss made the best of that additional disappointment. He was now a "seagoing Marine" but he was, like the ship, going nowhere.

He became acquainted with his shipmates and soon was offered a drink. His response was, "I am not drinking. But if I had all the liquor I've drunk I could float this ship out of drydock." That may not have been a true statement at that time but it wouldn't be long before it was. In time drink became his only relief from boredom. Later it became a serious problem, as it did for so many others.[16]

Less than a month later Bearss was detached from the *Prairie* and assigned to the USS *Michigan* based on Lake Erie, berthed at Erie, Pennsylvania. On his way north he stopped off briefly to thank the Steeles for their kindness and support. Then he made his way to his new ship. Upon arrival Bearss quickly discovered that this duty station was worse than the previous one. It was not a warship of the line but an old paddle-wheeler used mainly to train naval reservists. One of the important naval reservists who at times commanded the USS *Michigan* was a local politician named Edwin "Ned" Denby.[17] A treaty with Canada prohibited the berthing of more than one warship on Lake Erie and this was the one. Fortunately Canada and the United States had not been engaged in any serious unpleasant relations for many years.

The officers slept aboard the ship in staterooms and the crew in hammocks below. What was peculiar to this ship was the drill. Cutlasses were kept sharp, presumably because it wasn't known when a Canadian boarding party would force their way onto the USS *Michigan* and it was best to always be prepared. Fortunately, if the Canadians had ever decided to give it a whirl, the Americans had rifles (not muskets) on board. The ship would occasionally paddle around to different ports on Lake Erie. Its home port was Captain Gridley's hometown. Gridley was the same "fire when ready Gridley" of Manila Bay fame.[18]

At some time during this period, Bearss was enticed, without too much difficulty it appears, to take leave with Louis Mason Gulick and William Belo Lemly, both second lieutenants and both to make future reputations for themselves.[19] The three Marines arrived in Washington, D.C., and stayed at the Regent Hotel, then a model of decorum — that is, until Lemly and Gulick commandeered one of the elevators. With it they had quite a time for themselves. One would propel it upwards and leave the other on any floor. The latter would immediately signal to be picked up and the "driver" would stop at whatever floor he happened to be at and turn, up or down, to gather in the other — sort of an elevator game of hide and seek. This went on for some time until the management threatened to call in the commandant to relieve the hotel from further abuse. What part Bearss played during this affair isn't clear, but we can assume that if he wasn't falling down drunk he was well immersed in the hell-raising that was going on.

But the war was now over and the Marine Corps was going to have to settle back into its normal routine. Most of the recruit officers were soon mustered out. Hiram Bearss, 2d Lt. U.S. Marine Corps, was detached from the *Michigan* on 10 February 1899 and sent home to await further orders. Everyone at Ridgeview cheered when he arrived, resplendent in his uniform — as though he had won the war and all by himself. They were proud of him, but he was not proud of himself. He believed, very strongly, that the gods were against him. He felt even more that way on 21 February 1899 when he received his honorable discharge. He was no longer a Marine, or so it seemed. What he did at that point other than to commiserate with himself in his misery doesn't seem to be on record. But he didn't have long to wait. The latter war had encouraged Congress to loosen up the purse strings. The U.S. now had an "empire," though many Americans found that word tasteless. Actually, it still was not secured. The U.S. Army and Marines would continue to have much ground action and heavy expense in the Philippines before it was settled. Protecting the Philippines would require a very strong naval base at Hawaii, then army troops to protect the navy base. Then there was always the constant threat of Japan, a nation that would soon destroy a Russian navy and army. Most planning for the defenses of our newly gained bases in the Pacific would, of necessity, require planning for a contest with Japan. Most army and navy officers had decided, even that early, that the Philippine archipelago was undefendable if Japan made a decision to attack it. However, the president and his advisors saw fit to complete the conquest and the occupation.[20]

Four decades later, the original concept was proven.

3

Life Begins Anew

Our new territory, mostly in the far reaches of the Pacific Ocean, had to be protected. That required an expanded navy, which in turn required an expanded U.S. Marine Corps (some might say, to protect the navy).

Bearss' world came alive once again. On 2 June 1899, he was appointed a regular first lieutenant in the Marine Corps. Bearss would serve continuously until he was placed on the retired list as a colonel of Marines in 1919.[1] The alacrity with which he accepted his appointment would have overwhelmed a lesser organization than the Corps. As the saying goes, he found a home and they found a man.

Exactly two weeks after Hiram's initial discharge, Commodore Dewey had requested a host of additional Marines for duty in the Philippines. At first he wanted a battalion to defend Cavite, an important naval installation ten miles south of Manila, which he and his fleet had acquired. It was important to the Asiatic Fleet, which required that or a similar base in order to remain in the far Pacific. When Dewey destroyed the Spanish fleet in Manila Bay on 1 May 1898, the Americans were in a superb position to also take Manila, the Pearl of the Orient. The commodore didn't have sufficient Marines for the job. No one had expected such a rapid and complete victory over the Spaniards, and consequently only the small U.S. Asiatic Fleet was on hand.[2] The few troops he had available were the smattering of Marines in the various ship detachments. There were 189 in all— nowhere near enough to impress the Spanish troops occupying that city. Taking Manila would have to wait for the arrival of troops of the U.S. Army, which were on their way. Brigadier General Thomas M. Anderson, USA, showed up on 30 June 1898 with slightly more than 2,400 troops. They were immediately landed at Cavite, with Dewey's guns as Anderson's main protection. This lack of substance would reflect badly upon the United States' acquisition in its early stages. It would cause much bloodshed and anguish amongst both the Filipinos and the rest of the world—

and especially among the anti-imperialists in the U.S. On 17 July, 3,500 additional officers and men of the U.S. infantry arrived. They were under the command of Brig. Gen. Francis V. Greene, USA. With the Filipino leader Aguinaldo's reluctant agreement, Greene was allowed to land two miles north of Manila. At that point in time there were approximately 6,000 American troops in the vicinity of Manila.

In the meantime the Marine ship detachments had taken over from the army the role of guarding Cavite. Cavite had become useful for the fleet storage and as a place of repose for any foreigner fleeing the increasingly combative natives in the interior. The ship's detachments would remain there until an infantry unit of sufficient numbers arrived from the States. Actually, it would be a Marine battalion composed of 15 officers and 260 men armed with Lee straight-pulls,[3] plus two Colt machine guns and four three-inch guns. Colonel Percival C. Pope, their commanding officer, and his second in command, Major William F. Spicer, arrived with their troops at Cavite on 23 May 1899.[4] Before the end of that year the Corps would provide another battalion of about the same composition, and then a third. More would continue to follow until the Corps' representatives in the Philippines would numerically far exceed Marines based anywhere else.

Upon arrival at Cavite, Pope had barracks and officers' quarters built to accommodate 1,000 officers and men at the naval station. He was also in command of San Roque and Caridad, plus numerous other outposts where some of his men were stationed. Among his other good works were the establishment of a native police force and municipal courts plus enforcement of sanitary conditions among the natives.

The second battalion requested by the navy was formed at the Marine Barracks, New York Navy Yard, and it left Jersey City, New Jersey, for San Francisco by special train on 11 August 1899. In command was then Major (and soon to be lt. col.) George F. Elliott.[5] The battalion consisted of 350 enlisted men who would be joined by 12 additional Marines from Mare Island, California. Upon arrival at Cavite, this brought the total Marine contingent in the Philippines to 25 Marine officers, two USN medical officers, and 644 enlisted Marines.

Pope made the decision to divide the two battalions in such a way as to have two companies of the newcomers merged with the 1st Battalion and two of the old-timers merged with the 2nd. The colonel stated that he had made this decision so as to provide the needed steadiness to both battalions. Because Elliott ranked Major Spicer, the two traded positions; Elliott to command the 1st Battalion and Spicer the 2d Battalion. Their numbers would then be sufficient to create the 1st Regiment of Marines.

They wouldn't be the first nor the last regiment to bear that distinguished appellation.

There continued to be much moving about for the Cavite Marines. On 3 October 1899, with Capt. Henry C. Haines commanding, a detachment of five officers and 84 enlisted Marines plus a Colt machine gun and crew left Cavite under orders to report to Brig. Gen. Frederick Grant, USA, for duty at Bacoor. Upon arrival they were joined by Capt. John T. Myers, USMC,[6] with 20 Marines and 24 sailors, under the command of Ensign Albert W. Marshall, USN. All the latter were from the nearby USS *Baltimore*. The Marines plus troops from the USA joined together to successfully assault Imus the following day.

Trouble in the Philippines would require many more Marines to help the U.S. Army quiet the natives. Before too much time had elapsed, six battalions of Marines in all would make their way to the islands. The 4th and 5th, and later, the 6th, were sent directly to China to partake of the hospitality of the Boxers and their cohorts, the regular Chinese army. After that turmoil ceased, most if not all of the "China" Marines would be transported back to Cavite for service during the ever expanding insurrection in the Philippines. Before the end of 1901 there would be 58 officers and 1,547 enlisted Marines serving in the Philippines with sufficient activity to fill their days, and nights. For the still relatively small Corps, this was a large unit (about half of the total) to be committed overseas. The numbers would remain substantially the same for some time to come.

But where was 1st Lt. Hiram I. Bearss, USMC? Well, he was back on the East Coast where, on 6 June 1899, he had been assigned to duty aboard the USS *New York*.[7] That cruiser was lying in the harbor of the same name. Bearss reported aboard on 13 June. He was evidently quite happy with this assignment since the ship had been Admiral Sampson's flagship at the battle against the Spanish ship *San Diego* in 1898.

When he arrived, the Marine detachment was under the command of Major Thomas N. Wood. Duty, at least for the officers, was casual to say the least. The primary occupation of the ship and its crew was to sail up and down the East Coast, stopping every so often at delightful ports of call. The crew called it the "Pink Tea" cruise. Boston, New York, Philadelphia, Baltimore and other equally attractive cities were honored by its presence on an irregular basis. It was during one call at New York that Bearss was to make a very important acquaintance.

Everywhere the ship tied up, there were citizens to cheer the ship and crew. Like Bearss, many of the crew members were probably not the celebrated warriors of the late war, but someone had to suffer the pain of adoration. After a bit, in order to please the visitors, their stories of combat became quite elaborate and even more lurid than the real thing. The entire crew was verbally engaged in winning the late war, and the war was won by the present crew of the *New York* and none other, or so they would have the visitors believe.

For many of their admirers these officers represented the U.S. Navy and Marine Corps. In their marvelous white uniforms with buttons shining, some of whom, including Bearss, were even mildly handsome — what members of the fair sex could defend themselves from falling madly in love with the "bravest of the brave"? Not many, it seems. But there was still time for the Bearss-style gags. One medical officer, Assistant Surgeon Raymond Spear, designed one that pleased Bearss. He would inflate a rubber glove and toss it over the side. Then the attention of the visitors would be gained by someone yelling "man overboard." That hand would bob about a bit. The screams and suggestions of how to rescue the drowning man were provided by nearly everyone, including the crew members, who were in on the gag. At times efforts would be made by owners of small boats to rescue the unfortunate, all to no avail. This sort of nonsense continued for some time but eventually wore out its welcome.

While the ship was at anchor in New York harbor, Bearss met Miss Adelaide Louise Madden, daughter of Ambrose Madden, a businessman of Allentown, New Jersey. She was a lovely young thing of but 16 years and Hiram was smitten at once. That she was a beauty seems to be incontestable, according to reports from other than the bewitched swain. She in turn seems to have fallen for him in much the same degree. In fact she soon wrote a poem about him which is so charming it will be repeated:

> I first beheld Hiram on board the USS
> New York. The ship was magnificent,
> spotlessly clean, freshly painted, its deck
> burnished and resplendent.
>
> My older sister had been invited as the guest
> of an officer for tea, and my mother, as escort,
> allowed me to accompany them.
>
> The gentility and courtesy of all on board was
> of the highest order. As we proceeded up the
> gangplank, I saw for the first time a young man
> in white uniform and cap, with gold buttons and
> a shining silver bar on each shoulder.

It was Hiram, I may say now, but to me the vision
of this figure took hold of me completely. I
cannot say that I was in love at first sight, but
it doubtless was so.

He was not tall, but tall enough, slender, but
not slight, handsome in face and manner. He was
assisting the officer of the deck and immediately
asked permission, which was granted! That he be
permitted to join our party.

Never was anyone so attentive. Perhaps I affected
him in the same manner that he did me. I do not
know.

Bearss was enraptured. He asked her mother if he might conduct her charming daughter to the theater. Her mother was no less enchanted than was Louise. The response was, "Yes, you may take my darling daughter to the theater," or words to that effect.

Their first social engagement was truly her first. He was somewhat more jaded but nonetheless it was an exciting evening for him as well. She was, according to them both, very excited but did her best not to appear so. When he arrived at her home, resplendent in his white uniform, she came downstairs dressed in the current fashion — the hem of her dress reaching well below her knees. Her hair was worn in the latest fashion — tied in curls and down her back. They took a cab to the theater and watched the play and, not making any massive errors in deportment, she grew more confident as time passed. How Bearss behaved isn't recorded but we can assume it was creditable. After the closing curtain fell and they left the aisle, six Marine officers stood by at attention as the two departed. She felt that they were honoring her. This made her even more self-assured. But one of the six yelled, "Look what's there. Bearss is robbing the cradle." The evening wasn't quite ruined but later, at dinner, Louise's deflation was such that she had difficulty in partaking of the splendid repast set before her. She knew, and Bearss knew, that the evening had been shattered by a casual and stupid remark from an ignoramus.

The next day his ship weighed anchor and headed south. Was this to be the end of the romance? Not likely. Some days passed, and she was in despair, but lo and behold there came a knock on the door. To come back to her, Bearss had gone absent without leave all the way from Norfolk, Virginia. One thing led to another and within moments they were in each other's arms—mother not being there at that moment. Lucky Bearss made it back to Norfolk without running into the gendarmes and without collecting a disciplinary action.

Back to New York went he, aboard his ship of the same name, and so did Admiral Dewey. The honors bestowed upon the hero of Manila Bay were the most that New York City could bestow. Bearss managed to obtain three tickets for Louise, her mother and sister in the reviewing stand for the great parade, from which they could watch the line of march. Bearss was, of course, parading and as he passed he smiled and gave them a wink from the corner of his eye. To Louise, that was the big moment of the day. Never mind old Dewey; it was Bearss who won the war.

On 25 October 1899 1st Lt. Hiram Bearss, USMC, received his first line assignment.[8] His orders directed him to remove himself from the USS *New York* and proceed to the newly organized Third Marine Battalion where he was to report to Major Littleton Waller Tazewell Waller, USMC. Waller, a fighting Marine of very great distinction, was the son of a governor of Virginia and descendant of a long line of fighting Virginians. If you were going to war, then Waller was the fellow you wanted to go to war with.[9] Like so many other Marine officers, Bearss would learn a great deal from Waller. The names of his "students" would be legion and most would be from the fighting component of the Corps.

Hiram and Louise decided to marry—just like that. No serious thought was given to the future, if there was one, just the present. Fortunately Mother Madden had enough sense to talk them both out of what might have been a major blunder. Louise must remain at home. She and her hero could be engaged to be engaged. It wasn't much but Hiram, at age 24, finally managed to grow up a little bit. He realized that marriage between the two was not immediately in the cards and accepted the refusal with as much grace as he was capable of.

He met Waller in plenty of time for the departure. The other Marine officers in the battalion included 1st Lt. James C. Breckenridge, battalion adjutant; Capts. Herbert L. Draper and Philip M. Bannon; 1st Lts. Hiram I. Bearss, Louis M. Gulick, William H. Parker, Logan Feland, and William H. Clifford, Jr.; and 2d Lts. Norman G. Burton, Frederick M. Wise, Wirt McCreary, Wade L. Jolly, Stephen Elliott and Louis Little—most of whom would be long-serving members of the Corps. In addition, Assistant Surgeon Richmond C. Holcomb, USN, took care of their physical well-being. There were 325 enlisted men organized into four companies of eight squads composed of ten men each. They carried weapons of substance: two Colt machine guns, four 3" guns, and their Lee straight-pulls.

On the morning of 1 November 1899 the two companies formed at

Major General Littleton W.T. Waller received a direct appointment as a second lieutenant of Marines in 1880. During the following 40 years he served in many places and earned the respect of his fellow Marines as a courageous and talented officer who led his Marines from the front. A notable occasion was his leading the Marines while crossing the island of Samar. His major award was the coveted Brevet Medal.

New York left the city by train and reached Washington, D.C., late that same afternoon. Within an hour of their arrival, two more companies formed at Washington joined them at the railroad station. Then two companies of the battalion boarded another train and were on their way across the continent at 1530 hours. The other two companies, aboard another train, followed the first within a half hour. The officers were in Pullman sleepers while the troops were in regular passenger cars. They even had a dining car in which, the commandant reported, "they were fed three good meals a day." Their journey took a week. It was moderately comfortable for all hands and the food was outstanding. In addition, at least for the moment, the troops were on their best behavior. They arrived at Oakland, California, on 7 November and were immediately transported to Mare Island, which is located opposite the town of Vallejo.[10] There they awaited sea transport to their ultimate destination, the Philippines.

Soon after the battalion's arrival the USS *Solace* was ready and another Marine battalion was on its way to Manila. On 11 November the *Solace* weighed anchor and plowed through the great San Francisco Bay out toward the sea. Fritz Wise later described the ship this way: "I have been in one or two hell holes in my life. But the USS *Solace* wins the blue ribbon." He claims that the ship had begun as a no-comfort hospital ship and became worse as a troop transport. Describing the

Solace and the USS *Mercy*, he said there was "no solace on the *Mercy* and no mercy on the *Solace*."[11]

Shortly after leaving San Francisco the ice machine broke down and the food supplies began to spoil. The men were packed in like sardines below, with no room to move about except topside. The seas presently began to be rough and topside wasn't a good place to be. The *Solace* rode the seas like a cement bucket, arising with each wave and sinking with the undertow. Up and down the ship went and so did the stomachs of the passengers. Sleep in the dismal and cramped quarters, especially for those with weak sea-legs, was nearly impossible. When the seas allowed movement on deck the men's systems were still unable to settle well enough to take advantage of the good weather. It was a rough and dirty ride most of the way to Honolulu. Men were brought to the upper deck to attempt recovery from their *mal de mer* but had to be tied to the stanchions so as not to be washed overboard. One of the Marines asked, "Is this a hospital ship, sir? If so I hope never to sail on a transport."[12]

Wise and Bearss became good friends during that terrible voyage. Wise described him so well I have incorporated his impressions entirely:

> It was on the *Solace* that I first did duty with Hiram I. Bearss, then, like myself, a second [sic] lieutenant. There never was another like old Hiram in the world. Wild as you make them. Irresponsible to an incredible degree. Absolutely fearless. Seldom in funds. Always with some scheme afoot. He never had the proper clothes. He was forever playing practical jokes. His energy knew no control. He was always borrowing anything and everything from everybody he could. Yet always he was lovable beyond words to describe.[13]

He mentions that Bearss became seasick. To help his new friend he tied a piece of salt pork on a string and swung it before Bearss' eyes, but just beyond his reach, proving that he was a swell guy. Some of the time Bearss was able to make it to the wardroom assigned to the Marine officers for meals. There were two, with one for the exclusive use of the naval officers and the other for the Marines. There, Major Waller dominated all conversation, not so much because he was their commanding officer but because he told such wonderful tales of the "old Corps." He knew the history of his beloved Marine Corps and managed to pass along his feeling for it as a high and holy thing to his juniors. From every source it is clear that the young officers were thrilled and entranced with his tales. Some, including Wise and Bearss, never forgot them. He may have "flavored" them a little bit, but mainly just told the truth. In addition, there were poker games in which it appears that a small bit of money changed hands.

Bearss, finally on his feet and up to his usual practical jokes, was now aided and abetted by his new pal, Wise. When the ice machine broke down, they used broken glass as substitute "ice" for cocktails and seawater for the gin. The prank was soon discovered by the intended victims but instead of beating the perpetrators they tried it out on some new patsies. It went the rounds and eventually everyone became the goat. This clearly indicates that not all life aboard the scow was dead.

One day, after seven afloat, the ship's company saw the island of Oahu, one of the major isles of the Hawaiian chain. The city of Honolulu was not far away. There they would find hotels with dining rooms—no more ship's chow for at least a few days. Drinking and carousing would occupy their time ashore. They all had grandiose plans for liberty. But then the ship's executive officer, Lt. Comdr. Frederick W. Coffin, USN, doing what some naval officers enjoyed doing to Marines, told some of the junior Marine officers that they wouldn't be allowed ashore. Depression quickly overcame even the high-spirited Bearss and Wise. But, according to Wise, Bearss responded by expressing himself as any Marine should: "That damned good-for-nothing Navy bastard!"[14]

At that moment, their hero Waller, always to the rescue, went to town on the navy and that onerous decision was reversed. They would, after all, be allowed liberty from the floating hell hole; not only the officers but the enlisted Marines as well.

The Marines were landed and given an opportunity for exercise, drills, and target practice, being quartered in the drill hall of the Honolulu National Guard. This made an agreeable break in the monotony of the long sea voyage.[15]

Given the opportunity, Hiram and Fritz Wise made for the nearest bar, which happened to be in the famous Hawaiian Hotel, where every drink then cost a quarter. Friends took them to several clubs and then back to the hotel bar. Back and forth the two and their comrades trod until their collections of quarters were all gone—and they had a considerable number of them to begin with. According to one source, the "following morning" they made their way back to the lovely *Solace* and were poured aboard before the ship sailed.

The trip from there to their next stop, Guam, the then-pesthole of the Pacific, was over glassy seas with no one, now that they had their sea legs, suffering from *mal de mer*. Guam, which had been taken by U.S. forces shortly after Dewey's famous victory at Manila Bay, still provided the worst possible conditions for human habitation—or rather, lack thereof. Or, as Wise stated, "It was Guam, the Hell of the United States Marines."

Guam had already had several Marine units flow through with only a few miserable people remaining on a more permanent basis. Whosoever served there seemed to agree that it was a sordid and very unhappy affair. One group going through spent 16 months in that disaster posing as a U.S. possession. That group of Marines, led by Major Allan C. Kelton, a Marine since 1869, had arrived aboard the USS *Yosemite*. The unit also included Capts. Clarence L.A. Ingate, John H. Russell, and 1st Lts. Henry W. Carpenter and Robert E. Carmody.[16]

There seems to be some confusion as to the numerical designation for this battalion. It isn't numbered in the commandant's official report for 1899 but the quartermaster of the Corps named it the 3d Battalion in his report (Waller's battalion was also designated the 3d). At any rate their sojourn at Guam led to a mutiny of the men. Conditions were so bad that the island commander, a navy officer, treated with them and eventually conceded some points to them. The gist of the story is as follows:

The men were worked to death or at least into terrible fevers in the hot sun. Six privates died, as did Captain Ingate. As it appears in Clifford's book, there was the semblance of a mutiny—"the governor[17] arranging everything convenient for us; so we went back to work and soon completed our long job."[18] Some of the Marines stole some whiskey from medical stores and went into the hills to finish it off. At a formation in which the governor, Comdr. Seaton Schroeder, lambasted them for the theft, Private John Riordan, USMC, stepped out of the rear ranks and shouted, "That's enough from you, you muzzle faced ould walrus."[19] And, if you can believe, nothing happened to him. Guam affected everyone that way. Those unfortunate Marines of Kelton's battalion were retained on the island until November 1900. They suffered many abominations and vicissitudes, including a tidal wave that sank the *Yosemite*. The crew was saved from being shark bait when picked up by a smaller vessel and brought ashore. The Marines and sailors were immediately put to work rebuilding the shattered portions of the island.[20]

The visit by the men of the *Solace* was short but even that was never to be forgotten. Wise seems to believe that most of the officers who weren't dead or dying had already lost their marbles. The governor prescribed punishment for anyone cutting a notch in any coconut tree. Among the natives, drunkenness from their national libation, "Tuba," was rampant. The sailors and Marines grew to know that splendid brew and how to make it. Wise claims that Kelton was strongly preaching his version of evangelism to all who couldn't escape him. One officer, Carmody, had been ordered to Yokohama, Japan, to a mental hospital just prior to the arrival of the 3d Battalion. Carmody's last words when leaving the island were, "I hate this damned island so much I wouldn't even commit suicide on it." He waited until the ship got out to sea and then jumped overboard.[21]

Bearss made the most of his stay on Guam. Every opportunity that he had was spent in hiking over much of the area, observing the natural flora and fauna and possibly the native girls as well. He enjoyed hiking and after their long stay aboard the old scow he took every opportunity to exercise his legs. The local girls are mentioned because, at least at that time, the women were quite liberated and allowed familiarities not usual in so-called civilized nations.

Four unlucky officers, Lts. Louis M. Gulick, James W. Broatch, Edwin A. Jonas and William W. Low, who had been traveling with the 3d, BN., were assigned to the island. It was not truly a death warrant, but close enough to send the four of them into spasms. As Wise puts it, "They were a sick looking trio [sic] as we steamed away."[22]

But Bearss' crowd got on their way without any further ado. The sea was calm and the balance of the voyage was relatively quiet. In about a week the ship entered San Bernandino Strait and passed between the lovely rain forests on either side. Once out of the strait the *Solace* headed northwest through the Sibuyan Sea, sailing between many islands, then through the Verde Island passage between Mindoro and Luzon. Finally, the *Solace* entered Manila Bay and headed eastward to Cavite. This would be home to Bearss and many of his friends for several years to come; sometimes Cavite, perhaps Olongapo, or worse, the island of Samar. It was here in the islands that Bearss and his comrades received their first serious schooling in war, and it was mainly against guerrillas who were ferocious and had long training in the "arts" against the Spaniards. Bearss and his buddies would learn but in so doing, almost by necessity, they became as cruel as their opponents.

The Philippine archipelago consists of about 115,000 square miles of land on 7,083 islands scattered over an enormous space in the South Pacific. Of those many islands, less than ten are easily identified. The others are usually so small as to be practically nameless to anyone other than a geographer or perhaps a local. The climate is hardly satisfactory to people from more temperate and less wet conditions. It is very warm and humid and because of that, it was difficult to serve actively, especially in the bush—the primary home of the guerrilla and where the American forces had to go to get them. It was a difficult learning process for the latter.

Luzon is the largest island, and that is where most of the earlier American activity had taken place. It is the most accessible and the easiest on which to travel about. South of it lies Samar, a very inhospitable place that will occupy much of our story. It was where the guerrilla operated almost entirely without interference and where he did so much damage to both army troops and afterwards, the Marines. Leyte joins Samar and it became

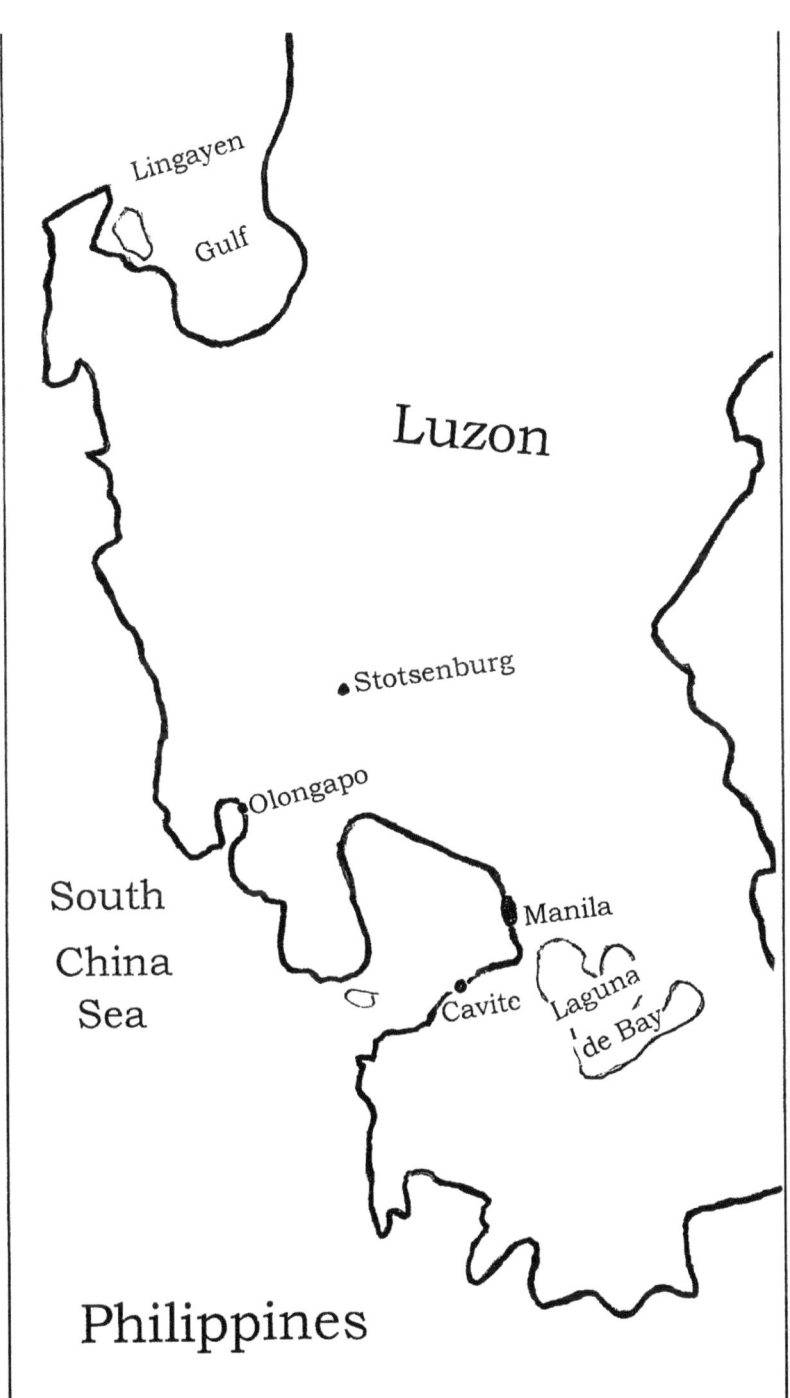

Luzon, the Philippines

famous during WW II. Samar, where Bearss was to spend so much of his time, is about 120 miles long north to south and nearly 70 miles at its widest point in the north. The island of Leyte joins Samar with but a narrow river, the San Juanico, separating both. None of these come into our story quite yet.

4

The Philippines: Operations on Luzon

U.S. forces had been seriously engaged with Filipino rebels for many months when Waller and his Marines arrived at Cavite. Initially, the two sides were able to keep their political differences under control. The Filipinos had been wrestling with the Spaniards for some years. Now that the Americans had helped them drive the Spaniards out of the islands, they expected to gain control over their lives and the islands. But the Americans had been given control over the islands in a settlement with Spain, and their latent imperialistic tendencies came to the fore, although many derided that direction. Imperialism had been and still was to many a dirty word in the United States. Only Britain, France, the Netherlands and a few other seafaring nations were guilty of that activity, and most Americans wanted no part of it. But Americans changed, or at least its government did, and rapidly it seems. The U.S. grabbed what it perceived as its right under the nation's "manifest destiny." Unfortunately for the Filipinos they didn't understand nor agree with that declaration. There were many years of turmoil on the horizon.

There are many opinions on why the United States assumed control of the islands. Located many miles from the continental United States, the islands would require a first class naval force in Asiatic waters to protect them, plus the added expense of naval shipyards prepared to supply and repair damaged ships. If the U.S. had not jumped in, there were many other nations waiting in the wings to do just that. Germany's naval force was there, hungry for new dominions. Japan wasn't there at that time but had shown a great interest in assuming that encumbrance if the U.S. hadn't. Britain was as close as Hong Kong, and whenever a new potential colonial expanse appeared, Britain was always willing to assume the "White Man's Burden." France wasn't much farther away — it had Indochina and would have been pleased to also own territory on the other side of the South China Sea.¹

So the prime argument was, "If we don't, who will?" And the answer was, "They will!" Looking back from a time 40 or more years later, it hardly seems likely that we believed we could hold the islands against other regional powers. There was no recompense earned by the U.S. in "owning" the Philippines, but plenty of expense. Taking the islands was a mixed blessing then and became even less of a benediction as we tried to paralyze the rebels during the next few years.

Because the warlike Filipinos were tough, the Spaniards hadn't been able to stop their rebellion. They were a mixture of people, who had settled those islands more than a thousand years before. Mostly they were Roman Catholic, from the Spanish friars' earnest and dedicated efforts to convert them. But there were enough Muslims to place Mecca as high on the scale as Rome. The difference seemed to be that the former knew when to quit, while the Muslims didn't. Hence there was a dirty war that developed in the southern islands and which continued until at least 1912. Several U.S. Army officers made a reputation in attempting to suppress those rebels, including "Black Jack" Pershing and others of later AEF fame.

At the arrival of Bearss and friends, the war between the conquerors and the "conquered" was in full swing, but it had degenerated into a guerrilla war rather than one of positions. The Filipinos had tried to fight European style and took a severe beating. Like most national liberation armies they then tried another way. By employing guerrilla tactics they were able to hold on for many more, very bloody, years.

The incoming soldiers and Marines were full of vim and vigor, straining at the bit to get at the GuGus,² as the Americans had come to call their small, brown skinned opponents. The Marines were also straining to get out of their steel trap and do something productive. Limbs long unused were weary. Even the beautiful sea was tiresome. The stench below decks had irritated the nostrils of even the most dedicated enlisted Marine.

Initially the Marines were ensconced in an old building at Cavite called Fort San Felipe—but it was a fort in name only. Built many centuries before, it could not have stood off an attack by properly trained Girl Scouts selling cookies. But it was only intended to shelter the officers and men from the weather, nothing more. For the first three months it was Bearss' home. There, he and his comrades faced the usual daily activity of a Marine—reveille, chow, and drill. Upon arrival, Lt. Col. George F. Elliott commanded all Marines at the station.³ Elliott had been in command when on 8 October 1899 the Marines joined their army comrades in the attack upon Novaleta. Two columns of Marines assisted, one led by Ben Fuller and the other by Henry C. Haines, described by Smedley Butler as "rugged, gentle, and strikingly handsome."[4] Both were subordinate to Elliott. To make the attack on time the Marines struggled in mangrove swamps in water up to their armpits. When they arrived at the point of contact, they carried their portion of the enemy's defense, as did their comrades of the army coming in from another flank. Eleven Marines were killed or wounded and a great amount of personal bravery was shown throughout the command, so much so that Elliott commended his officers and men for their bravery. He later complained that though his officers, especially "Thorpe, Gilson and Porter," had shown more aggressiveness than they should, he wanted them admonished by the admiral in command for excessive "bravado."[5] Most probably this was his technique for getting them some attention.

After this, the Marines in the Philippines were limited in their exposure to the rebels until December 1899 when Capt. Herbert L. "Spud" Draper chased "ladrones, held elections, collected taxes and generally pacified the region."[6] A company of Marines led by Capt. Dion Williams, along with the detachment from the USS *Oregon* led by 1st Lt. Randolph C. Berkeley, moved in and took Vigran without difficulty. There they found an American naval officer who had been a prisoner of the rebels. Apparently life wasn't all that harsh for the captive. He needed money to pay off his liquor bills in the cantinas about town. The poor fellow had run out of his own personal funds.

Elliott was subsequently relieved by Col. Robert L. Meade, another Civil War veteran and a nephew of the famous George Meade of Gettysburg fame. He has been described as being very much like Elliott in requiring the strictest unquestioning obedience to his orders. Punctuality was another fetish — obedience at the proper time, including hour, minute and second. Meade made some interesting enemies during his career as a Marine (more on that later).

Waller continued in command of the 3d Battalion. Under his direction he now had Maj. Randolph Dickens as his second in command; as well as Capts. Charles G. Long, Ben Fuller, Austin R. Davis, Henry C. Haines, Philip M. Bannon, William B. Lemly, and Henry O. Bisset; 1st Lts. Hiram I. Bearss, Smedley D. Butler, Stephen Elliott, Robert F. Wynne; and Capt. Cyrus Radford, quartermaster.[7]

At this time there were about 1,200 Marines at Cavite. Their daily existence was not all that disagreeable, especially for the officers. The weather was always rank in the islands but being near the bay helped a great deal. There was a parade ground, which was not only used for close order drill but for Bearss' old delight, horse racing. They had a bar and at night played cards, notably poker in which, as could be expected, some officers won and others lost while some got drunk. That problem was to become a nightmare for commanding officers in most overseas stations in which the Corps was based — that is, if the CO himself was sober.[8]

In the early spring of 1900, Bearss was transferred to the naval base at Olongapo on Subic Bay. It is located on Luzon, just to the northwest of the Bataan peninsula. The station was enclosed on the land side by a wall. They were fortunate in that the old Spanish officers quarters still remained and were usable. Captain "Spud" Draper commanded the 350-man Marine detachment. It was a dismal place and here Bearss was destined to remain for close to a year. Suffering with him at Olongapo were 1st Lts. Charles S. Hill, George Thorpe and Logan Feland. The only positive thing they had going for them was a surfeit of GuGus to keep them from going stale. In fact nearly every day the Leathernecks would have to chase small groups of the *insurrectos*, as they were also called, through the *bosque* undergrowth. That growth nearly strangled everything in its path including the mountains that surrounded the base.

It was during this period that so many of Bearss' comrades were sent from the Philippines to China to assist in reaching the besieged legation at Peking. That China service in the spring and summer of 1900 created many Marine heroes. Among them were names like Waller and Butler, but not Bearss. He was to remain where he was, in the outback of Luzon with the unfriendly natives but without the interest generated by the more colorful conflict in China.[9]

While there Bearss developed and perfected a method of his own, which technique fixed many GuGus before they fixed the Marines. Right from the start, it was his object to get his men to where he wanted to be as rapidly as they could travel. No matter how far the march, nor how difficult the countryside, he usually accomplished his mission in rather short order. When he caught up with the *insurrectos* he found that if he could hold them in one spot and circle around them with part of his force the rebels would fold up. The surprise at finding their enemy before them and behind them was more than the ill-trained natives could absorb. The result usually was raw panic, which led to a rapid disbursement of those that could escape. It was during one, or perhaps several, of those rapid moving escapades that Bearss gained his famous sobriquet, "Hiking Hiram." The euphony of the two words lent color to him and his reputation early in his career, and far beyond his comrades in arms.[10] It was repeated over and over and would become known far and wide to enemies and friends alike. Most likely it was spread by the sergeants, with whom, then and later, he seems to have always had excellent rapport. At any rate, the appellation stayed with him throughout his career, including his time with the U.S. Army. But then he was sometimes called "Hike 'em Hiram."[11]

Life in that outpost was rough and tough at its easiest. The enlisted men were not as well educated as they would later be. They were a difficult bunch at best. So, of necessity, most officers were strict disciplinarians. Bearss never tolerated insubordination. But he also never failed to assist a "good Marine" in trouble. His favorite admonition was "put him in irons, but keep it off his record." Most Marines of that time appreciated what that stood for. With no marks on your record, you could always remain a "good Marine" no matter where you went.

In one case, a recruit Marine named Hatfield walked up to the toughest sergeant on the base and slammed him on the back with a "Hello, you old son-of-a-bitch," which caused some difficulty. Sergeant McCoy (rightfully, it was later acknowledged) hit the clown and flattened him. Getting up off the deck, the recruit ran to his barracks, got his rifle and came back to shoot the sergeant. The rifle, however, was knocked into the air, thereby saving the sergeant's life. Charges were preferred and the culprit went to a court-martial. It seems that the boot was from a part of the country where that "greeting" was considered good manners. During the recruit's trial Bearss came to Hatfield's defense. It came out that the Hatfields and McCoys were in the midst of a feud that had been going on and would continue for many years more, and that was the way honor was settled: "Shoot the bastard if he hit you." Hatfield told the court that if you didn't call a man a "son of a bitch" where he came from, he would have thought you didn't like him. Bearss was his defense attorney and based his defense on the fact that no ill will existed on Hatfield's part — and he somehow managed to pull out of his hat a lesser sentence than anyone had a right to expect. After a relatively short period of brig-time Hatfield was back as a full-fledged Marine.

On 9 March 1901 Bearss received welcome news. Orders read, "Promote to captain with rank from July 23, 1900, by and with the advice and consent of the Senate." But life as a captain was almost the same as life as a lieutenant, only with a little bit more money to lose in poker games and at the bar. Promotion and added money, however, meant responsibility, which meant that Bearss was now commanding a company. At that time a company was composed of 75 enlisted and a couple of officers to back up the skipper.[12] The Marines at Olongapo were beating the bush for the recalcitrant Filipinos, those who still hadn't gratefully and gracefully accepted as rulers the new occupiers of their country. Guerrilla bands roamed all over the backcountry, mostly living off the peasants who, for the most part, gladly shared their own food with them. If not, the *insur-*

rectos intimidated peaceful natives until they did. The peasants also gathered weapons and ammunition along the way, and more importantly, they gathered information about the Americans to pass along to the rebels. On one occasion word was received at Olongapo that a group of "bandits" were camped in a wooded area, not many miles away. Apparently they intended a lengthy stay because they had improvised fortifications for defense while raiding the locals for anything not nailed down. Captain "Spud" Draper organized a detail to root them up and out. Bearss and Captain Robert H. Dunlap[13] were assigned to this task as Draper's subordinates. Their mission: jump the bandits — kill them or drive them out.

Draper, Dunlap and Bearss planned for Dunlap to advance upon the rebels from one direction and Bearss from another. The two would converge upon the natives in a pincer-like movement. Draper would be in overall command of the operation. Bearss started from the base with his company and in the dead of night crossed the Calacan River. This was so that he and his men could reach the rear of the enemy's encampment by early morning. Like all rivers in the Philippines, it was subject to instant flooding. The Calacan river bed was supposed to have been dry at this season, or at least, wadeable. It hadn't been raining when Bearss and his men began their journey, but when they reached the river it was a raging torrent, much too deep for wading and much too swift for swimming. Regardless, no delay could be permitted. The success of Draper's operation, especially Dunlap's attack upon the *insurrectos'* stronghold, was contingent upon Bearss' successful advance from the opposite direction.

What to do? This is a fine illustration of Bearss' notable adaptability. Perhaps he was not an admirable "book" soldier, but he was an outstanding natural soldier. He ordered his men to remove their blanket rolls from their shoulders and had those encased in their waterproof shelter halves. They were then tightly wrapped in their rubber ponchos. Each looked like a short log when the process was completed. Rafts were then formed by roping each of the short "logs" together, creating a stable platform of considerable buoyancy. The area was overgrown with vines of the Bahuca tree. One vine was cut down and looped about the body of a Marine able and strong enough to swim the treacherous river. That Marine then plunged into the torrent and made his way over to the opposite bank where he tied the end around a stout Bahuca tree. On Bearss' side the end was tied to the raft, on which the ammunition belts and various other articles of necessary equipment were drawn across the river. The nonswimmers clung to the raft and were dragged across in several trips.

Bearss showed there was no need to rely upon your seniors to make decisions for you when you can make your own. He was never known to ask why nor even how when he received orders. He may, on occasion, have asked when. Nor did Bearss ever complain that something was too difficult or impossible.

After successfully crossing the river, Bearss and his company hiked the several torturous miles to the rear of the rebels' position. Rope lines had to be used in the dark to enable the men to keep up with the man in front. The jungle undergrowth seriously slowed the trip and was nearly impassable. About daybreak they finally spotted the natives' position. Bearss looked about but fortunately didn't see Dunlap and his company. If he had, then so would have the rebels. The company set out guards and then set to wait for a notice from Draper.

Not long afterward messengers found Bearss and gave him Draper's latest instructions concerning the attack. The enemy's position was on a height of ground which was almost impossible to climb under fire. At the rear were insurmountable, precipitous cliffs. Bearss made his decision. After quickly outlining what he wanted to do, the men were formed up and Captain Bearss led his company up and at 'em. Yelling every imaginable curse that Marine minds could conceive, up the hill they went, scaring the living hell out of the superstitious Filipinos. Although now it seems reckless, this kind of audacity frequently managed to unbalance Bearss' opponents. The Filipinos, numbering upwards of 100 men, fled unceremoniously before this assault by the American devils. Down the cliffs they went with the aid of Bahuca vines, which had been strung in advance for just this kind of emergency. If it hadn't been for those vines the Marines would have slaughtered most of them. Guerrilla warfare can make honest men very nasty when they are the targets of the unseen. Dunlap's part in this whole event is unclear, but we have to assume that he and his men came from the opposite direction because Dunlap would never have allowed anyone else to do the fighting when he was around.

Bearss ordered his men to cut the vines so that they could not again be used for the same purpose. In addition, they destroyed all food and other captured supplies as well as the natives' quarters. Nothing of any value was left intact. Bearss believed that the natives would come back to such a fine defensive position. Therefore, he requested of Draper that he and a dozen of his men be allowed to remain for such a contingency. Draper, considering it too risky, refused the request. Both companies returned to their post at Olongapo. Shortly after the Marines left the area, the GuGus did return and they reoccupied their splendid heights. But Draper had sense enough to realize that Bearss might just be right, so he had his gunners establish the range by measurement, and through the use of a three-inch field piece they made the position permanently untenable.

Other natives in the area realized that the *Yanquis* were there to protect them, and when the bandits returned to their carefully chosen site, the Marines were the first to know. With the gun only 3,000 yards away as a crow flies, it was quite easy to keep the rebels off the hill.

On 18 July 1901, Capt. Rufus H. Lane and a small detachment from Olongapo went after two infamous *insurrectos*. The group included Bearss, 1st Lt. Fritz Wise, 2d Lts. James T. Buttrick and John W. McClaskey, and Hospital Steward Fred Stewart (a corpsman) plus eight native policemen. Joaquin Soriano, one of the villains, had been at Cabatogan, but when the Marines arrived he disappeared. Lane split his force into two factions with Bearss leading one of them. Bearss and his lads found Soriano and seven of his followers, capturing all eight plus five rifles and a hundred rounds of ammunition. Lane gave Bearss all due credit. Bearss' report congratulated "Lieut. Fred M. Wise, Jr. and serg't of Native Police [Juan Salano]" and added, "I wish to commend [Wise] for his bravery and coolness." Commandant Colonel Charles Heywood also added his endorsement on 5 September 1901 "for file with the record of Captain Hiram I. Bearss, USMC."[14]

Captain Hiram I. Bearss, c. 1902, following his return to the United States from the Philippines. Courtesy Special Collections, Norwich University, Northfield, Vermont.

Olongapo had been home to Bearss and his fellows for a lengthy period when the Marines returned from the China expedition; all except for the casualties, which included Captain Austin Davis, the only Marine officer killed there. He, a redhead with a smiling face to go with his southern accent, remained behind forever. In the meantime, Waller, who had been brevetted a lieutenant colonel at the siege of Tientsin, and his battalion were at the Cavite Naval Station, all 1,678 Marines straining at the leash — especially a young, newly brevetted captain, Smedley D. Butler. They wouldn't have long to wait for action.

There were now enough Marines in the islands to constitute a brigade and Lt. Col. Mancil C. Goodrell, USMC, commanded it.[15] Marines were situated in other places in the Philippines, including at Olongapo guarding captured Filipinos, at Cavite guarding the naval installation and others elsewhere in numerous small detachments. About 100 Marines were stationed at Port Isabella on the island of Basilan while a smaller detachment of 50 protected Pollac on Mindanao. The 1st Marine Regiment was based at Olongapo and the 2d Regiment and Brigade Headquarters was at Cavite. Captain Hiram I. Bearss had been recently transferred and was now with Waller at Cavite. For about one year after the return of Marines from China to the Philippines, the area around Subic Bay had been under navy and Marine control. The Marines at Cavite were stationed at various local spots doing their collective best to keep the natives happy, or at least, not disgruntled. Mostly, they were successful.

Down south at the island of Samar, the 9th Infantry, which had also recently returned from China, had been "entertaining" the locals. Part of the entertainment, however, included the near massacre of Company C, 9th Infantry, at Balangiga, a village of 200 Nipa huts located on the south shore of that isle. On 28 September 1901 the company had taken a walloping from local guerrillas, mainly Pulahane bolo men led by General Vincente Lukban, assisted by the villagers of Balangiga. The story of that horror show affected every soldier and Marine then in the Philippines. Marines recently returned from China had fought side by side with the 9th Infantry on the march to Peking and felt for them as for brothers and kin.[16]

The U.S. Army transport *Liscum*[17] had delivered Company C to that southern village on 11 August 1901. Increasingly of late there had been violence perpetrated upon Christian Filipinos and Americans by the native Muslim population on Samar and Leyte. The company commander, Captain Thomas W. Connell, a 28-year-old West Pointer, made every effort to make friends or at least pacify the locals. He even suggested that his troops help clean up the village. That was the downfall of Company C. The locals brought in helpers who maneuvered freely about the village and for some reason raised no suspicion amongst the infantry. On Saturday the 27th, some of the soldiers noticed a number of small coffins being brought in by women. When questioned, the ladies responded that they bore the remains of children who had died of cholera. No one wanted to touch the wood or the bodies so the women went forward with no hand against them.

The following morning, Sunday, was more or less a day of rest for the infantrymen. It allowed them to reread their letters just received the day before from home. That kept most of them busy. Some went to breakfast, carelessly leaving their weapons behind. The attack began after most of the soldiers were in their mess hall. Few weapons were available except for those horrifying bolos in murderous Filipinos' hands. Many of them had gone into the tents and grabbed the infantrymen's rifles. It was a massacre. Of 74 soldiers only 36 survived, with at least 30 of those being badly wounded. Captain Connell was one of the dead.[18]

Major General Smedley D. Butler served as a Marine officer from age 16, beginning in 1898, until he retired in 1931. He was the recipient of two Medals of Honor, a Brevet Medal, and numerous other awards of distinction.

Down south, the U.S. Army and ships of the U.S. Navy were being kept busy. Samar, as already mentioned, was a particular hotspot. Following the slaughter at Balangiga, a detachment from the 17th Infantry was sent there as the replacement unit. Following that, Waller and a battalion of Marines were dispatched from Cavite to aid the army at Samar. This was at the express request of the local commander, Brig. Gen. Jacob H. Smith, USA. Smith, a Civil War veteran and Indian fighter, was more commonly known as "Hell Roaring Jake" and for good reason, as we soon shall see.[19] From this point onward, Waller and the Marines would come directly under Smith's benevolent command. His orders were to be followed to the letter, which would cause Waller some serious problems in the months ahead.

Samar

Samar and Leyte islands were part of the Visayan group in the Philippines. Samar is about 5,000 square miles of rugged and generally still unmapped territory. Waller called it "an evil-looking humpbacked island." It was a terrible place for men to hunt down men and then, worse, to have

4. The Philippines

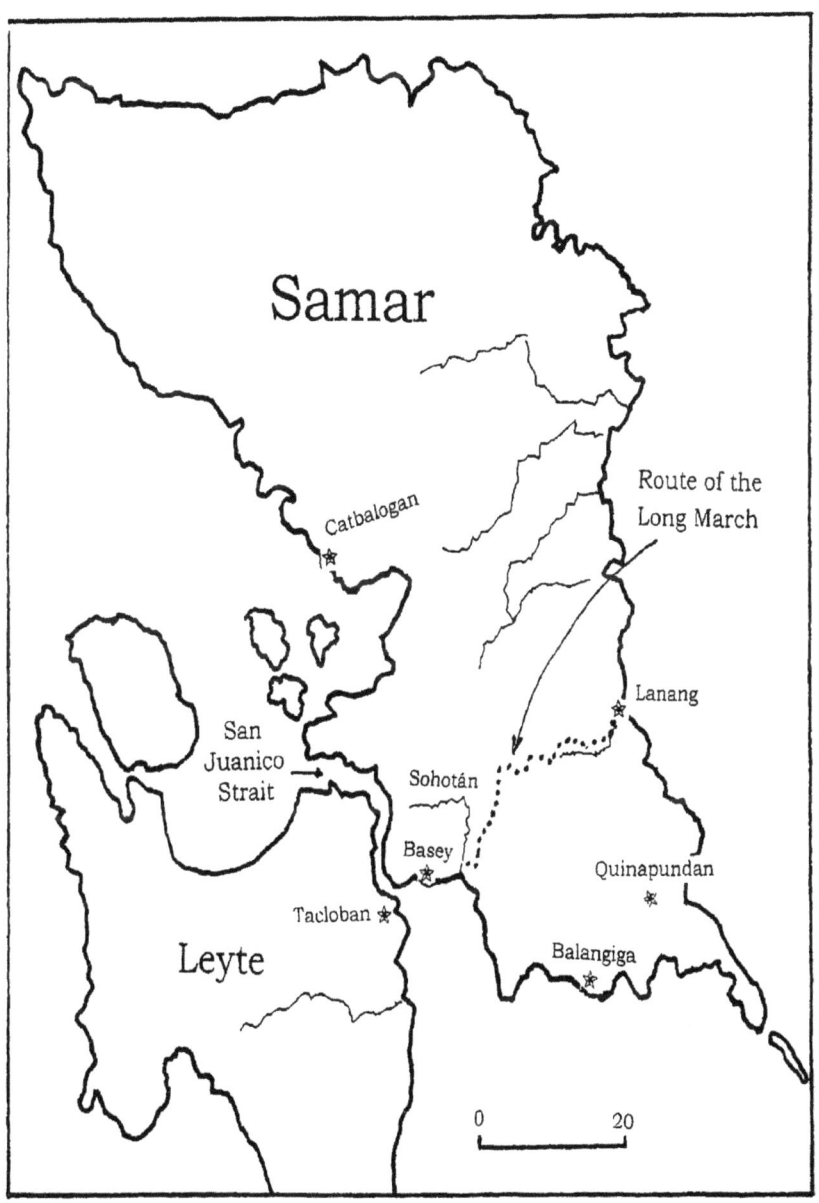

USMC OPERATIONS ON SAMAR 1900

Samar

to fight them. The situation on Samar was so bad that during the Spanish era even table knives had been outlawed because they could and would be turned to death tools against the Spaniards.

Rear Admiral Frederick Rodgers, USN, senior squadron commander, Asiatic Squadron, issued the order for the battalion of Marines to reinforce Jake Smith's troops on Samar. It was Rodgers' intention to provide logistical support for the Marines even though they would be temporarily under the army's jurisdiction. On 20 October 1901, Companies C, D, and H of the 1st Regiment and Company E of the 2d Regiment, 300 enlisted Marines in all, embarked at Cavite aboard Bearss' old "Pink Tea" cruise ship, the USS *New York*.[20] We have no record of what Bearss thought of being back aboard but can assume he renewed old acquaintances, especially those bearing bottled gifts. Rodgers, for some reason, had a fortunate change of heart and on 22 October sent Waller instructions that precluded the Marines' being detached from the 1st Brigade of Marines. As before, they would continue their affiliation with the navy. That was probably the best thing that happened to Waller during his service in the Philippines.[21] On 23 October, Brigadier General Smith met with all the Marine officers of his Marine battalion. After Smith's address, he then turned to Waller, who later admitted being shocked when his new superior told him, "I want no prisoners. I wish you to kill and burn, the more you kill and burn the better you will please me. I want all persons killed who are capable of bearing arms in actual hostilities against the United States."[22]

These were words that would encourage the belief that the U.S. military leadership could be expected to run amuck in its new preserve. That was the way Smith and his cronies had been treating the American aborigines, and it was the way they would treat the Filipinos—that is, until the anti-imperialists back home found out about it.

On 24 October the *New York*'s stop was at Catbalogan, located on the northwest coast of Samar. The ship and crew, less the Marine passengers, remained at anchor. The admiral traveled aboard the USS *Frolic*, which also carried General Smith and both staffs southward. However, Waller and his Marines were on the USS *Zifiro*. Down they went through the San Juanico straits between Leyte and Samar to Tacloban on the island of Leyte, then on to Basey, which is located about five miles east of Tacloban, in the San Pedro Bay, not far from the southwest tip of Samar.

Waller's first act was to relieve a detachment of the 9th Infantry at Basey. Then the *Frolic* and *Zifiro* delivered Captain David D. Porter with his company of 159 men to Balangiga, where it relieved the detachment of the 17th Infantry. The vicinity was tense—the massacre was still on everyone's lips, native as well as Yankee. Porter's orders were to clear the area of any enemy, and the more punitive the manner the better; destroy all food supplies, leaving barely enough for the local populace. The less available supplies for the rebels, the better Smith and Waller would like it.

At Smith's urging, Waller did the same at Basey.[23] Several strong Marine patrols went forth searching for troublemakers. Several engaged them in battle, although they only occasionally could find the *insurrectos*. Porter was doing the same thing. Both groups were finding uniforms and equipment previously owned by Company C. The patrols lasted through the first two weeks in November, when the deleterious effect upon the native population began to show. Food supplies were being destroyed as were unregistered boats, and the natives were screaming. But the Marines continued with little letup. Unfortunately, as could be expected, the more successful were the Marines, the more hatred was generated.

From that time forward the Marine patrols were kept busy searching in every direction — taking native supplies of all kinds, but mainly destroying food when they came upon any caches. They did the same with any weapons or useful tools. While all of this was going on, the rebels were also busy. They were coming into Basey with the help of the town's presidente, Seradio Elcano, to recruit and obtain food. Waller confronted Elcano with what information he had. His reply was that he didn't know any GuGus. Waller knew this was a lie. Waller tried martial law, but as anticipated, that was only partially successful.

The pressures forced many Filipinos to come in to take the oath of allegiance to the United States. During this period, Captain Edwin C. Bookmiller, USA, supplied intelligence that the rebels were in action around San Antonio and south of Basey. Captain Bearss was sent with one detachment to clean up the mess as rapidly as possible. In the course of his travels they came across a small village with a group of at least 20 bolo men whom they routed, managing to capture two. That base was largely one to supply local guerrillas, so the Marine hastened to destroy it, including buildings and food. About 50 natives took that opportunity to emerge from their forest to take the oath of allegiance at Basey. In the meantime information was flowing in, describing an enemy strong point located not far from Basey. It was identified by the natives as a position that was "impossible to take." One Francesco Chemilla came in and professed great loyalty to the United States, and added one very important bit of information. He told of a "great fortress" 13 miles upriver that he, as a captive and forced laborer, helped to construct. Another native verified those facts but added that the position was not 13 but 15 miles upriver. It was said to be located in the vicinity of Sohotón. Waller found this information exceedingly interesting. It would behoove the Americans to knock out the position before it became a greater headache for the Marines. Indeed, just the night before, many bolo men had penetrated as far as the outskirts of Basey to inflict pain on the residents and Marines of that town. They had only turned back when they learned that Waller had two guns in the town. Waller decided that he and his Marines would have to go out to take the "great fortress."

The Sohotón Cliffs

The next stop for Waller and his Marines was the Sohotón area, located up the Basey River.[24] For several weeks expeditions of Marines from Basey had been going into the interior to harass and kill *insurrectos* in the Sohotón region. Hiram had led some of these. Therefore, the terrain wasn't entirely unknown to the Marines. By the middle of November they had cleared most of the area surrounding Basey, but there was still that venerated position farther up the river. It was also learned that there the rebels had developed fortresses on cliffs above the river that were "impossible to climb." Further information described the walls of the cliffs as volcanic rock, specifically pumice. On top of the two main cliffs, which rise nearly straight up approximately opposite each other, were prepared positions, fortified over several years by forced native labor. The cliffs rose at least 200 feet above the raging river. The jungle approaching the base of these cliffs was almost impenetrable. The few narrow pathways and trails were lined with pits in which poisoned spears had been implanted for that unlucky Yanqui who fell in. There were many other traps leading to the cliffs but the dense jungle precluded much transit by the uninitiated. Death was everywhere for those who tried.

The pumice cliffs were burrowed without great difficulty and many holes had been created in their faces. Within those holes, the natives could disappear in times of trouble only to reappear in another place equally difficult to reach. Bamboo ladders led to the top, but only for the invited, in which group the Yanquis wouldn't be included. Tons of boulders were perched atop the cliffs in woven baskets. These were held in place by vines for immediate release with the simple cut of a bolo. There was almost an equal volume of smaller stones set aside for the natives to hurl at any fool attempting to climb the nearly sheer face. On top the natives had constructed numerous bamboo cannons. The bamboo was already hollow and thick enough to survive a powder blast. They were uncomplicated guns and only required powder and some pellet of a substantial girth to create an unpleasant experience for the recipient. These people had thought of nearly everything, and possessed a well-founded sense of security. It was a sense of protection only those not previously subjected to a U.S. Marine attack could appreciate.[25]

Waller knew that to dislodge the natives from those positions would require an excellent plan and enormous energy. He also realized that the Marines must knock them out of both places in order to gain the moral edge. Face was important in the Orient and the loss of such highly touted positions would entirely change the attitude of the Filipino people. It would change from hatred, or even ambivalence, towards a desire for peaceful relations with the United States— that being the nature of all human beings. The natives were convinced that no one could accomplish the job.

Waller's plan was to send two companies against the cliffs while holding a third, commanded by himself, for mopping up. The first two were to travel by boat partway and then overland, while his group would make the trip slightly later and entirely by boat. Captain Porter was to command one of the companies, Bearss the other, but with Porter, the more senior man, in command of the ground forces. The two were to travel separately via the shoreline and coordinate shortly before the attack was to begin.

On 15 November the two attack companies moved out toward their target. Bearss and Porter were (as it would now be called) on the fast track. Both were young and full of vim and vigor. Porter was the lineal descendent of numerous professional American fighting men of that name. He was also 14 points in grade ahead of Bearss and for that reason would sometimes overshadow his contemporary. But Bearss would catch up and eventually pass Porter, especially during his service in World War I.[26] Porter led the first column. Bearss' bunch, following, went by boat to Odac and then by trail to Lirnan. There they were able to join Porter. Meanwhile, on 16 November Waller began his advance on the river. Both land companies ran into the worst possible traps. Dug pits covered with loose branches, leaves and dirt, with poisoned stakes implanted in the bottom would rapidly reduce one's life span. So would the poisoned spears fastened to tree branches, hauled taut like a bow, and fixed to spring forward at the slightest touch. In addition, the advance guard had to always be prepared for a deadly ambush at any time. Fortunately, during the advance there don't appear to have been any casualties among either company. It has been recorded that Bearss took absolutely no chances with his men's lives during his approach. Each and every native village passed was completely destroyed. In all 165 huts were burned and at least 50 natives were killed. Probably Porter was equally cautious, and for the natives, it was equally calamitous.

Coming northward along the west bank of the river, the column, now joined, completely surprised a parcel of rebels. The natives attempted to fire off one of their bamboo cannons but Acting Corporal Harry Glenn rushed forward and yanked the fuse. The attack of the Marines killed 30 natives and completely routed the balance. After driving them from their positions the Marines now crossed the river. They used Waller's boats, he and his men having arrived upon the scene.

Porter and Bearss were both to advance to the base of the Sohotón cliffs while Waller proceeded upriver by boat. Porter and Bearss' contingents, opposite each other, were at least 200 feet above the river unit. Somehow messages between the three were garbled. Waller's group misinterpreted one message, which they thought said the river was not navigable farther up, so they set up camp for the night. Bearss and Porter continued along the shore heights and discovered the enemy's trail on the morning of the seventeenth.[27] Along this trail were buried the usual pits and spears.

When Company C reached the base of the cliffs Bearss and his men ran over and placed the already prepared bamboo ladders against the wall. Bearss was the first to climb. When asked later why he didn't let one of his men go first he replied, "That came from having indulged in so much hot air. I had blown my mouth so long to the men that I wouldn't order them anywhere I wouldn't go—that I didn't have the guts to tell the fellow behind me to go first!"[28]

Some of those who followed Bearss up those bamboo ladders were Cpl. Harry Glenn and on the opposite wall a famous hero from Guantánamo, Gunnery Sergeant John Quick. Porter's Company E began the ascent at about the same time as did C. As they continued up the ladders, they were all subjected to fire from homemade muskets, arrows, spears, boulders and stones. Fortunately, the enemy's aim was largely ineffective. But the rebels did engage the Marines in some hand-to-hand combat and for men still on the wall it was hairy at times.

After they reached the top of their ladders the climbers had to move up the face as best they could. The pumice of the cliffs soon cut through the Marines' shoes and tore their hands. It wasn't long before many of the men were practically barefoot. The Marines made their way from handhold to handhold even though their hands were bleeding profusely. Upon reaching the top Bearss pulled his pistol from its holster and blazed away at the enemy while Glenn again rushed forward to pull fuses from as many of the cannons as possible. Bearss was a dead shot so there were some native casualties from his fire. Glenn's action was one of the most important of the entire battle. Many lives would have been lost had those guns gone off.²⁹ Among the first Marines on top with Bearss were two machine gunners, Tom Pendergast and Bill Slattery, who, with their gun assembled, began hammering away at the *insurrectos*, quickly clearing a wide area in front of them. It took guts and hard work to haul that heavy piece up those cliffs but it paid for itself many times over.

After climbing to the top, John Quick did what he always did in a fight — he went straight towards the rebels. First Sergeant John Grogan, also of E, kept up a verbal diatribe at his men all the while they were climbing the cliffs. If you've ever heard a top sergeant lecturing, you know what it sounded like. Communication between the two companies was, when possible, managed by waving signal flags. Porter's crowd discovered cooked food that

Major General David D. Porter, scion of a distinguished military and naval family, was directly commissioned a second lieutenant of Marines in 1898. He served in Cuba, the Philippines, and China. He transferred to administrative service and remained with the Adjutant and Inspectors Department until he retired in 1937. He and Bearss both received their recommended Medal of Honor from President Franklin D. Roosevelt. Porter was also a recipient of a Brevet Medal for services in the Philippines.

had been left behind in the *insurrectos*' rush to survive the madmen. Porter's men were also equipped with a Colt machine gun, and with native porters' help managed to get that up on top. Private Walter Campbell, of Company E, was commended for good work in his operation of the Colt.³⁰

The defenders didn't wait too long. Startled by the audacity of the climbers, they fell back precipitously. It wasn't long before they were defeated. At the conclusion of the fighting the Marines set about destroying anything that might be useful. When they had completed their job, the cliff tops were nearly barren except for Marines. The report of Major Waller gives important details relative to the entire operation. Meanwhile, Waller, extremely agitated because he didn't have the opportunity to lead his men, came up to Porter's position and started to say a few harsh words. But, being the gentleman he always was, he instead congratulated both officers on their conduct of the assault. Surprisingly, there were no Marine casualties. After the assault and capture of the position the men and officers dismantled all the various traps in the immediate vicinity, being especially careful to avoid the poisoned parts of the stakes and spears. Supplies were, however, badly needed, as were shoes and other clothing torn in the bush and on the cliffs.

Brigadier General Jake Smith was especially complimentary about the work done by Waller's battalion. His message to Waller was as follows:

> The brilliant success of your command, both men and officers, has my highest congratulations. There is nothing impossible for the American fighting man, and your work in the Sohotón Province is an additional proof of that fact.[31]

Admiral Rodgers telegraphed his compliments from the *New York*:

> Well done, marines. The senior squadron commander sends hearty congratulations to you, Captains Porter and Bearss, and your command. They are doing what I predicted for them, and are maintaining the reputation of the corps.[32]

Major General Adna Chaffee, USA, telegraphed Waller from Manila:

> Have just read your messages to General Smith, dated 19th. Thanks to officers and men. Assure each of my cordial regard and my highest appreciation of the manly heart and soldierly spirit which makes light of obstacles and is never daunted or satisfied while service can be rendered to our country. I hope kind Providence will guide the footsteps and take the part of American soldiers battling for peace in the wilderness of Samar.[33]

Smith was ecstatic about Waller's success, since it reflected well upon himself, and ensured that his own recommendations were sent forward to the secretary of war and then to the Secretary of the navy. His were laudatory of the entire Marine battalion, but especially of Waller and the several officers and men he had commended. It was shortly after this time that Smith sent Waller a special communication—one which indicated his desire that Waller make a march from Basey across the island to Hernani on the east coast, for the purpose of selecting a route for a communications wire to span the distance. This was a distance of only forty miles as the crow flies. But as it always turns out, no self-respecting crow would ever consider flying that 40 miles. This was not only unmapped territory but, for the most part, completely uninhabited by human beings, for good reason.[34]

4. The Philippines   53

The one thing desired by Waller and his men was maps, good solid maps of this country they were operating in.[35] He soon learned that there was no such thing. In the meantime, minor clearing operations were carried out during the balance of November. Waller with Porter and a selected crew took a cutter and went down to a point near Nipa Nipa to intercept and capture rebels and their boats, which were communicating with Leyte. Second Lieutenant John Gridley led a patrol to Iva, killing some of the enemy and capturing many of their krises — bolo weapons much feared by the Americans.[36] In December there was more activity. There was a two-column march of Marines to Balangiga, one led by Waller along the coast and the other by Bearss marching about two miles inland. Nothing untoward happened and before a week had passed the units were back at Basey. The upper Sohotón River, beyond the cliffs, was tentatively explored. It was learned that the river disappeared into the Loog Mountains and reappeared some 100 feet below. At times footprints were discovered in the muddy banks that were determined to be of American shoes. Other items found were scraps of paper, sometimes letters or even birth certificates, all American and all Company C, 9th Infantry. In a modest way, their Marine comrades were getting even for the massacre. There was no question that the enemy was completely disorganized and now operating in bands of two or three men who seemed to be simply looking for food in the jungle. The *insurrectos* on the island of Samar were on the run. As expected, the Marines had been the main cause of it.

However, Waller's Marines weren't in any shape to make another major effort so early after Sohotón. There were the beginnings of a malaria epidemic and a serious eye infection had developed in many men. They were still, for the most part, physically exhausted. The tiring journey across country, the crossing of the raging river and the severe climb up those cliffs under the most trying conditions had worn the men out. The debilitating climate and rugged terrain were nearly impossible to overcome by men from the Occident. This would continue to be a problem for American soldiers and Marines for many years to come.

In the first week of December something significant happened between Smith and Waller. First Lieutenant John H.A. Day, Waller's adjutant, came into Waller's office and placed a single sheet of blue paper before the major. On it was written, "The interior of Samar must be made into a howling wilderness." That was it. No signature and nothing additional by way of explanation. Waller looked at it and asked Day, "Where did you get this?" Day replied that Smith had given it to him as instructions for Waller. At the time, Waller had been giving Porter and Bearss their instructions, so he turned and showed them what was written on the page. He went so far as to tell them to be guided by those instructions and then tossed it into the waste basket. That was a major blunder.[37]

A few days later Bearss was told by a native that a local *insurrecto* leader, Juan Colinares, was hiding with 20 of his men in a village only 20 miles away. They were armed with bolos and four rifles from Company C. Off went Bearss and 50 Marines. The majority of the villains had disappeared but two natives remained. One was identified as an *insurrecto* leader and the other a member of his team. Bearss had both shot on the spot and the village burned. This wasn't the first execution of natives by Americans, and it would grow to huge proportions, becoming a major propaganda problem for all Americans concerned.

A few days before Christmas 1901 would find most of the Waller battalion near the rebel stronghold at Quinapundan, located at the south of the island, and not more than ten miles from Balangiga. In order to successfully approach the town the force had to travel upriver in small rowboats. They were subjected to rifle fire emanating from the dense jungle that lined both sides of the river for the entire distance. Sometimes they could scatter a sizable force with their Colt machine gun, which naturally had a prime position up forward in one of the lead boats. Finally, by late December 1901, Waller was as close to being ready to make that trip across the island as he ever would be.

General Smith had made known to Waller his wishes that the island be crossed, west to east. It was his aim to locate a path for telegraphic wires to be strung and communication established between both sides of the island. Waller and his Marines were to make the reconnaissance. Why he picked Waller's Marines is anyone's guess. Certainly the various army units, located mainly on the east coast, had traveled within the island, at least in their sections. Anyway, off the Marines went to the east coast. For some reason not readily apparent, Waller had instead decided to travel east to west.

The March Across Samar

This could just as easily instead be entitled "The Ill-Fated March Across Samar," for that is what it became. Bearss was intimately involved, though not in a direct leadership position.[38] At best, it is a very complex story and events should be followed closely.

The gunboat *Arayat* brought Waller and his party to the east coast town of Lanang,[39] at which they arrived at on 24 December. Lanang was garrisoned by Company K, 7th Infantry, Captain James N. Pickering, USA, in command. Pickering and Lt. Kenneth Williams, also of the 7th Infantry, tried to talk Waller out of his intended mission, but without success. Williams had recently tried to make a trip through but failed. So had Capt. Edwin Bookmiller, USA, the intelligence officer, the year before. Williams spent 12 days out in the boondocks and was convinced that no trail led to Sohotón. But Waller was adamant. Smith wanted it traversed and as far as Waller was concerned, an order from a superior was to be obeyed without question.

As finally constituted, the Waller party included Capts. Porter and Bearss, 1st Lt. Alexander S. Williams and 2d Lt. Frank Halford, all USMC.[40] According to a later report, each of the officers had "begged to go." In addition another volunteer, 2d Lt. DeWitt C. Lyles, USA, also accompanied the Marines. Gunnery Sergeant John H. Quick was to supervise the 50 Marine enlisted men. The men selected were the strongest and most stable of the entire Marine battalion. In addition to those mentioned, seven enlisted men from the 7th Infantry accompanied Lieutenant Lyles. Capt. Arthur J. Matthews and the remaining Marine officers who were not selected to make the trip, plus their men, were sent back to Balangiga across country by way of Quinapundan. The only medical officer available, Assistant Surgeon Brister, was unable to hike. He, lucky fellow, was suffering from swollen and blistered feet. Two natives from Basey were "induced" to come along as guides. The names assigned to them by the Marines were "Slim" and "Smoke." Slim, also a member of Lieutenant Day's native police force back in Basey, was the only native man known to have been trained in the use of a rifle.

On the morning of 28 December the party, which included 30 or so native carriers, made their way down to the riverbank to load the *barotos*

Sergeant Major John H. Quick became a Marine in 1892 and followed the usual path of enlisted men until service at Cuzco Wells, Cuba, in 1898. He then went to Samoa and the Philippines. He was with Waller, Bearss, and Porter on Samar, Cuba, once again, and then Vera Cruz. He went to France with the 6th Marines and was awarded a Distinguished Service Cross followed later by a Navy Cross. Quick retired in November 1918.

(a native boat), which were to carry them partway up the river. Waller's plan was to follow the river westward as far as was possible, perhaps 15 miles, and then continue through the mountains and jungle to the Sohotón cliffs, then on to Basey. That sounded easy enough but was to prove to be one of the worst disasters that the American military ever inflicted upon itself. Before leaving Lanang, Waller had, via the *Arayat*, sent word to Captain Dunlap back at Basey to set up a supply camp near the cliffs, bringing supplies that much closer to his hiking Marines. Dunlap was to leave 1st Lt. James T. Bootes in command at Basey. Dunlap would follow orders and then would wait at the site as directed. As it turned out, he would have a long wait, and a very difficult time of it while he waited.

Both Pickering and Williams made one more attempt to dissuade Waller, but to no avail. His mind was made up. Smith wanted it done and it would be done. Waller was well aware that if they once started they would never be able to turn back. The white man's face, like his Asian counterpart's, had to be protected. Therefore, no matter what problems they might encounter on this trip, which nearly everyone expected to be hazardous, they must succeed. Consequently, to continue was one of the most important decisions that Waller ever made.[41]

Off they went. On the first day the weather was good. The sun shone brightly and the men felt good. They made 17 miles paddling on the winding Lanang River to a point where the river branched off. The next morning Waller decided to move up the north branch and they made eight miles that day. The rapids forced them ashore at the village of Ligtao. Waller then decided to ship the boats downstream using the soldiers of the 7th Infantry as their crew. One source states that they then marched toward the Suribao River, which is complete nonsense, since that river is located at least ten miles out of their way in a northerly direction. It is more likely that they were six or seven miles from the coast, having traversed a winding river and were still, on a direct path, at least 35 miles from Sohotón.[42] As they made their way several of the officers made maps of each mile they traveled; their accuracy was later found to be outstanding. The information was used years later by army units attempting to neutralize the insurgents inland on Samar.

Meanwhile, Dunlap was doing everything correctly. He based his camp as directed and then set out to find the approximate direction that Waller could be expected to come from. He even set out markings that would tell Waller that he was headed in the correct direction. Dunlap was also subjugating any natives in the area who were, or seemed to be, *insurrectos*. There still were quite a few in the neighborhood.

The next day the men were on foot. It was the 30th day of December and Waller was concerned. Their movement was going too slowly. By his own calculation, and he was too extravagant, they had moved halfway or so to Sohotón. Going westward and northward and sometimes southward, they crossed and recrossed the now swollen river several times. Each time, their clothes were soaked and because the sun hardly penetrated to where they were, never dried. After a while their wet clothes, constantly rubbing, caused severe chaffing on different parts of their bodies. This would become one of the major problems of the trip. Each time they crossed some men and officers slid on the slippery rocks into the river. Besides the hurt from the fall on rocks and the dampness from the river, it was embarrassing, especially for the young officers who always tried to maintain a proper decorum before the troops. The troops may have paid little if any attention, because they were suffering the same indignities. Back and forth they continued. The path, never worthy of the name "trail," kept ending, and because the trees dropped their branches so close to the river bank there was nothing else to do but cross over again. Downpours were a regular affair. They often made the river a raging torrent that was hard to walk beside and worse to cross.

Because of extreme dampness caused by the incessant rain, they had a fireless camp that night, which added to their misery. Waller also decided that they must shorten their daily ration since there was no telling when food would again be readily available. With that he cut the portion to one half of the regular issue. Waller told his officers to make sure they said nothing that would depress the enlisted men. He even had to chew out some of the young officers who were hurrying the men along. They were too anxious to be at the front of the column. Waller told them that their proper place would always be with their men. They were all quite young. Bearss was the oldest of the officers and he was only 26.

On 31 December they followed a stream bed so severe it was almost like a waterfall. They did not reach the crest until nightfall. The climb had been particularly brutal, the men were worn out and they still had to clear a place for their bivouac. The level portion of the hilltop was only about 20 feet wide, which made it very difficult for many of the travelers to lie upon flat ground. Because the food was uncooked, it was tasteless and unsatisfying even though they were all extremely hungry. In addition, Waller had reduced the ration once again. Each man, officer and enlisted, would receive half of the previous issue. They were now down to quarter rations and had barely begun their trip. The hard bread was all gone. Now it was only coffee and bacon, and little enough of that. Another day passed. The men were beginning to become restless and murmurs of discouragement were overheard. At this height the winds coming from the ocean were especially harsh and the group, mostly in wet clothes, felt in their bones the drop in degrees. It was a rotten New Year's Eve for everyone. Waller now calculated that for each four or five miles' distance they had covered it cost them up to 15 or 20 actual miles. He also decided that he must assume total control of the march. They were not doing very well and he believed that the younger officers were too anxious to exceed their fellows, thereby causing some problems with maintaining discipline. He also decided that the interior of Samar was desolate of human beings for the most part, and made such notations in the journal he kept. Waller had expected to find the beginnings of an old Spanish trail at about this point but none appeared. Everyone was exhausted and no sentries were posted. The reader can well imagine the seriousness of that happening in a military organization in the field.

It was a new year, 1 January 1902, and though the sun shone brightly, it began terribly for Waller's Marines. Food was in very short supply, the officers and men were being used up at a rapid rate, and the native bearers were becoming increasingly surly. Although they may have had a magnificent view over many miles of the countryside, it was covered over by the forest below and only certain mountain peaks and rivers could be clearly observed.

At this time Waller took a compass bearing, west by southwest for the day's march. Down the mountain they went. Why they had gone up is best left to conjecture. He had considered his alternatives. One of course was to return from whence he'd come. That, for Waller and his officers, was tantamount to admitting failure — something a Marine would not consider, ever. Another was to again reduce the amount of their rations and push on as before. Now, according to calculations, they were down to an eighth of the original rations each day. The Marines were now starving.

Because of the terrible undergrowth to be hacked with their machetes the journey downward was extremely difficult. After a bit they came upon another stream but it was flowing in a northwesterly direction. After a conference with his officers, not something that Waller was prone to do on a regular basis, it was agreed that the column should follow it. That night of 1/2 January, camp was established once again. The men's feet were in terrible condition. There were more sores on their bodies and many additional leeches had attached themselves to the Marines' flesh. Blood lost from the leeches and the tearing of flesh began to become unbearable. The sores were festering because of the difficult sanitary conditions and becoming increasingly painful. Waller's men were now struggling forward mainly because they realized there was nothing else to do. To stop meant death—continuing onward probably meant the same. Better to go forward than to rot. At least their officers were going forward. The enlisted men's continued confidence in them probably had as much to do with the forward movement as anything else. The next morning, 2 January, they set out again.

The stream continued and expanded; in fact, it rapidly grew to be a good sized river. At noon there was no food. The river was nearly westerly in direction but it was impossible to cross. They continued forward until late in the day. The stream they had been following emptied into a much larger stream which in itself flowed almost due east. Now they were hemmed in between two large streams, neither of which was possible to ford. In order to get beyond this calamity it appeared that the men would have to retrace their steps back to the mountain from which they had descended. Physically, they were unable to add that much more effort onto themselves. The situation was worse than extremely serious. The spirit of the men was now neither plus nor minus, it was neutral, which was the beginning of being completely down.

That night, 2/3 January, they stopped along the trail to rest. A semblance of a camp was set up. After several fruitless attempts to build a fire a single slice of uncooked bacon was handed to each officer and man. Waller then called his officers into a council. Where the night before it had still been possible to turn back, now there was no one who considered they could even find Lanang. They probably couldn't even have found the place from which they had started the day before. The party was lost. Waller was convinced that every individual's life hung on what was to be done, and he needed their input to stave off disaster.

They sat apart from the men in order that their words wouldn't be heard and possibly misinterpreted. Waller expressed the thought that they were on the Suribao River.[43] He told them it was his intention to go on but that he wanted every officer to participate in a democratic solution. Therefore he asked that each, even the most junior, give his own opinion as to what their course should be, after which a vote would be taken. The majority would rule.

As it finally turned out, none of the officers were willing to make any final decision that would be contrary to what Waller wanted to do, so he made the decision anyway. It was to build a raft of bamboo and ride the river northward to some point from which a march to Borongan could be made. That town is on the east coast and many miles north of where they were or had started from. It is obvious now that the Waller was terribly incorrect as to where they were actually located.

The next morning, on 3 January, they attempted to build bamboo rafts but each sank before it could be used. But by then Waller had devised another plan — one that would divide his command. This decision he made himself, with no input from his juniors. He told them that he would take Lts. Halford and Lyles and 13 of the men in the best physical condition and strike west to find Dunlap and his station on the Sohotón. Then he would send a fresh party back with sustenance for the Porter group. Porter was to be left in command with Bearss as his second. Waller would leave a trail marked plainly and Porter would follow it. To Waller, and perhaps some of the others, it seemed like the best plan to follow. It might have been, if everything had gone according to plan and everyone had followed directions.

Waller was the first to make alterations. He and his group headed west but by midmorning had made such poor progress he decided to turn back toward Lanang. Waller sent a native carrier to find Porter and give him a message to again build rafts for another attempt to propel themselves to the coast on the "Suribao" River. Waller and his party would join them there and they would head for the coast together.

Porter received Waller's message and did as he was told. The rafts they built were as unsuccessful as the previous group. Meanwhile, Porter began to have serious trouble with the carriers. He told them to cut bamboo with their bolos but they refused, saying it couldn't be done. John Quick took a bolo and showed them how. Then the natives began to give Quick some lip. Now angry and using his fists, he knocked two of them on their rears. That didn't change any minds; they still refused to cut.

Bearss came up with a solution. He said that he would make a raft for two persons and that he and Lieutenant Williams would float down the river to Borongan to get help for the main body. Porter refused that, saying, "I can't spare two officers at this time." Shortly afterward, Bearss countered with a plan to take Cpl. Joseph J. Murphy and locate Waller. Fortunately for Bearss and Murphy, and our story, this time Porter agreed. Off the two went, following without great difficulty the trail left by Waller.

On 4 January Waller and his group were making slow process. Then Bearss and Murphy made their appearances. Bearss told of Porter's dilemma on the river bank and how he was still unable to create effective rafts using bamboo. In the meantime, Waller and his group had themselves made a discovery that could save the lives of all his men if only he could get the word to everyone. They had walked, or rather stumbled, into a grove of bananas, sweet potatoes and coconuts. After everyone had a genuine feast, Waller set about to try to communicate with Porter by starting a fire in the grass using his field glass lens under the bright sun. Apparently Porter never saw it. If he had, what might he have considered it to mean, and what would have been accomplished? He was still waiting for Waller to return.

Waller sent a guide named Victor to tell Porter that the game plan was again being changed. This time they were going to go to Basey; Porter should head west until he found the grove of edibles. Porter was to rest at the grove and wait for Waller's party to return for them from Basey. Waller did describe the route, and everything might have worked out if Porter had ever gotten the message. Meanwhile, Porter and his men continued to starve.

After they had digested their edibles, Waller sent Bearss and Lyles out to scout ahead in a large clearing. Bearss soon returned with the news that he and Lyles had found a native hut just beyond the clearing. Although he could not prove it, he did sense that there were humans about and probably within the hut itself. Waller then moved his group about a mile further on, found the hut and surrounded it. Five natives were captured. Two were adult males, two were adult females and one a boy of about ten years. As Waller later described the incident he said that those ragged, filthy and bearded Marines must have scared hell out of the poor Filipinos. Two of them, an adult male and the boy, admitted that they knew the way to Basey and agreed to take Waller there. Three were given their freedom while the man and boy were placed under guard.

Victor returned sometime later with the story that the *insurrectos* were so numerous that he had been unable to get through to Porter. It was a very suspicious report and Waller knew it. He had noticed that the natives were becoming quite unruly as the Marines became noticeably weaker. Waller had considered all natives to be treacherous and had no reason to change his attitude now. As the trip had become more and more difficult his belief had been strengthened by the increasing surliness he witnessed about him. Victor was undoubtedly lying. What would happen next and what could he do about it, anyway?

Bearss told Waller that he believed that Porter would follow instructions and continue his journey westward. Porter had, after all, told Bearss that he was going to continue in that direction. This was what Waller wanted to hear so he accepted Bearss' story without further question. Waller and his group again started to Sohotón and Dunlap. But no word of that change was sent to Porter, who, apparently, was still expecting Waller to return.

That night, 4/5 January 1902, Waller, encamped at the top of a mountain ridge above the Loog River valley, received more proof that something sinister was brewing. Bearss had no sleeping blanket with him and Waller kindly agreed to share his. The two men lay down and within moments Bearss was asleep. Waller found the location uncomfortable and decided to move over under a tree. But he couldn't awaken his sleeping junior so he dragged him, still within the blanket, to his desired position. Waller always slept with a bolo hung on his waist, but he found that the arrangement wasn't very comfortable so he placed the bolo next to him outside the blanket. As he again went back to sleep, he felt the bolo moving along his leg. He cautiously raised himself but by then whoever had taken the knife had disappeared. Waller woke Bearss and told him what had happened. Just then he spotted a dark object nearby that looked, in that dark rainy night, just like his hat. He grabbed his pistol and reached over to find that it truly was his hat and with a native under it. Indeed, the native also had Waller's bolo knife in his possession.

With a curse Waller kicked the native, then with his hands around the man's neck jerked him to his feet. He then pushed him through the center of the encampment toward where, under a Marine guard, the other natives were located. With one more kick for good measure the native joined his fellows. Waller had recognized the native: it was Victor. He told Bearss to make sure that he was punished when they arrived at Basey.

Early the next morning, 5 January, the officers and men were up and as ready as they could be. The boy, who (the father professed) knew the way to Basey best, was put out front. Off they went as soon as the first light of dawn appeared. The lad led them to a trail that they had just left, turned to the right and followed familiar ground — across the same two rivers that Waller and company had previously traversed. At one point the boy, without hesitation, leaped into the river as did the following Marines. All walked up to their necks in driven water, against the current. At length they reached the Sohotón River, but it was so swollen that they were forced to wait several hours until it receded. By the use of Bahuca vines and a log they managed to cross it. On the opposite side they found evidence of a trail. It was thought to be the old Spanish trail that was often referred to but, up till now, never seen by any Marine.

Waller was so anxious to make Basey that he continued the trip far into the night. Near midnight, realizing that they would have at least one additional day on the trail, he consented to camp for the night. They were wet, all suffering from sores and chaffing, and, of course, starving. Everyone bivouacked as best as each could but none were remotely comfortable.

The morning sun arose and each officer and man was again handed a single piece of uncooked bacon. On this sixth day of January this group of Marines was going to be saved. As soon as everyone had eaten their meager breakfast the party marched down a steep bank to the village of Banglay, which lay at the junction of the Loog and Caacan rivers. They were now nearly home, if any of them could consider Basey as such. The village of Banglay was deserted but they found rice, sweet potatoes, and coconuts. Soon the rice and potatoes had been cooked and eaten and the coconut milk drunk. They then rested. Within two hours they were on their way again. The group crossed the river and located Dunlap's camp. He wasn't there but returned about an hour later. All climbed into Dunlap's cutter and headed downstream to Basey.

Poor Dunlap had his tale of woe and they patiently listened to all that had happened to him while he had been waiting for them to arrive. He had already lost two camps to raging waters. The first time he had built his camp too close to the river and a tidal wave had taken everything with it. Although he had rebuilt farther back from the river, the same thing happened.

A little after noon they arrived in Basey and all were hysterical with relief. As Waller later said in a report, "The men realizing that all was over and that they were safe and once more near home, gave up. Some quietly wept; others laughed hysterically ... most of them had no shoes. Cut, torn, bruised and dilapidated, they had marched without a murmur for twenty-nine days."[44]

Waller was very proud of his men. They had endured privations known only to the group that Porter was leading. Waller's men were almost entirely without shoes. Their feet were bleeding, sore and swollen and their eyes in terrible shape from the various bites received, mainly from leeches. The rest of their clothing was almost nonexistent. But they had accomplished what no other white men had ever done. They had crossed the most uninhabitable locale on the earth — a place that may never have been crossed since. Courage and endurance are the marks of brave men but this entire expedition was contrary to all common sense.

The balance of this horror story, the trials and tribulations of David Porter and his company, does not include Hiram I. Bearss directly so it will only briefly be covered. This conclusion is very important to what happened after the *Sturm und Drang* of the march. It affected nearly every Marine officer on the island of Samar.

Major Waller was barely back at Basey when he sent Lieutenant Day and Surgeon Lung with a party back to search for Porter. Two days later, as sick as he was, he joined them and led that party along the trail. All traces of the path followed had been eliminated by heavy rains. After seven days of searching, the new group was also beginning to get into bad shape. Leeches and fever were of epidemic proportions. Finally, on 11 January, Waller himself returned to Basey. There he was immediately placed in the hospital, where he collapsed. He was suffering from a severe fever, his eyes were swollen shut from leech bites, and one of his ankles was twice its normal size from a sprain. At 45 Waller was much too old for this kind of punishment. He would never again be the same healthy man he had been before Samar.

After treating Waller, Dr. Lung went on to some other patients and Waller asked the attending corpsman to swab his hugely swollen right ankle with iodine. The corpsman complied and by the next morning the right ankle was much more serious than the untreated one. In fact, it looked so bad the doctor believed that Waller had gangrene. Thoughts of amputation were seriously bandied about. But the doctor wasn't a butcher and he managed to treat Waller without any cutting. Waller was terribly sick with an extreme fever and would continue to be so for some time to come. Because of this, his direction over his battalion wasn't as meticulous as it should have been. The lack of supervision was not due to anything but his illness.

Dr. Lung made Waller's junior officers aware that he was in tough shape and that they should do everything possible to relieve him of onerous duties. Dunlap tried. He climbed out of his bed and did move about trying to take on the commander's load but he too was ill and was forced back to bed. By 18 January, Waller's fever varied between 101.2 in the morning to 105 degrees in the afternoon.

But what had happened to Porter and his group since Bearss and Murphy had left them? He had, briefly, remained where they had left him awaiting Waller's return. In the afternoon he had sent one of his men to look for the Waller party. That man returned in two hours and told Porter that he could find no trace of them. Porter was now reduced to one officer, Lieutenant Williams, and 40 Marine enlisted men, two native guides and two dozen bearers. His remaining supplies were down to a couple of cans of bacon and one ration of coffee. Porter and Williams had a powwow. It was obvious that Waller's party was delayed and might appear the next morning, but then again, they might never show up. It was then that Porter made the decision that was contrary to Waller's implicit instructions. He decided to head back toward Lanang taking the same route that they had coming out. Since he was in somewhat better physical shape than was Williams, Porter split the party once again. He would take Sergeant Quick and a detail of the six strongest Marines plus six carriers with him. Williams and his party were to slowly make their way back as best they could. Porter's intention was to make a rapid return trip with supplies for the men left behind. Porter left a message for Waller in a tin can tied to a tree, telling him what had transpired. Of course, the message was never received.

After a few hiking days of horror, Porter left several men in his group, who were unable to continue, at Arasares. They were left besides a small sweet potato patch which Porter was convinced, correctly, would provide them with sufficient food until he returned. Porter's detachment was now split three ways. On the evening of 11 January, Porter, Quick, and two other enlisted Marines fell into Lanang. Captain Pickering immediately formed a rescue party led by Lt. Kenneth Williams, USA, consisting of two corporals, eight privates and a medical corpsman. They brought shelter halves and 300 rations.

The first day, 12 January, a swollen river rose to extreme heights and swept the boats back down to the ocean. River conditions limited them severely. On the fourteenth of January they were able to make another attempt and during the following three days they finally reached the point that Waller had made on the first day. There they found the four Marines that Porter had left behind. Weak but alive, they were saved.

Meanwhile, Lt. Alexander S. Williams and the main party, after resting for an hour again marched eastward toward Lanang. Over the mountaintop they went. What had taken them but a few hours to descend a few days before, now took two and one-half days to climb. Descending on the eastern side took up the next two days. Here Williams allowed the men a day and one-half of rest. This included time to collect any food they might find in the jungle. Meanwhile, the natives were becoming a severe disciplinary problem and intensely worried Williams. Williams spoke some Spanish and had been able to converse with the guide named Slim. But Slim seemed no longer to be able to understand what Williams was saying. In addition, he was convinced that Slim and the other natives were gathering food and holding out on giving any to the Marines. At this point the Marines rifles were so encased in rust and mud that they were practically worthless.

During his tenure as commander on the march, Williams did everything humanly possible to control the natives, but their surliness became quite extreme. By this time the Marines were close to their end and it appeared that the natives realized that. Each day the Marines would march for a few hours and then fall down in huddles to sleep. At one point Williams was attacked and badly cut by the bolo-swinging bearers. He also lost his pistol to one of the natives who by good fortune didn't know how to use it. Sergeant John McCaffery and several other Marines came to his assistance but were too weak to even pull the bolts on their rusted rifles. Their three attackers got away across the river and disappeared into the brush. Williams didn't have life threatening cuts and was able to gather his Marines together to discuss the matter. They decided that they must kill all the natives before they themselves were done in.

They spent a terribly restless night, expecting an attack at any moment. Fortunately on the next morning, 18 January, they were discovered by Lt. Kenneth Williams' rescue party. But they had been greatly reduced. Ten Marines had fallen by the wayside during this most terrible portion of the "Long March." Upon arrival at Lanang, Williams, from his sickbed, told a still very ill Porter how badly the native bearers had treated them. The natives made their way down to Lanang via one of the boats and, at Porter's orders, were immediately arrested. On 19 January the Marines were all loaded aboard the *Arayat* and the following day they arrived at Tacloban.

This was the end of the march but was just the beginning of what developed into a major cause célèbre and created a worldwide demand for Waller's head. The liberals in the United States were also anxious to get the head of him and every Marine in the Philippines, and they nearly succeeded.

Of the officers Waller left behind at Basey, 1st Lt. John H.A. Day stands out as the most controversial figure.[45] Day was the only Marine officer whom Waller never commended. He has also been considered to be the officer whom Waller wrote of as causing many of his problems. In his final report on the Samar campaign, he wrote of "the vain boastfulness of one of my officers" as leading to his ultimate problem — the Army court-martial. Day must have had his own agenda but exactly what it was has never been made clear.

With Waller missing someplace between Lanang and Basey, and Dunlap up near Sohotón, day-to-day operations were directed mainly by Lieutenant Day. A serious morale problem was created with the unpopular Day in command. In addition, the recent massacre at Balangiga and swarms of natives estimated in the thousands around and about Basey caused a declining esprit among the enlisted men. These and other problems would face Waller upon his return and would require rectification.

Capt. Robert H. Dunlap, in actual overall command during Waller's absence, was away on the Sohotón River preparing for Waller's return and had no direct control. The other officers, Surgeon George A. Lung, USN, 1st Lt. James T. Bootes, the quartermaster, and 2d Lt. John P.V. Gridley, went efficiently about their business. Day, the battalion adjutant and commander of the 20-member native police force, had, on nearly a daily basis, direct access to General Smith. He was the officer who brought Waller the message from Smith about creating a "howling wilderness." He would also be the officer who would bring the wrath of the civilian population back home down on the army in the Philippines, and eventually on Waller himself.

During the major's absence there were many rumors floating about as to how the local *insurrecto* leader, one Juan Colinares, was threatening to attack Basey; that he would do to the Marines at Basey what he did to the army at Balangiga. It was a load of hyperbole but it sounded bad to the inhabitants of the town. Dunlap had tried to find Colinares' camp but had been unsuccessful. On 20 December Gridley had gone out with a 20-man patrol south of Basey. On the return trip 1st Sgt. James Murphy noticed that one of the carriers was staggering under what was obviously an excessively heavy load. Murphy tried to help the man and was stabbed twice in the back by an iron spearhead the man was carrying under his shirt. Mur-

Brigadier General Robert H. Dunlap was a direct appointment from civilian life in 1898. He served in the Philippines, China, Samar, and at Vera Cruz. Later, as an artilleryman, he became CO of a U.S. Army artillery regiment in France. In 1931, Dunlap was sent as a student at the French military school *L'Ecole Supérieure de Guerre* in Paris. He was killed while saving a French woman who had been overwhelmed in an avalanche.

phy gave him what for—two quick rounds from his pistol reduced the scoundrel to a heap on the ground. Marines and many of the native carriers were now more jumpy than ever before with the fear of a native uprising. The more peaceable natives no more wanted death and destruction than did the Marines. Most of them wanted the Americans to get the hell out of their homeland but weren't willing to kill or die for it. Most of the Marines wanted to live as long and safely as was possible. But, as is so often the case, the innocent, or the nearly so, are always targets for someone more aggressive. No one could label the Filipinos lethargic. If anything they were high-strung even at the most peaceable times, possibly the result of Spanish overlordship for so many centuries.

The situation at Basey remained calm but uneasy. Nothing of substance, other than Dunlap's departure for Sohotón, happened during the next few days—except that Day returned from General Smith's headquarters at Tacloban with a most interesting five-page circular. It was typewritten and dated "December 24, 1901" and addressed to all station commanders in the 6th Separate Brigade, which of course included Waller. It wasn't marked for "eyes only" so Day had read it and had also shown it to Bootes. As an officer Bootes didn't rate very high in Waller's estimation and consequently had been given nondemanding roles.[46] Below is a portion of what Smith had produced. Perhaps Bootes wasn't a topnotch Marine, at least at this stage of the game, but he could read and this is what he saw:

> The policy to be pursued in this Brigade, from this time on, will be to wage War in the sharpest and most decisive manner possible....
> Every native ... will be regarded as an enemy until he has conclusively shown that he is a friend....
> Short, severe wars are the most humane in the end. No civilized war, however civilized, can be carried on a human basis....
> In waging this war officers will be guided by the provisions of General Order Number One Hundred, 1863.[47]

General Order Number One Hundred is the rule that Abraham Lincoln promulgated and issued for the treatment of the South and which was the basis for German control of conquered France at the end of the Franco-Prussian War. General Smith had fully adopted and implemented Sherman's theory that "war is hell." Bootes and Day read it. Each quickly understood the rules for their future conduct and the treatment to be meted out to the Filipinos. The balance of the five pages was a diatribe against all natives but most especially against the wealthy classes. It wasn't all that different from Smith's diatribe of 23 October. It just reinforced the message. When Waller was capable, he was given the above message to read and implement. He was still under the shadow of his exertion and perhaps didn't clearly realize the implications of what he read. Technically, it was Federal policy, but far from what the American public would accept from its representatives.

During an interrogation by Major Edwin F. Glenn, the Army judge advocate of the Basey region, rent collector Petronillo Jacosalen implicated Joaquin, the town's *presidente*, in his devious undertakings. This information flowed (pardon the pun) from the results of the water-hose treatment on Jacosalen. When his belly was gurgling and near bursting he blurted out Joanquin's name as a collaborator. Day was quite close to the *presidente* and this outburst was, to say the least, very embarrassing. Out went the police, and Joaquin was soon in the hoosegow for the same water cure.

Joaquin lasted about as long as did Jacosalen. Several other names of leaders were brought out during the interrogation. One was a man named Acevedo, as it happened another embarrassing "friend" of Day's. The location of a store of weapons in the town was even more troubling to Day who had readily accepted the friendliness of all those who were now listed as scoundrels. The final result was that the town was to be subjected to a massacre just like Balangiga. Only this time, instead of the unprepared 9th Infantry it was to be Waller's incapacitated Marines. Day wasn't personally involved but this pointed out his carelessness in conducting his office as police chief.

Major Glenn ordered Joaquin, Jacosalen and Acevedo shot and the local priest, who was also part of the conspiracy, thrown into the local hoosegow. The three ringleaders were duly executed on 6 January 1902 but, seemingly, even that did nothing to soothe the nerves of Day and Bootes. Even Waller's commiseration with them upon his return accomplished little. But he had little time to spend with those two. His men from Lanang, as we have already seen, were in bad shape and needed his attention.

Private William J. McCanless, one of the men who had traveled with Waller, passed along important information to his commander. He had heard some voices speaking of "Captain" Victor, he who had tried to steal Waller's bolo, as being with the raiders of Balangiga. Victor was arrested by the sergeant of the guard and thrown into jail to await the return of Waller from his search for the remnants of Porter's party.[48]

On 15 January, after a conference with General Smith, Waller ordered Bearss to take 46 Marines to garrison the town of Quinapundan.[49] Bearss was one of the few in the Samar party to have survived and was still able to serve on active duty. The order was worded:

Samar, January 16, 1902.
Captain H.I. Bearss.
Company D, First Battalion
First Regiment, U.S. Marines.

Sir:
1. You will take your company and proceed by [the] *Panay* to mouth of Quinapundan River, disembark, march to Quinapundan [town] and garrison that place. Take all company property, buzzacoat [?] — 30 days supplies for troops, with 30 days additional supplies for native carriers, one colt's [sic] gun with 10,000 rounds of ammunition.

Necessary equipage and medical supplies will be furnished you.

2. Arriving at Quinapundan, form your camp and stockade it, or tear down walls of the burned church and fortify it. Camp. Clear all of the grounds and territory of the insurgents supposed to be there. Make weekly reports of all your expeditions.

By command of the Major Commanding

J.P.V. Gridley, 2d Lt. Adjutant.[50]

Other than excursions into the field from Olongapo, this was the first independent command held by Bearss. On the same day, Waller also sent an order to Capt. Arthur J. Matthews, who now commanded at Balangiga, to provide Bearss with an additional 25 noncommissioned officers and men when the *Panay* arrived. These men were for duty at Quinapundan and were to be placed under the direct command of 2d Lt. Frank Halford, but as part of Bearss' overall command.

Shortly after having given Bearss that order, both Dunlap and Dr. Lung tried to get Waller to reverse himself. They believed, and rightly so it seems, that to send Bearss away would weaken Basey to a dangerous degree. With 30 Marines in the hospital only 45 men would be left to garrison Basey. In the event of a forceful attack by a determined enemy Basey might very well fall. Also, Bearss seemed to be the one senior Marine officer of the battalion who was in good physical shape. He took with him 1st Lt. Charles C. Carpenter and Assistant Surgeon Richard B. Williams, USN. This reduced the healthy and competent officers at Basey to just John Horace "Horrible" Arthur Day. As always Waller was adamant, refusing to alter his orders. As directed, Bearss moved out towards Quinapundan.

At Quinapundan

Shortly after arrival on the coast, just a few miles below Quinapundan, the Marine column was attacked twice and each time drove the attackers away. On 19 January a camp was established at their destination after which they were again attacked. It was estimated that the natives had about 12 rifles but didn't know how to use them very well. Lucky Marines, unlucky *insurrectos*. Lieutenant Carpenter was camping in a nearby area and arrived during this latter disturbance. He and his 15 men managed to outflank the natives and soon routed them. According to reports of the time, Carpenter was a six-footer and physically huge. Someone, perhaps Bearss, made the statement that Carpenter could have easily lifted the much smaller Bearss with one hand. Perhaps an exaggeration, but he was just the kind of fellow to have around during a fight.

They named their base Camp Goodrell, in honor of the Marine brigade commander. Their next moves were to clear all the brush about the place and then to dig trenches. Several times on the twenty-first they were fired upon. Again Carpenter with some men got around their flank and let them have it. At this point Gridley let go with his Colt, which also made quite an impression. The bodies of the dead were buried without pomp or circumstance.

The next day Sgt. Bryan McSwiney with 15 Marines went out and scouted the countryside. He returned with a quantity of Nipa with which Bearss had a kitchen and mess hall partitioned off in the local church. Hiram then sent 1st Sgt. John S. Lipscomb out with a detachment to scout in the opposite direction. At some great distance they were fired upon but without casualties. On the twenty-fifth, Lts. Carpenter and Austin C. Rogers, with 30 Marines, engaged in some patrolling activity in the nearby mountains. They were fired upon but managed to kill four natives. For the next few days it rained constantly, limiting Hiking Hiram's favorite exercise, but by the twenty-ninth the weather was clear. So, out went Bearss and Carpenter with an expedition consisting of 25 enlisted men. They hiked in a southeasterly direction and captured two carabao. Sgt. Lipscomb went out with a detachment and captured four more carabao. Most probably there was a barbeque that night and for several more thereafter. A couple of days later Lieutenant Rogers also went out looking for game and found some. In the process they nailed five bolo men. As Bearss' report said,

> The heavy volleying was heard in camp, and I at once started to Lieutenant Rogers' assistance. By the time I arrived, he had so thoroughly done his work that I was not needed.... The entire command has done excellent work. I cannot speak too highly of Lieutenant Carpenter's conduct on the night of January 21 and the conduct of Lieutenant Rogers this day. They have been as valuable in camp as out of camp.[51]

In further reports to Waller, Bearss described the other events occurring in his area. The bolo men had 20 rifles and put them to pretty good use with volley firing. Company D's Sergeant McSwiney was shot in the hand and groin and later would expire because of these wounds. In addition, a native guide was wounded during the same period. So far American casualties were moderate and would continue to be, but conditions were abhorrent.

Like his mentor Waller, Bearss was quick to note his subordinates and their work, including Surgeon Williams. He was also quick to mention and credit the U.S. Navy and Army forces helping the Marines in that area — usually praising their efforts to the highest degree. If one's subordinates and associates are doing well, then obviously they are well led. And Bearss was doing very well. He would always give his officers and men credit, which helped create a meaningful level of loyalty toward him throughout his Marine career. This was his first major operational command and his men were doing vicious things to the *insurrectos*, which was what he, and they, were being paid to do. He received official compliments for his handling of the area and rebels in the 1934 award ceremony when he was awarded his Medal of Honor. Part of his citation stated, "Colonel Bearss also rendered distinguished public service in the presence of the enemy at Quinapundan River, Samar, Philippine Islands, on 19 January 1902."[52]

Upon arrival at Quinapundan one of the first orders Bearss issued was that no native be allowed to fish, except by special permit. This was, of course, a terrible hardship since fishing was the primary source of their food and livelihood, even more than hunting or planting. Fish was plentiful while game might not be and crops might easily fail. Bearss had his reasons. The law-abiding native had no trouble getting a permit, while those suspected of providing supplies and food to the *insurrectos* had a difficult lesson to learn. Of course, anyone that could, disobeyed the order. That was their first mistake. They didn't need to make any more. Bearss was a great teacher.

One day, shortly after the order was posted, when Bearss returned from "hunting," he spotted numerous natives out in boats about a mile or so offshore, fishing. Not many permits had been issued so obviously some who were fishing were in troubled waters. He called Gridley and told him to cancel the fishing. Gridley at once had the Colt machine gun and two three-inch pieces set up on the beach. This was the same Gridley that Bearss had met while on duty aboard the USS *Michigan* on Lake Erie. He was also the son of Dewey's famous naval captain at Manila Bay. So, Bearss reportedly commanded, "You may fire when ready, Gridley." The story is that Gridley caused much anguish and discomfiture to those within the boats. They paddled in every direction and some, those that found themselves in "hot water," so to speak, swam for the shore. It was the last time anyone had to entice any native to obtain a permit. As a consequence, the rebels noted a rapid decline in their fresh fish supplies, and there was soon a decline in the numbers of bands operating in this area.

Back to Basey

In mid–February after Bearss' expedition returned to Basey, he soon had other duties to perform. One such was an unsuccessful effort to flag down the commander of a gunboat whom Waller desired to speak with. When Bearss was called upon to stop the boat it was well along on its journey toward the San Juanico straits. Out into the bay went Bearss, in a native *banca*, propelled by four natives. Not knowing of Bearss' attempt to contact them, the gunboat just put on steam and hauled off about as fast as it could go.

Bearss was now out in the bay, some distance from shore, with four natives who were clamoring to head toward Leyte, which was now much closer. Bearss was no dummy. He realized that he could have been in great danger if he allowed them to proceed to where there were no Americans he could rely upon. Somewhat desperate by this time, he gave orders for the boat to return back to Basey. At that point he saw one of the rowers lift his paddle so as to strike him over his head. Bearss pulled his revolver and jumped to the back of the boat. Then he ordered the natives to row back to Basey, "or else." The pistol was sufficient inducement. Acting as his own coxswain, he compelled the crew to obey. Back to Basey they headed. In the meantime it was apparent to Waller that his young officer was in serious trouble. He immediately had the town's *presidente*, the man who selected the rowers, thrown into the hoosegow with a threat that if anything happened to Bearss it would cost his head. This didn't really help poor old Bearss out there on the briny, so Waller sent Dunlap out with several boats loaded with Marines. That rescue party didn't make contact with Bearss until later that evening but by then he had the "situation well in hand." When they finally returned to Basey the four rowers were added to the *presidente*'s party.

Things were happening to the native population at Basey and trouble was expanding for Waller's Marines. As the adage goes (and it is especially true in the old Marine Corps), first an officer or enlisted man was decorated for valor and courage and perhaps for winning a battle, or even victory. Then he was court-martialed for disobedience or for exceeding his authority in execution of the deed. This is what happened to Major Littleton Waller Tazewell Waller. It also swept up John Day in its talons. But if any Marine was guilty of enlarging what could easily have been a modest difficulty, Day was the man to do it.

As previously mentioned, the victory over Spain was celebrated far and wide in the continental United States. Letting poor little Cuba make its own way in the world was exactly why the United States went to war, but taking and holding the Philippines was not satisfactory to many Americans. For many years citizens of the United States had been complaining about the other imperialist nations: Britain, France, the Netherlands, even little Portugal, among a few others. With the acquisition of that island archipelago, the United States was now down in the mud with the rest. The nation had "sunk that low" and many Americans didn't like it.[53] The attitude of stateside Americans is important in understanding how and why Waller was tried at court-martial and how that impacted on Hiram Bearss and his future as a Marine.

Elihu Root, the secretary of war, put pressure on Major General Adna Chaffee, the U.S. Army officer commanding, to clean up the growing mess in his army. Chaffee, in turn, put pressure on Jake Smith, commanding the 6th Brigade on Samar. That came rattling down hard on the fighting men. Waller was the most active commander and consequently was the goat. His Marines were fighting and winning on Samar and Chaffee's army hadn't been overly successful there. Besides, Chaffee wasn't all that fond of Marines, so was unsympathetic to Waller's plight.

While Bearss was at Quinapundan, there was constant unrest in and around Basey and Balangiga. As we have seen, while Waller was in his hospital bed with a raging fever, 1st Lt. John Day was in command of all the Marine operations in and around Basey. Many of the men were sick — some from their exertions, from Lanang to Basey. There were many others suffering from the rotten conditions in and around the two main Marine camps. The dilemma that Day and the surgeon, Lung, had to face at each sick call was whether those obviously sick men should be allowed to lie in bed to effect a cure, or instead sent out on various duties related to the protection of their respective bases.

Day never had enough Marines to fill all the places that required men. So he, too, was under a great deal of pressure to perform as expected of an officer of Marines. The problem was that he wasn't the right man and he was at the wrong time. There were times when old "Horrible," the men's nickname for Day, had to physically push and pull the men into formation or curse those who couldn't move. Of course, while this was happening, the natives were squatting and watching the deterioration of the command and daily growing bolder. From the surrounding countryside the Marines were being pelted with rifle shots from occasional snipers that caused little damage but helped to erode morale. Day had no extra men to send out to hunt the snipers down.

Day was essentially the only officer on duty therefore he was always the officer of the day. Gridley was often ill and Bootes wasn't yet fit to command. He slept fitfully every night, making at least five trips to each guard post to make sure the men were awake and alert. He was also every other duty officer, including provost and officer of the guard.[54]

The barracks, or what passed for them, were scattered all about the town of Basey. This made the positions even more vulnerable. Most troublesome was the guardhouse, with a flimsy door, where over 100 native prisoners were now incarcerated. It was located over 100 yards from the headquarters building and guarded by a lone, usually ill, sentry with only his rifle to maintain order.

One day the new *presidente* of Basey brought a prisoner in to see

Major Waller, who, as sick as he was, made every effort to fulfill his function as the commanding officer. Day spotted the activity and rushed over to make sure nothing was put over on the Major. During the course of the interrogation of the prisoner it came out that the man was a subordinate of the infamous Joaquin, who had been executed, although he wasn't aware of that. Day, quivering with rage at this information, requested permission to execute the prisoner at once. As the surgeon later testified, Waller wasn't able to coherently listen and make that kind of decision. According to Day's testimony, Waller "ordered me to shoot the man as a spy."[55] Obviously, someone was less than truthful.

Day pulled together a firing squad with the only two men immediately available. They were Privates Omer Kresge, a cook, and James McGee, an orderly. The three men with the prisoner in between them marched him down toward the river and had the prisoner stand, back to them, a few feet from the water. Kresge fired at his head and McGee at his back. Then with his pistol Day gave him the *coup de grâce*. Day then ordered the local native chief of police to leave the body on display for all to see. He believed that would intimidate the natives. Day told a delirious Waller what he'd done and then spoke to Lung and Bootes, and later to Dunlap and Gridley about it. Interestingly, none of the officers mentioned ever admitted that they had any personal knowledge of that killing on 19 January. Later it came out, under questioning, that Lieutenant Day had several times mentioned to 1st Sgt. James Murphy that he would like to "kill every goddamn GooGoo in town with the cannon and settle our scores once and for all."[56] That kind of talk would not have surprised any Marine because for the most part they all felt much the same way. Being subjected to guerrilla warfare can make regular troops very cruel and bloodthirsty. Besides, he wasn't stating anything very different from what the area commanding general had been spouting off.

The following day the *Arayat* arrived with the load of sick Marines from Lanang. As soon after arrival as possible, Captain Porter had Sgt. John Quick deliver a verbal message for Major Waller, describing the events of Lieutenant William's tribulations with the native carriers who had done some wicked deeds to the Marines on the trail. While Quick was waiting to see Waller he met Captain Dunlap and told him the story about the carriers. Somewhat altered and enlarged, the story swept the Marine compound. According to the rumors ten Marines had been slaughtered by the natives, ten more died of starvation and Lt. Williams was in the local hospital, near death from the wounds inflicted by those same carriers.

As soon as possible, Quick was ushered in to see the still very sick Waller where he recited Porter's story verbatim, including the proposition that the natives be shot. "What would you recommend, sergeant?" Waller asked the superior noncom. Quick responded, "They should be shot, sir, I would shoot them all down like dogs."[57] There was obviously no question in Quick's mind, and probably the same could be said of all the other enlisted men and officers.

Waller was obviously impressed. Both his closest subordinate, Porter, and his most trusted noncommissioned officer, John Quick, had no hesitation about executing the recalcitrant carriers. He then called in Dunlap and Day who, when told what Quick and Porter had said, both agreed "the natives should be shot." As sick as Waller was, he didn't enter lightly into execution of prisoners. He needed and wanted advice and support. After this session Waller remembered Victor, the man who tried to carve him up with his own bolo knife. It was time to settle accounts.

Calling together Private McCanless and Cpl. John H. Carroll, who spoke Spanish and would interpret, he then called for Victor. An attempt was made to interrogate him but he would say nothing. As Waller later said, "He just stood there and trembled." Waller then ordered Victor to be shot with the others. Day took both Kresge and McGee with Victor and executed him in the middle of the street. The lieutenant then left him lying dead — it was the same warning as with the previous unnamed prisoner.

Since Day was the officer upon whom the heavy responsibility fell, we should take a quick look at the condition he was reported to be in at the time of these executions. Later reports from some of the enlisted men indicate that he was constantly and heavily under the influence of alcohol. Because he was fatigued from being on duty nearly 24 hours of every day, it wouldn't be farfetched to believe that he relied upon the bottle for comfort. Day later admitted that when he met the boat carrying Porter and his badly abused troops on 20 January, he was "trembling with a cold rage." He was extremely excited and easily agitated. Whatever his physical condition was, he was reputed to have relished the entire bloody business.

The executions continued on. Quick identified two natives as being "OK!" and they were released, but many of the others were on the receiving end of the Lee rifles. The charges against the natives were never committed to writing though there was continual reference to charges being brought against them. In other words there were no records of any trials, nor even physical interrogations, like the water torture so commonly used. They were executed in groups as well as singularly. Some of the Marine survivors made their way to where the executions were being held and reported that they enjoyed every minute of it. This sometimes callous surveillance was later brought up during Waller's trial so as to indicate the injudicious manner in which the executions were held, and probably to add for the record how beastly all Marines were. There is little question that senior army officers, including Chaffee, were out to ensure that it was going to be Marines who paid the price demanded by the press back home.

By 21 January, Waller's temperature was down to just 99 degrees and he was capable of making a report to Jake Smith at brigade headquarters. The telegram read, "It became necessary to expend eleven prisoners. Ten who were implemented [sic] in the attack on Lt. Williams and one who plotted against me."[58]

Although the telegram reports 11 executions, it appears there were others who weren't being counted. Chaffee somehow learned of Waller's telegram and of the executions. Without delay he arrived at Tacloban on 23 January, breathing hellfire and brimstone. "Smith, have you been having any promiscuous killing in Samar for fun?" Smith said he didn't understand what Chaffee was getting at and added, "No, sir." Chaffee then reported that he'd heard tell of killings in Basey. Smith baldly stated, "I knew nothing of it until then," waving the telegram. He then added that he would personally look into the matter.

Chaffee didn't give him any opportunity to do so. In a few days a member of the U.S. Army inspector general's staff appeared with written orders from Chaffee to take over the probe. Smith smelled a plot to make him the goat and, as soon as he could, warned Waller of the impending investigation. Waller, who was just about recovered from his terrible exertions, was less concerned. He was too busy writing his report of what transpired on the long walk. He apparently had no idea of what was coming nor the seriousness of the problem.

In his report, Waller acknowledged that ten marines had died during the ordeal and two more had since died in the hospital, 12 in all. In other words, he lost nearly 25 percent of his original command of 50 men. Those were heavy losses without sufficient and appreciable gains. For obvious reasons, neither Smith nor Waller cast a poor light on what transpired nor on the value of the crossing. Perhaps the two dozen casualties, Marines and executed natives might have told a different story had they been interviewed.[59] On 19 February an order arrived from 6th Brigade Headquarters: "Upon arrival of the transport *Lawton* and the embarkation thereon of the Battalion of the U.S. Marines under the command of Major L.W.T. Waller, U.S. Marine Corps, this battalion will stand relieved from duty in the Sixth Separate Brigade."[60]

In other words, the Marines had paid their dues. They were now going back to what must have seemed like heaven compared to the experiences of the previous four months. On 26 February the *Lawton* arrived at Tacloban and the Marines embarked. Smith was there and had kind words to say for his friend Waller and his command: "You are as fine a group of soldiers as has ever served under my command and I have been an officer for forty years."

As their ship proceeded north and passed Catbalogan the USS *New York* was in the harbor. The entire crew stood at attention and as their colors were dipped the band played the Death March in memory of the Marine dead on Samar. The latter ship then joined the caravan and escorted the Marines to Cavite at which they arrived on 29 February. A cheering crowd welcomed them while Colonel James Forney, now commanding the Marine Brigade in the Philippines, granted them a full month's pay and five days to spend it in.[61] He also allotted them the best quarters in town to enjoy themselves and become civilized once again. But as the saying goes, "It ain't over until the fat lady sings."

Waller appeared before Maj. Gen. Adna Chaffee to report in, and was welcomed with, as he later said, "a charge of murder." The charge was for killing 11 natives of the islands and his court-martial would begin within three weeks.

Waller was in serious trouble. Someone had to pay for all the ruckuses in the United States. Congress was in an uproar. That "someone" selected was the man on the spot.[62] Waller followed Smith's orders, although he could be accused of not being selective enough in those he accepted. Waller was not always well served by the officers surrounding him. Someone should have advised him not to indiscriminately carry out those orders from Smith. His physical and mental state were not of the highest measure immediately following the march. Simply stated, he didn't have anyone with sense to aid him. Most if not all his officers urged him to execute the natives and then stood aside, disclaiming any knowledge of the proceedings. Only those officers who were detached, such as Bearss, were not there and escaped any censure, then or now.[63] The only other officer who was also on the spot was 1st Lt. John H.A. Day. He had been duty officer and responsible for carrying out orders from Waller.

The Courts-martial

On 5 March 1902, Waller's trial began. It was convened by direct order of the president of the United States, who was under great pressure back home. Brig. Gen. William H. Bisbee, USA, like Smith an old Indian fighter, presided over the court as president. Major Henry P. Kingsbury, USA, was judge advocate. The charge was murder in violation of the 58th Article of

War. It was a long specification covering everything so consequently the trial lasted a long time. The army was going to "get" Waller so they built up a number of specious charges. Major William P. Biddle, USMC, was a member of the court and has also been accused of "going after" Waller because they were both candidates for the post of commandant of the Marine Corps.[64]

The *Manila Times*, a local English language rag, even went so far as to print a story that the natives had been excruciatingly tortured for days before they died. The Marines who had been there were furious and completely astounded by that story since that, at least, had never happened. In the newspapers back in the States, Waller was being called the Butcher of Samar and other equally affectionate epithets. The press had already tried and convicted him and were demanding his head. But he still had good use for it and managed to keep it for a while longer.

Captain Hiram Bearss was a witness for the defense. He was called to the stand on 25 March 1902, the fourth day of the trial. His testimony was primarily about the efforts of Victor to relieve Waller of his bolo and probably his life:

> Major Waller and I were sitting leaning against a tree. The major had kindly offered to let me have part of his blanket and I had fallen asleep. Suddenly the major jumped up, wakened me, and said someone had taken his bolo. I immediately got up and in looking around we found a native, one Captain Victor, just behind the tree. The bolo was found on the ground where the native had dropped it.

"Why did you give Victor the title 'captain'?" Hiram was asked.

> He was known among the natives as a captain, and had been a captain of insurrectos, so I was told.

The advocate asked Bearss a question which the defense counsel told the court was a leading question. It concerned Waller's statement that Victor was trying to assassinate him.[65] Then Bearss continued with his testimony:

> After finding the bolo there and the native nearby, the Major and I discussed it in an offhand sort of manner and we decided that he [Victor] must have intended to kill one or both of us as we were sleeping together.[66]

Bearss went on to say that Victor had been in the guard house when he left for Quinapundan on 17 January and he was aware that Victor had been shot while he was gone. That was the end of his testimony and he stood down.

Two things came up during the trial that put a different complexion on the entire mess. One was that Waller and his Marines had never been formally detached from the U.S. Navy when assigned to the U.S. Army. Consequently the U.S. Army had no legal jurisdiction over him or any Marines. Only the president of the U.S. could make that transfer, officially. The second, even more important in many ways, was General Smith's position. He initially betrayed Waller by claiming no knowledge of the orders to burn and kill, but was eventually forced to come around and admit that he had devised the instructions and had officially ordered Waller to carry them out.

On 8 April, the fourteenth day of the trial, it was Waller's turn to describe what his orders had been. He mentioned the orders he had to "kill and burn" and he also brought forward the information about the "Howling Wilderness," which Porter, Bearss and Day had witnessed. During this part of his defense he mentioned Admiral Rodgers, who he believed was present during several meetings with Smith. This set Bisbee off on a tirade. In order to preserve interservice harmony, Waller had to equivocate on that point. Once more, Waller's officers testified to having seen the message and having Waller explain that it was from Smith. Kingsbury didn't even bother to cross-examine them.

Smith was finally held up as the guilty person and the court was forced to release Waller from all charges. Despite his acquittal, this trial and the subsequent publicity destroyed any chances Waller might eventually have had to be the commandant. Instead, politically well connected Biddle was the man selected. Even after Biddle's sojourn, when Waller was once again up for serious consideration, someone placed a demeaning article in a national magazine rehashing the story of Samar. That finished Waller for ever. As Smedley Butler once said, "The doctor reported he had a stroke. What he really died of was a broken heart."[67]

Bearss received orders effective on 15 May 1902 detaching him from the 1st Marine Brigade and returning him to the United States via the U.S. Army transport *Kilpatrick*. He was glad to leave. He had enough of the Philippines to last him for quite awhile. Hiram had been gone from all his loved ones, including Adelaide Louise Madden, for two and one-half years. He was now a very experienced 27-year-old captain of Marines who had earned plaudits for his leadership and ease in assuming responsibility. Notre Dame, Purdue, DePauw and Norwich were his training grounds. His raising of a band of volunteers to fight Spain was now four years past.

5

Recruiting, Panama, Marriage and Back to the Philippines

Bearss' ship reached San Francisco on 19 June, and he immediately reported to Mare Island, remaining there until 27 June. His orders that date directed him to entrain for New York, which he reached on 23 July after a delay en route at Ridgeview. As could be expected, his folks and friends were glad to see him. Rumors abounded of his having seen great action. Bearss was making a name for himself on his home ground. No one at Ridgeview, nor even those in Peru who knew him, were greatly surprised. He had been a hell-raiser, and no one expected that he had changed all that much. Some, perhaps, felt sorry for the Filipinos.

His first post was at the Brooklyn navy yard, at which he remained only one week. But even in that short period he quickly became, depending upon one's interpretation, a boon or bane to the commanding officer. Colonel Robert L. Meade had met this young man, so he was somewhat prepared for what to expect. Duty at the navy yard was largely drill, guard mount and parades. Meade was a character of the old school, hard and bitter towards his subordinates and superiors. Besides being the nephew of the famed Civil War general he had a brother who was an admiral, with whom he also didn't get along. At this particular time he was encouraging the intense dislike of the president of the United States, Theodore Roosevelt.[1]

At this time, Marine Corps personnel were below quota, and the commandant put heavy emphasis on recruitment. It was necessary to obtain volunteers for the expanded Corps.[2] His report to the secretary of the navy said in part, "Vigorous measures are being taken to stimulate recruiting, additional substations being opened to the regular recruiting districts, and offices established in Chicago, Illinois and — another in Indianapolis, Indiana."[3]

Insofar as Chicago and Indianapolis were concerned, Bearss constituted the "vigorous measures." On the 30th of July, he was detached from the Brooklyn navy yard and proceeded under orders to Chicago for the purpose of establishing a Marine recruiting office in that city. From that base he also established recruiting substations in Milwaukee and Indianapolis. His arrival in Chicago was delayed until 14 August 1902 by another stop at Ridgeview.

The selected office in Chicago was located on Clark Street, on the second floor of an old building with outside stairs to climb. No doubt the rent was cheap. Bearss' recruiting detail was composed of him and perhaps a second officer, along with several noncommissioned officers and privates. Recruitment was conducted under U.S. Navy regulations, which irked Bearss. As part of the naval service, the Marine Corps was, it seemed, always getting the dirty end of the stick. The navy doctors made sure that few, if any, prospective Marine applicants were physically acceptable. Amazingly, all those Marine rejects made their way into the navy. Since there were no doctors in the Marine Corps the navy supplied all those required. Hiram requested that the local doctor be "surveyed and condemned, then thrown on the dump." How that all turned out isn't known but you can be quite sure that Bearss didn't lose out. He never did. Evidently, after this imbroglio, the Corps began receiving its share of recruits, at least in his district.[4]

By late fall he had completed his task in Chicago and was also headed toward success at Indianapolis. Russell Harrison, a Bearss family friend and son of the former president, Benjamin Harrison, located space for him in Indianapolis. During this period Bearss obtained a 15-day leave and had a chance to go to Ridgeview for the Christmas holidays. The *Peru Journal* and *Chronicle and Republican* gave him a headline worthy of any Marine: "Hail the Conquering Hero Comes, Sound the Horns, and Beat the Drums." Bearss loved it. He strutted about town in his dress uniform — it was a joyous yuletide for him. Meanwhile, Louise wasn't far from his thoughts. He sent her a five-pound box of candy, an opal brooch, and gloves.

At 27 he had held several important posts in the Marine Corps, in combat and in administrative duties. But he also found time to promote himself and the Corps. Back to Indianapolis he went to address the convention of the Military Order of the Loyal Legion. This was at the special invitation of a certain General Ketcham. While there he managed to meet with Booth Tarkington, the novelist and one of Indiana's most famous sons. He also had time for several well-known politicians and newspaper owners and editors. It was heady stuff and he was growing found of the spotlight.

5. Recruiting, Panama, Marriage and Back to the Philippines   83

On 21 December he was detached from recruiting duty, which was finished for now. He was ordered back to Brooklyn and Colonel Meade. He reported in on 9 January 1903. From now on there would be plenty of time for his Louise. They attended parties, went to dances and other festivities, and Hiram paid her compliment with many flowers. She loved them and he loved buying them for her. They were in love, and it would last through many years of trial and tribulation and many forced separations.

Shortly after his arrival they announced their engagement. But true love, for a Marine and his loved one, never runs smoothly. On 29 May he was detached from the Brooklyn navy yard Marine Barracks, and ordered to the USS *Panther* for duty with the Marine battalion already aboard. This time Bearss and his battalion would go down to the island of Culebra for training exercises in landing and establishing advanced bases.

The battalion of four companies of 104 enlisted men each was established at Philadelphia as directed by the General Board, an instrumentality of the U.S. Navy. Its function, though not as yet firmly established, would be to take and hold advanced naval bases. In order to hold the bases it was decided that the troops engaged must be trained in the following exercises:

> (a) The construction of field fortifications, gun emplacements, gun platforms and magazines.
> (b) The transportation of guns less than 8 inch caliber from ship to point of emplacement and the mounting of same.
> (c) The construction and operating of field telegraph and telephone lines, signal, searchlight and rangefinder stations.
> (d) The planting of mines, countermining and the operating of torpedoes for harbor defense.[5]

When the battalion arrived at Culebra, the Marines immediately set to work, and hard work it was, too. There was much digging of emplacements and it was all done by shovels wielded by enlisted Marines. Hauling five-inch guns up from their landing rafts to the newly prepared positions in that intense heat induced fatigue and thirst. How the enlisted men satisfied the latter isn't known, but the officers had access to some spirits. According to Smedley Butler, the navy only assisted the Marines with verbal advice.

This was a time in which there were serious clashes between the Marines and navy.[6] One such occurred to Bearss after he had been warmly entertained aboard Rear Admiral Joseph B. Coghlan's flagship. Although it wasn't the admiral himself doing the entertaining, it was royal and the warmth of the libations even made him feel warmth, temporarily, toward the navy. He was even courteously escorted back to the *Panther* via a motor launch. Unfortunately for Marine-navy relationships, the *Panther*'s duty officer was Lieutenant Edward H. Durrell, USN. For some time, there had been bad blood between the two men. Durrell had a history of anti–Marine activities during his 20-odd years in service. This time he was going to hang one Marine captain for some reason, any reason he could find. And the odds were in his favor.

After Bearss' arrival and the usual saluting of the flag, they exchanged a few heated remarks and then Bearss went below to his quarters. Durrell then betook himself to the ship's captain and reported Bearss as being under the influence of liquor. Bearss' mother hadn't raised any stupid children. He had freely imbibed of the admiral's liquor and if called upon would not have been able to walk a straight line. Down to his quarters he raced, removed his uniform and quickly got into the shower, as cold as he could make it. Removing himself and putting on his finest uniform, he waited for the call he knew would come.

Fit as a fiddle he reported to the captain as directed. When Hiram passed a startled Commander James P. Parker, USN, he was asked, "Why are they sending for you? There isn't anything the matter with you." Nevertheless, after a brief interrogation, the captain ordered Bearss to return to his cabin under arrest for being inebriated. In response, Bearss accused Durrell of being drunk on duty. Durrell had nearly fallen down as he had been making his report. Durrell was indeed sent to his quarters under arrest but Bearss was recommended for court-martial. Durrell, who had been drunk on duty, was suspended from duty for three days. The three-day restriction was (and may still be) used to get someone off the hook. In the service, once you have been punished for an infraction you cannot again be liable for the same "crime." Therefore, three days was enough to get Durrell out of jeopardy forever. But Bearss was in serious trouble. This was naval justice in action, which was another reason for the bad blood between the two services.

There was collusion. Durrell and the captain were in league one with the other and were determined to get Bearss. Upon receiving the recommendation for a general court-martial the admiral sent for Bearss. The admiral referred the papers to him and asked for an answer to the charges preferred against him. Bearss had been in plenty of scrapes before this. He, if anyone, would know how to get out of this mess. So he wrote on the paper with the charges, "Undoubtedly from Durrell's action, the *hospitality* of his [the admiral's] flagship had been too much for me" (Emphasis added).[7]

Admiral Coghlan read the notation and had Bearss appear before him

5. Recruiting, Panama, Marriage and Back to the Philippines

once again. He said with direct emphasis, "That was a hell of a note, to add that in." Hiram agreed but added, "The admiral was there when I left his ship and he is aware that I was then in reasonably good shape, as the admiral can attest." He added that he had nothing further to drink on the launch going home. The admiral admitted that Bearss was correct; he wasn't drunk when he left. After explaining what had really transpired aboard the *Panther* and how the captain had set him up with Durrell's help, the admiral restored him to duty. He also sent for the ship's captain. There is no record of the conversation between those two, but we can well imagine what some of it was. Admirals do not like to be set up by navy captains. We do know that the captain admitted that several days before the incident Bearss and Durrell had had a heated argument. It was about the relative merits of the navy and Marines. Other than that we can only imagine what might have been said between the two. Bearss was suspended from duty pending investigation between the seventeenth and twenty-second of August 1903.

Trying to nail Bearss was not the only reason the navy and Marines were at Culebra. The training exercises were designed specifically to develop a navy/Marine team that would be able to take and defend naval bases. This was a new navy, one which would have to project itself around the world in order to enforce the will of the United States. It needed muscle ashore that large shipboard guns couldn't provide. And it needed troops to make short work of any fools who tried to defend ground the United States wanted. So, in the course of this period, Marines set up gun emplacements and pretended to beat off attacks by another naval power.[8] It was a very hard time for the Marines on the ground as Bearss and Smedley Butler could affirm. Work on the ground required pickaxes, sledges, crowbars and dynamite. The guns had to be removed from the small boats and manhandled across the beach and then up to the high ground where they were to be installed. Mostly it was man-killing work in a very hot and humid environment. It had to be done — defending any bay from an attacking fleet was the end result. But the navy seemed anxious to make life for the Marines at Culebra very difficult. They were extremely successful in that endeavor. It left a lot of ill will between the services that has required many years to heal. Bearss was on that site for several months but left before the work was completed. Needless to say, he didn't enjoy this part of his service life.

Panama

Later that year the new president, Theodore Roosevelt, encouraged the people of the Isthmus of Panama to declare their independence from

Colombia. They did, and Colombia prepared to do what the northern part of the United States did in 1861. This time, the U.S. insisted it wasn't right to force any people to remain within a commonwealth if they didn't want to. Funny, that wasn't what Old Honest Abe had said. But here, just 42 years later, another president said it was OK to declare independence. And, he was going to send the muscle to make sure that the people of Panama could be "free." Bearss and his Marine battalion were the muscle.[9]

On 23 October 1903 Captain Bearss and the Marine battalion were transferred from the *Panther* to the USS *Dixie*. Their ship sailed from Philadelphia with Major John A. Lejeune in overall command of the Marines. The ship first proceeded to the island of Jamaica and while there received its orders to continue to Panama. It was all done in a clandestine manner. The *Dixie* went out of the harbor and headed north for one hour beyond the sight of land, to allay any speculation that newspaper people might have as to their destination. This alteration en route caused the ship to arrive off the coast two hours later than had previously been agreed upon, and the Panamanian rebels were concerned. So, as we can see, this was all prearranged. Teddy was an imperialist at heart no matter how much he damned Britain and France for that same practice.

Bearss' company was landed at Colón. They were advised by the street urchins crowding around that they were already two hours late. That delay would cost 4,000 U.S. dollars. An agreement had already been reached with the Colombian soldiers to not attack Colón. They were to board ship instead, receiving the four large ones if they did. Bearss' Marines had a very easy time landing, with little or no difficulty from any organized resistance. They first occupied the warehouses adjacent to the wharf and other public buildings. Then the American consul showed up. He was past 70, wore whiskers and hobbled with a cane. Bearss declared later that neither the consul, nor his black driver, who was at least as old as he, nor their bony old horse, would be much good in a fight. The consul directed the Marines to occupy the old offices formerly housing the French canal company, which they did. That, in fact, was the end of the "fighting." A few Colombian generals were arrested and their troops taken into custody, possibly for disturbing the peace. Colonel George F. Elliott showed up a bit later and assumed command from Lejeune.

Many of Bearss' pals were there: Waller, now a lieutenant colonel, Smedley Butler, and a host of other old friends. Almost immediately, when things settled down, Bearss engaged in his usual raucous behavior. While on horseback, he managed to have himself invited to dinner at a fine home. Leaving the horse tethered outside he went in and had a fine meal with his host and friends. Somehow the horse became free and waltzed up the staircase to where the diners were enjoying themselves. Needless to say, he and horse were no longer welcome. "Get the hell out and never come back," were the reported sentiments. On his return he stopped at Waller's encampment and engaged in several impromptu horse races—with side bets, of course. Then on (he must have been falling down drunk by now) to Colonel Elliott's headquarters. Knocking on several doors, including Elliott's, he said, in a changed voice, that they were wanted at the "general's quarters at once." And they all went, which raised the general's ire.[10] The entire camp was aroused. Hiram made his getaway by sliding down a hill on his horse. At the bottom he decided he had to cross the open-trestle train bridge. His horse stepped very gingerly from one tie to another. One mistake and down would go the horse and his rider. Even to a drunk the ravine below must have looked less than tantalizing.

The general seems to have seen all this and was so enraged that he allowed himself to say, "If the so-'n-so makes it across I won't do anything to him." He did, and the general didn't.[11] That was Bearss' luck. Riding on past the bridge for another three miles, he discovered a barroom, the Three Friends. It supplied the Marines with poisonous rotgut. He rode up and had his horse kick the bar down. Marines were slopping up the joy juice and he ordered them to their quarters. Bearss suspected the owner of running guns to the filibusters in Cuba. In those days, just to suspect gave you some authority.

It wasn't all fun and games. Sometimes they had to work. He and 1st Lt. Frank E. "Pat" Evans ventured out on a scouting party.[12] Its purpose was to determine if Colombian soldiers had come back across the border. In addition they were to also discover what the condition of the country was and whether there were any supplies that could be scrounged up. It was soon learned that no Colombian army could make it north through the jungle.

Nicholas Biddle, a *New York Herald* newspaper man, wrote of a great battle in which "hundreds of Marines were killed." Most of the story was written at a bar in Colón. According to his own reports, Biddle had started more revolutions than any other man in Latin America. His flexible fingers could deduce a bit of trouble anywhere, without benefit of seeing it himself. It was safer that way. He sent in a story on how a "Captain Hiram I. Bearss has killed a certain General Huerta." The truth was less complicated than that. Bearss had drunk Huerta under the table. Finally, when Huerta became paralyzed, Bearss ordered Pat Evans to throw him down the stairs. Pat did and enjoyed his assignment. That was the extent of the general being "killed." Biddle was lots of fun. He was well thought of by

Bearss and his pals. He could be counted upon to do whatever was right, when it suited him.

The American consul mentioned above came into the middle of something that was brewing by demanding that Biddle notify his papers that the navy and Marine officers were playing roulette and poker — gambling while on duty, oh my! Biddle told the consul that he understood that the consul had certain local gambling interests. "Think of my wife and children," the consul exclaimed. "Why don't you think of their wives and children?" was Biddle's response.[13]

Bearss once stole Biddle's clothes. They all had gone into a swimming pool and while no one was looking, Bearss grabbed Biddle's clothes and disappeared. Biddle was forced to walk back "naked and unadorned." That was a trick that Bearss had picked up on the banks of the Wabash, long ago and far away. Other things happened to brighten everyone's day. His old pal 1st Lt. Charles Carroll Carpenter from back at Quinapundan, was enjoying himself dining in a Spanish-type restaurant when a big fellow came in and made some nasty remarks about his eating habits. Carpenter, also a big fellow, hit the troublemaker smack on the jaw and knocked him cold. The proprietor came over and remonstrated with Carpenter, who in turn chased him out of his own restaurant. It didn't pay well to be in business where Marines were your customers. There was a load of overhead involved.

Another friend was Jimmy Haight, founder of the Stranger's Club. He elected himself vice-consul, mainly because he was the only man on the isthmus who had evening clothes. He was sort of a gent. He not only formed the Stranger's Club; he became the only voting member, because he was the only member. When he ran a local restaurant he would give a free bottle of expensive wine to any customer who proclaimed that it was his birthday. He had a lot of customers and most, at his expense, had many birthdays. There were many other situations and people like that, and Bearss must have had fun.

Thus, the intervention in Panama came to an end. It didn't include much shooting and killing but other than that, many of the Marines did have a good time while it lasted.

On 7 March 1904 Bearss received orders to return to the States aboard the *Dixie*. Once reported aboard he requested and was given permission by the captain, Comdr. Greenlief A. Merriam, USN, to return to shore one last time. When he arrived, a farewell party for him was in progress at the Washington Hotel. At about 1700 when he started to leave he noticed that the good ship *Dixie* was already moving out to sea. The attendees tried but failed to attract the crew's attention. He had missed the boat. Admi-

5. Recruiting, Panama, Marriage and Back to the Philippines

ral Coghlan, his old friend from Culebra, gave him special orders to "proceed north on the first available transportation." That saved his bacon. Bearss was having more and more close calls and sooner or later he was going to get into serious difficulties because of them.

But for now, his fabulous luck held. He managed to obtain booking on a faster ship also headed for New York, which would arrive before the *Dixie*. He landed at New York in the midst of a heavy snowstorm. His tropical weight khaki uniform without an overcoat did little to protect him in the extremely cold weather. Taking a taxi to a hotel he had a minor problem with the desk clerk who checked his records to see if Bearss was a wandering deserter or some other heinous character. Bearss managed to obtain a suit of civilian clothes and notified the Marine commandant of his troubles. He was ordered to report to the Brooklyn navy yard when his uniforms appeared on the *Dixie*. Otherwise, his first task was to see Louise.

On 18 March he again reported, in full uniform, at the Marine Barracks. At that time Maj. James E. Mahoney was in command but he would soon be replaced by Col. Mancil C. Goodrell, Bearss' pal from back at Cavite.[14] Goodrell was a stickler but an efficient commander. Perhaps he could not be compared to Col. Meade but he had his own likes and dislikes. They weren't as extreme but were every bit as quotable. While Bearss was in attendance, U.S. Marine Corps headquarters sent an inspector with limited experience and few years compared to Goodrell's 40. Goodrell was extremely vexed at this. Goodrell at once had the "Call to Arms" sounded, which meant, "Come as you are, but come at once." Officers and men responded with great dispatch—cooks in undershirts and others in whatever they were wearing. Goodrell turned to the youngster and said, "This is my command, go ahead and inspect it." The younger man's report was greatly unfavorable but it was accompanied by Goodrell's endorsement which read, "This officer's report is comparable to his ideas of orientation." So much for young inspectors.

One time, when Bearss was officer of the day, two miserable looking privates, Thomas F. Pendegast and William Slattery, were reported by a young officer of the guard as "intoxicated." Both men were effective machine gunners but more importantly, both had been with Bearss at Sohotón and over the route across Samar. In order to save their hides Bearss had both of them sent to his office to await his return. He was then engaged in an inspection that would take a long time. His sergeant, another old-timer, knew enough to fill both bums with hot coffee and fresh air. More than an hour later, when Captain Bearss finally reappeared, they were both in fair shape. Bearss gave them a warning not to do it again, then let them go. That was what it was like in the "old Corps." Do what you could because good men were hard to find and those two, drunk or sober, were worth their weight in a fight.

Marriage

On 1 May 1904, Captain Hiram I. Bearss and Miss Adelaide Louise Madden were joined in holy matrimony at the Little Church Around the Corner in New York City. The Reverend Houghton was the Episcopal rector who performed the service. After the ceremony, during the handshaking and congratulations, the rector happen to ask Bearss, "How come you got a pronunciation like 'Barce' out of Bearss?" To which Bearss is reported to have replied, "It is just the same way you get 'Hooten' out of Huffton."[15]

The newlyweds' honeymoon was delayed for two weeks, and they were compelled to live in a New York hotel room before he could obtain leave. It was finally granted and on 15 May they headed toward Ridgeview by train. Whenever something of importance happened to him, it was always back to Ridgeview.

After his return Bearss had, as of 2 April 1904, command of the Marine prison guard detachment aboard the USS *Hancock*. The ship was a receiving station through which men came and went—a sort of clearing house for sailors and Marines. It was also a military prison, but that was actually located in a frame building on the wharf called the cob dock. That prison was Bearss' main responsibility. This duty would continue until 17 February 1905 and it was definitely not his cup of tea. He was cut out for active duty and, to his mind, watching prisoners wasn't active duty.

When he arrived, the Marine guard had been subjected to numerous negative commentaries from the navy officers, and from one in particular. Within a week after Bearss' assumption of duty, that same officer reported that the guard was proficient. How that came about was quite simple. After a certain hour the ferry from the navy yard to the cob dock ceased running. The naval officers and men were forced to then come back via the land side—which, in turn, forced them to present themselves to the Marine on guard, for admittance. The first night that Captain Bearss was running the show some naval officers were halted by the Marine and refused admittance because they didn't know the password. Word of the problem was passed along from guard to sergeant to officer, and during this time, the navy officers were required to wait. It was snowing and a bit chilly for early April. It was uncomfortable. The officers were not ensigns and were not used to being so treated by "mere" Marine guards. Criticism

5. Recruiting, Panama, Marriage and Back to the Philippines   91

of the Marines was rampant. But, the next morning, all was forgiven. The ship's commanding officer, Captain William Emory, USN, congratulated Bearss for installing a system that worked. Everyone else fell in line and he was now the darling of the post.

But that nice feeling of collegiality didn't last long. Captain Emory's wife called Bearss one day soon after and told him that she wanted a "Marine to show her eleven-year-old son around the ship and docks." Hiram carefully and courteously told her, "Nothing doing." Marines weren't baby-sitters. Those weren't his exact words, but you get the idea. Mrs. Emory slammed down the receiver. Shortly thereafter the telephone rang again. This time it was the commanding officer. Emory assured himself that Bearss had not been misquoted and then gave him a direct order to detach a Marine to conduct his son about the yard and ship. Bearss told him that it wasn't a proper order and the captain repeated it, loud and clear. Bearss then respectfully requested that the captain put the order in writing. This last was to give Bearss enough rope to provide an escape. If Emory had been fool enough to do as requested, Bearss could then reply *in writing* that the order was improper but that he would obey a direct command no matter how inappropriate it was. Emory didn't make captain in the U.S. Navy by doing stupid things. He refused Bearss' request and the matter was closed. Bearss' predecessor, Capt. Thomas C. Treadwell, USMC, had the "advantages" of being an academy graduate but had been unable to stand up to the navy. Consequently, he had been taken advantage of. However, this was a different Marine, this Captain Hiram I. Bearss. He was no academy graduate, and had no preconceived notions about the "senior service." He didn't back down when he was right and it made him many enemies, navy and Marines.[16]

On 17 February 1905 Hiram was transferred to the Marine Barracks, League Island, Philadelphia, arriving as of 21 February. There wasn't much pleasure at League Island for Marines, at least not then. It was drill, guard duty, colors and general garrison duty. It was either a jumping-off place or it was the end of the line. The dampness created an extremely uncomfortable cold that made guard duty dreadful for all hands, especially in the winter months.

While located there, Hiram and Louise made many excellent social contacts that stood them in a good stead for the balance of their Marine service years. Because there were no quarters available for officers, they took an apartment in the city. It was then that Hiram received his first physical injury. On an evening in March, Hiram, while returning home from a social engagement, was attacked by an unknown assailant. Whoever it was hit Hiram's head with a blunt instrument, causing him a concussion. He had little money so the attempted robbery went nowhere.[17] In the moving process from New York, Hiram, always impatient, became annoyed with a slow porter. He grabbed an oversized trunk and hurled it onto a truck and created a double hernia for himself in so doing. With the concussion still bothering him, on 16 March he turned himself into the navy hospital at League Island. Four days later he was released. But the hernia started acting up and on 22 March he checked into the navy hospital in Philadelphia. There, a surgeon friend successfully operated on 28 March. Afterward, Hiram begged for permission to leave and stay in his own bed at his apartment. The doctor and Louise discussed the situation outside in the corridor. After much soul searching, and with promises from Louise to keep him in bed, the doctor relented.

To home and into bed he went, but not for long. After lunch he asked Louise for a bag with some papers he had been working on. When she returned with the requested bag he had already formulated a plan for a trip to Indiana. He told her that there was a train that afternoon and insisted that if he could only get back to Ridgeview everything would be all right. He persisted, and she relented. She believed that he would mend much faster at his beloved home. Louise obtained a drawing room on the next train and off they went. He got home, spread out before the huge fireplace and soaked up all the nostalgia his home was capable of providing. In a very short time he was well mended and in fine fettle and they were on their way back to Philadelphia. You might say the trip was just what the doctor ordered.

Back at League Island by 19 April he found that things were humming. New construction, mainly barracks for the enlisted men, was going up all over the place. Cement walks had been laid, new bolts on the buildings would now keep the doors closed, and modern plumbing had been added. But nothing was being done about the decrepit officers' quarters, so they were still forced to rent apartments off base. The Bearss were just as happy to be away from too close observation by other Marines and their wives, so they thankfully stayed where they were. In October 1905, Hiram received new orders to return to the Philippines. But this would be different. Now he had a wife to accompany him.

On 20 October 1905 Hiram and Louise were on their way. First, though, they stopped off at Ridgeview for a few days. They reached San Francisco on 2 November where he reported, once again, to Marine Barracks, Mare Island. They boarded the USS *Sherman* on 6 November and prepared themselves for the long voyage. Hiram's sole official responsibility was in caring for the well-being of the 100 Marines aboard who were, like him, destined for service with the 1st Marine Brigade in the Philippines.

5. Recruiting, Panama, Marriage and Back to the Philippines

One situation of some interest and perhaps amusement occurred. A Marine's wife from Georgia refused to sail on a ship carrying such a name. She actually refused to board and demanded that her husband have her bags returned to the tugboat that had delivered them. Weeks later, she sailed on another, differently named ship. Such were the feelings of ordinary, sometimes intelligent people, about what had happened 40 years before.

The voyage to Hawaii was unpleasant for Louise. She was not a good sailor and was ill for most of that trip. At Honolulu, where the ship tied up and was to remain for some time, Louise refused a doctor's suggestion that she return to the States as soon as she could — she was going to accompany her husband no matter what the outcome. Louise insisted that she would be braver and stronger with him by her side. Fortunately the ten or so days and nights spent in Hawaii seemed to set her on the straight track. Louise appeared on deck and seemed very well when the ship was again prepared to sail. But she lasted about an hour after the ship sailed before falling apart again. Louise remained ill for the entire voyage. In later years it wasn't something that she remembered with nostalgia. In fact, it was the first and only time that she traveled with Hiram to a distant duty station.

Brigadier General Frederick M. Wise received a direct appointment as a second lieutenant of Marines in 1899. He served in the Philippines, followed by China. This was followed by service in Cuba, Vera Cruz, Haiti, and Santo Domingo, after which he went to France with the 5th Marines. There he participated in the Battle for Belleau Wood, later transferring to the U.S. 4th Infrantry Division where he commanded the 59th Infantry, later the 8th Brigade. He served in Haiti and on several bases in the U.S. before retiring at age 48 in 1926.

Meanwhile, while Louise suffered, Hiram was, as usual, having fun. There were two American women aboard, traveling gratis because they were married to British naval officers. One, a Mrs. Sigscee, asked Hiram how she could be sure that they had crossed the meridian. He carefully explained that if she were up and about at sunrise and watched, she would see two little red lights. Of course, she believed him and was up at dawn.

What she saw, most likely, didn't include the two red lights. At least nothing more was said about it.

The other woman was the wife of the chief of staff of the British fleet in Asiatic waters. Although Hiram got along with her very well, he did twit her a bit about the British navy. One question he asked was, "Why are most of the officers of the British navy Irish?" And the other, "Did she know if the British navy was using chainless anchors as the American fleet was doing." The first she couldn't answer but to the second she replied that she "was positive that the British navy was using chainless anchors." Anything the U.S. Navy was doing, the British navy was also doing, and probably better. She maintained this posture even after his description of what he had been talking about. He told her that the new system worked because they were using huge magnets to draw up the anchor. She accepted that theory without question.[18]

The Philippines

Upon reaching Cavite in Manila Bay, Hiram went ashore and reported his arrival and that of the detachment to the brigade commander. He also received immediate orders to proceed to Olongapo. He tried to get the very sick Louise to stay at Cavite until she recovered but she was adamant—she was going with him.

With the still ill Louise and 200 Marines who were assigned to Olongapo, Hiram embarked in a barge towed by a tug manned by a native Filipino crew. Off they went across Manila Bay northwest toward their new station. He had been advised that there would be a reception waiting for his young wife. So Hiram had Louise change into her prettiest dress so as to be ready when they arrived. The problem was that the barge and tug had been used almost exclusively to haul coal. The trip, which would normally take about two hours, was somewhat delayed. A terrible storm came up, the barge rolled about, and Louise was tied to the rail and forced to sit on the filthy deck. As they were approaching Subic Bay, the native skipper missed his turn. Hiram was very familiar with the waters, having been on them many times when he was chasing rebels in 1900. Taking over, he brought the boat about and into the channel. Instead of arriving at four that afternoon they managed to make it at 0130 the following morning, 4 December 1905.

When they arrived, six Marine officers were there to meet and greet them. But poor Louise was a mess. Her lovely white dress was dirty and torn. The party was all done, as was Louise and possibly Hiram as well.

5. Recruiting, Panama, Marriage and Back to the Philippines

But the night had changed and the stars and moon made everything, at least to Louise, just fine. She has been quoted as saying, "Isn't this the most beautiful spot in all the world?" After what she'd been through we can safely assume that it was.

Smedley Butler's version of what happened when they arrived bears repeating. According to his story Fritz Wise was already there:

> We both let out a few whoops when we learned that Hiram Bearss was coming. No one could be bored when "Hi" was in the offing. He kept things moving. He had just been married, and Fritz Wise and I went to the dock at Olongapo to meet him when he arrived with his bride, one of the prettiest girls I've ever seen. As they stepped off the tug, Fritz said, "I'll bet you a dollar, Hiram, that you're wearing someone else's undershirt."[19]

Hiram refused to bet or take the undershirt off. So they helped him disrobe. Sure enough, they later claimed, he was wearing a shirt marked "D.D. Porter." Butler added, "Hiram never seemed to have any clothes or funds of his own." He continued, "He was always borrowing ... but Hiram was so likeable that he could get away with anything. He was fearless, wild, always playing practical jokes."[20]

That was his welcoming committee. What Louise thought about her poor husband being abused like that is not of record. The poor thing was probably still too sick to notice. She had married a tiger and was always hanging on by his tail. What a ride that marriage must have been. But at this time, they appeared to be a happy couple.

Officers' quarters at Olongapo were built with a frame of wood and with a bamboo covering. The Bearss were assigned to one of them. All were very small and intended for one person. Their "residence" was the same size only it was divided into two quarters; the officer who occupied the second part happened to be away at the time. He was Capt. Jimmy Broatch, one of Hiram's old pals. The separating partition was of bamboo with a thin cloth curtain, about six feet in height, providing the door. For that night and a few days after, Smedley Butler and his wife, Bunny, invited Louise and Hiram to room with them until the matter was straightened out.[21]

Hiram had no intention of taking his bride to share such quarters with another man. He protested to Major "Uncle Joe" Pendleton, the post commander, questioning the morality and decency of the situation. Pendleton, who was well known as an affable and honorable man, answered that the situation was such that he couldn't provide any other quarters for Hiram and Louise. Space was so limited that similar situations arose continually. A correct arrangement was made by good old Jimmy Broatch himself. When he returned, he agreed with Hiram that if anything were to happen, he had to go. So he went. He and a bachelor naval officer moved in together, leaving the space for the newlyweds. Modesty prevailed and Hiram was happy.[22]

Hiram was given two companies to command for instruction and on the rifle range. His regiment, the 2d, was then commanded by Major Eli K. Cole. There was a great deal of laxity — most of the fighting was over in that part of the islands. Consequently, a good use for the men's time was athletics. At 30 years of age, Hiram was in prime physical condition and still in love with sports. As we have seen, baseball was always his first love, closely seconded by football, both of which he was superbly fitted for, as small framed as he was. Hiram was still the happiest of men when in competition with anyone. As a result, his companies won all but one of the athletic events. It was the same with the military events. Bearss and Butler were constantly engaged in "friendly" competition, one always trying to upstage the other, and frequently each alternately winning contests.[23]

He always found time for practical jokes. One of his best was with the cooperation of the post quartermaster. The quartermaster was instructed to walk by Hiram's quarters at about noon, the hottest time of the day. Hiram called out to him, "That water motor fan you gave me for cooling this house really does the job. Come on in and feel the coolness." The quartermaster responded, "If you like that one so much you can have the other one in the warehouse, which ought to cool you down twice as much." Loud voices — midday brutal heat with everyone indoors struggling against odds to attain some cool comfort, and then this. Hiram's voice, while not of the intensity of "Buck" Neville's, was still of the quality to be heard throughout the entire camp.[24]

In very short order, all of the other officers' wives came to visit Louise and see this magnificent water fan they had heard "so much about." But each had already sent their husbands over to the quartermaster's office to "get that other fan." At Hiram's place they demanded to see this wondrous fan. So Hiram took down an old hand-operated fan from the wall and showed the ladies how to drink a glass of water "for energy" and then he rotated the "water fan."

In his book, Smedley Butler tells of a march that he and his men made that was swift — so rapid that when they learned of it, headquarters demanded an investigation. How could he treat his men in so dastardly a fashion — what terrible condition their feet must have been in — and so on. Before too much more time had elapsed, Hiram decided to go Butler one better. Camp Stotsenburg, a U.S. Army cavalry post, lay about 50 miles distant, more or less as the crow flies. Hiram's company must make the journey in less time than Butler, whose expedition, to and fro, had taken five days.

Off they went over mostly poorly marked trails. Major Cole had earlier remarked to Hiram that he would be pleased if his men should beat out Butler's company, which just happened to be in Pendleton's regiment.[25] Hiram replied, "We'll make better time, sir." On 30 April 1907 Cole submitted a report of the ensuing march to the brigade commander. In it he described the events in detail but was somewhat confusing. According to the Commandant's Report for 1907 Hiram and his men made the trip to Stotensburg in approximately 36 hours, and we know he was back by the 27th. Butler and his men had made the trip and returned within five days, Hiram got there and back in four.

Hiram, leading his men and leaving very early (0645) sent a message to Cole the next afternoon: "Have just arrived, everything just fine, men in good condition." Up and down hills, over difficult terrain and in less than two days. The message caused quite a shock. It was received just as Cole and some friends were seated on his veranda watching the evening parade. It created a considerable stir. The pro–Butler faction thought it "an outrage" while Hiram's group was sure it was a "wonderful feat."

Remaining at Stotsenburg just long enough to sleep, Hiram's troop began their journey back the following day. But this time it was a trace more casual. Several days later they had returned and first thing upon arrival, Hiram was in a shower. It was then that orders from Major Pendleton, Cole's senior, were received ordering a complete physical of the Bearss men and especially their feet.[26] Cursing, Hiram got out of the shower and dressed. He then prepared his men for inspection. It was found that not one man suffered anything, let alone blisters. How could this trip have been made in such a short period of time without damage to the men? There was a simple answer. Hiram had been training his men to cover ground at a "jogtrot," not running but a slow trot. They were all prepared. The reports indicate that the men reveled in the notoriety of this victory as much as did Cole and Bearss. It was at this time that Hiram became more widely known throughout the Philippines and then the entire Corps by his nickname, "Hiking Hiram." Even the army and navy were soon aware of him, his record and his nickname, and used it.[27]

But it didn't end with the foot exam. Someone, perhaps Major Pendleton, demanded a court-martial. Major Rufus Lane, who was the inspector general of the Marines Corps in the Philippines, came up from Cavite for a board of inquiry. The men were again interrogated. All supported their "skipper." Again it was determined that the men were as "fit and solid as punch." A large number of them insisted that they would like to go out again and beat their own record. They all said that they could "out hike anyone in any service." There wasn't much else that could be dreamed up to do to Hiram so the entire matter died out. Just one thing remained alive and that was his nickname, by which he is still known today.

Cole was an officer who held Hiram in the highest regard. "If Hiram ever said anything couldn't be done, then it couldn't be done. The only way to keep him happy and out of mischief was to give him work to do." He accused him of completing a week's work in a single day if allowed to. For the most part, Hiram received reviews of that sort from his commanding officers.[28] He was a tough man to have aboard. The other officers found it quite difficult to measure up, but it was even tougher when he was gone.

Meanwhile, Louise had settled in and was enjoying herself. Then she started noticing certain things. She was suffering from morning sickness. Her stomach was notoriously weak anyway. But she had enough sense to quickly put herself in the hands of the naval doctor. It was he who told her she "must go to the hospital." She refused to accept that advice, so early in her pregnancy. It was only the first of March and she still had several months to go. One day the doctor happened to be passing their abode and discovered that Louise was still there and hadn't moved to the hospital at Cavite. He thoroughly frightened both Hiram and Louise about the consequences of delaying any longer. After all, there was that terrible trip by barge to consider. Louise remembered — so did Hiram.

Off they both went at 0300 the following morning, in a native tug with supplies and a 60-mile trip ahead of them. They landed without further difficulty and she spent that evening with Major and Mrs. Charles A. Doyen who were, according to reports, "lovely to her."[29] Within hours she was transported to the hospital at Manila where she remained for six weeks until time for her delivery. In those days, doctors insisted that pregnant women have as much care beforehand as was possible. Hiram came over to see her every week and fortunately was there when her time came. According to reports, it was the most grueling experience of his life. His nerves were almost shot when, at 0630, a nurse came to him and proclaimed, "Captain, you and Mrs. Bearss have a little daughter."

Louise and "little Louise" remained two more weeks in the hospital. Then Hiram made arrangements to bring both his ladies home. In the meantime numerous gifts were assembled for mother and child. One of the presents was a bassinet prepared by the mother of Capt. Henry "Harry" C. Davis.[30] Captain George C. Reid rushed aboard the boat and then he and Hiram proudly carried the baby ashore in the bassinet. Two stalwart Marines were needed to carry one little baby, but they did it with care and obvious pride. Many of the officers and their wives met the boat to welcome them "home." It was, they all decided, a very happy homecoming. And everyone was at least an undesignated godparent.

One of the wives was a nurse but had been away for three months on leave. Upon her return she immediately clamored to see little Louise. It was only about 0200 but having seen lights in the Bearss cottage she insisted upon seeing the infant at once. It was just as well that she did. After a quick glance, she realized that all was not well. Louise had been having serious misgivings herself. She had said little because she didn't wish to be any more of a burden than she had been already.

The baby was dreadfully undernourished, due to the lack of fresh milk and, among other things, the terrible heat working its way on mother and daughter. So, once again, Louise was outward bound to the hospital. For the next three months it was nip and tuck. The doctors gave up hope, as did Hiram, but Louise held on to her faith. She willed her daughter well. Two leading Army doctors, both of famous reputation, looked poor little Louise over and declared the infant without hope. It is said that she then began to smile and gurgle. Every doctor in the hospital who had anything to do with this mother and child was convinced that he had seen a miracle.

But now the mother was in a bad way. Her nerves were shot. She was, in fact, on the verge of a nervous breakdown. Her doctor insisted that she and her baby must return to the United States as soon as possible. Hiram agreed and asked for a leave of absence to take his family home. The family returned on the good ship *Sherman*. The baby spent her first Christmas on the high seas while daddy played Santa for all the children aboard. They arrived at San Francisco on 28 April 1906, just shortly after the great earthquake. Then on they went to Indiana where they were welcomed with great pride by the grandparents and aunts and uncles. Hiram's brother Braxton and his wife were there, as were sisters Lucy Bearss and Emma Muhlfeld and her husband, Oscar G. Muhlfeld, and their daughter. Louise spent 15 months at Ridgeview with her baby amidst Hiram's family while he returned to his duty at Olongapo. Louise and Hiram had brought a young Filipina named Islana with them to help with the baby. She was 17, and a convent bred orphan. Islana would stay with Louise during the first few years of their arrival in the United States. At times it would seem as though the still young Louise had two children to care for, since Islana would sometimes be a handful.

Hiram was always fortunate in his choice of commanders. The brigade commander who had given him permission for the special leave was Colonel William P. Biddle. Biddle was a reasonably good fellow, although no one ever considered him a fighting Marine. He came from a very wealthy and politically well appointed family, which greatly helped his career as a Marine. In addition, Biddle was a graduate of the U.S. Naval Academy. With that background, nothing could seriously harm him. As we know, he later became the eleventh commandant of the Marine Corps.

The following period, while Louise was in Ridgeview with the baby and Hiram was back in the Philippines, would be very lonely for both of them. Upon his arrival at Olongapo, Major Eli K. Cole had been detached and on 24 November 1907 Hiram was placed in command of the 2d Marine Regiment. He would continue in that role until detached to Headquarters Marine Corps, Washington, D.C., on 14 February 1908.

Unfortunately, he was delayed because of an epidemic of cholera aboard his ship, again the *Sherman*. The ship's crew and passengers were quarantined for five days at Mariveles, opposite the island of Corregidor, on Manila Bay. There were 400 officers and men aboard, as well as civilians, and it wasn't the most pleasant of times for any of them. Baths had to be taken daily and clothes put through a daily process to kill off the germs.

Finally the ship was allowed to leave and make its way back to San Francisco. Bearss found out, at Mare Island, that his new duty post would be the Norfolk navy yard. With an extra few days' travel allowance he was able to make his way back to his beloved wife and child at Ridgeview for a short leave. While there, he and Louise were able to spend a great deal of time together. Out they went, on hikes of all things, and boating down the Wabash. There were other diversions, which we are not at liberty to discuss. Soon, too soon, after his arrival he was forced to make his way to Norfolk. Upon arrival he learned that he would have to wait awhile for the quarters of an officer who was outgoing before he could send for his family. But in comparison to the last time he had been at Norfolk, the quarters were now downright lavish. When his wife and daughter arrived, Hiram was able to provide them with a lovely brick cottage, with screened-in porches, up and down. It also came with space for a garden, which Louise immediately began to plan and then plant with vegetables and flowers.

However, not all was well with Hiram. He had a reoccurrence of a fever he had picked up in the Panama expedition. It was Chagres, a version of malaria, and it would hit him with high temperatures of short duration. This same fever would trouble him for the balance of his life because those were the days before "miracle medicines." This illness, for some reason, doesn't show up in his medical record.[31] While he was doing his fever bit for Uncle Sam, the latter devised more trouble for him and a bunch of his fellows in Panama. It seems that an election was in the process of being held, and the State Department insisted that it be kept "clean and pure." Not at home, mind you, which was even then badly in need of "straightening out." Just in other countries.

Back to Panama

On 19 June 1908 Hiram and a detachment of Marines sailed south to Panama aboard the USS *Idaho*, a battleship of the Atlantic Fleet. Upon arrival, they immediately went into camp at Monkey Hill. There were now enough officers and men to create two Marine companies, all under the command of Major Ben H. Fuller.[32] The elections passed quietly. The Marines were posted outside each polling place to ensure honesty. Hiram's later comment was that "it would be a great thing to place Marines at polling places in the U.S." as well.

As usual, he was unable to keep himself from engaging in pranks, but this trip almost did him in. Hiram did something that was completely unnecessary and insulting to a brother officer. It was a prank but without the grace or innate fun that most of his seemed to have. There was no excuse for his behavior on this occasion.

Colonel Charles H. Lauchheimer was a graduate of the Naval Academy, always dedicated to the art of shooting,[33] and was well liked. At this period he was Marine headquarters inspector and had arrived at Panama to take a look at what was going on there. Hiram organized his company for the inspection and had each man pull his hat down over his ears "to make them appear Hebrew." Each answered roll call as either "Abie" or "Moses." There were other similar shenanigans. Lauchheimer went though with the inspection and said nothing about this unseemly action. He happened to be Jewish and that fact was well known but not, apparently, of any consequence to anyone except Hiram. The story rocketed up the line to headquarters and might have been the end of Hiram's career except for one thing. Charles H. was a man with a fine sense of humor and a high boiling point. He squashed the matter and later apparently bore no ill will toward Hiram.[34]

There is no question that this action was an unnecessary display of antisemitism and shows Hiram as a terrible boor, which he may have been on other occasions as well. Like many of his generation, he was obviously bigoted. It was a stupid trick to pull, and there was no excuse for it. He was rightfully worried for a bit. Although his famous luck held at the time, he added another nail to his eventual professional coffin, as we shall see.

The chief danger in Panama, at that time, was the Chagres Fever, a violent form of malaria. The Marine encampment on Monkey Hill seemed to be the headquarters for malarial mosquitoes. The officers and men were dropping like flies and with no previous warnings. As we have already seen, Hiram had previously been a victim and had seemed to become immune. But when he dropped he went all the way. He was so sick that he was packed up and shipped home at once.

Back at Norfolk his fever abated and he was soon back on active duty. Best of all, his old boss Littleton W.T. Waller, now a colonel, commanded the Marine Barracks. Hiram was at once assigned as post adjutant. But it wasn't long before he was again in the soup. Hiram was then, and always, a stickler for regulations, especially if it concerned the rights of a Marine. One of his officers, 2d Lt. Edward A. Ostermann,[35] for some reason was severely criticized by Capt. Edward D. Taussig, USN. The latter had no authority to criticize any Marine officer of the guard, no matter what the reason, and Hiram was angry. He wrote an official letter to the admiral in command of the station, Rear Adm. George A. Bicknell, and to the captain of the yard, Capt. Daniel D.V. Stuart, USN. Stuart upheld Taussig and overruled Hiram's objections. That raised further hackles so Hiram asked if certain regulations or orders from the Navy Department were enforced in the navy yard. The less than brilliant Stuart replied, "No." Hiram then wrote a letter through official channels, requesting that Stuart, captain of the yard, be disciplined and that a court-martial be instituted against him, citing his reply. Bicknell asked Waller to return from leave and handle the ensuing situation. Stuart only had a short time left on the active list before his retirement and Hiram was asked to withdraw his complaint. Hiram did and Stuart apologized for his actions. That ended the disagreement and the harassment of Ostermann.

During this tour of duty, Bearss commanded the Marine Battalion at Norfolk. While there, word was passed to him that there would be a parade in the city and that the "Naval Brigade and staff" would *walk* with the "battalion commander and staff." Hiram went to see the admiral, with whom he was now quite well acquainted, and the commander of the Naval Brigade. He informed both that the Marines would furnish them horses. Hiram was advised that no one of the Naval Brigade "cared to ride horses." Bearss retorted that Marine Corps regulations required that Marine officers be mounted on parade. Unless he and his staff were allowed to ride, he would be compelled to report the matter to the commandant at once. The outcome: The Marines rode horses and the navy walked. That was material for several jokes for the next few days.

This was a very depressing time for Marines in general and Colonel

5. Recruiting, Panama, Marriage and Back to the Philippines 103

Waller in particular. Secretary of the Navy Vaughan L. Meyer told Tony Waller that he would be the next commandant of the Marine Corps. It was nearly every "grunt" Marine officer's wish that Waller be promoted to that position. Unfortunately, politics reared its ugly head and he wasn't. Senator Boies Penrose of Pennsylvania put extreme pressure on President Taft to instead appoint his first cousin, Colonel William P. Biddle, of the Philadelphia Biddles.[36] This was very distressing to Waller, who most everyone agreed would have been the preferred candidate. And, it was almost as distressing to every Marine who had served under him at one time or another. There is no question that he was every fighting Marine's idol. It really came down to selecting a warrior Marine or a chair-bound Marine and the latter was the choice. This was the first of the latter chosen in the history of the Corps but it would happen a few times over the next few years. What it really boiled down to were the academy graduates versus all others.[37]

At this time a situation occurred that added another level of bitterness to the everyday existence of the Corps: the navy officers won their long-term fight to have Marines removed from navy ships. President Theodore Roosevelt issued the orders and the Marines marched off their ships while the sailors cheered. This was in late 1908.

At Norfolk, the various former ship detachments reported to Colonel Waller. They marched in resplendent uniforms with drums beating and flags flying to the Marine quarters at the far end of the post. No "tails between their legs," they were still Marines and would show that fact to any observer. But, Lord, they were bitter. American sailors all over the world didn't hesitate to let Marines know how happy they were at their seeming downfall. Catcalls from sailors to Marines were the order of the day. On shore, fights that may previously have been avoided were now a common occurrence. It must have been very difficult to have been a peace-loving man in those times.

But for all the challenges, free-for-alls, and name calling, within six weeks the Congress went to work and the Marines were back aboard the navy ships. For good reason, the admirals wanted the Marines returned. As one navy officer once said, "A ship without Marines is like a garment without buttons."[38] The Marines were ordered to refrain from any name calling, gloating and other fanfare. That they did, but barely. They may have grinned more than usual.

Nearly a year after the Marines returned to ship, Hiram was assigned to sea duty. On 5 November 1909 he received orders to join the USS *Louisiana*, a battleship then at port in Norfolk. The ship went absolutely nowhere, so Louise and little Louise remained at the Old Monroe Hotel located in Portsmouth.

When Bearss arrived on board, the first difficulty he perceived was the condition of the rifles assigned to his men. They were old Krag-Jorgensens. By 1906 they were slowly being replaced within the Corps with the marvelous new Springfield '03. These Krags were badly infected with rust outside and inside, probably due to the service aboard ship. Hiram refused to have his men saddled with weapons that might be defective. There might be serious difficulties should they be called upon to land and put out a "brush fire" war someplace. Bearss asked for a review board to survey these rifles. He was successful and as a result, the rifles were condemned and the new Springfields issued.

During this period he finagled a trip to Washington intending to gain a meeting with Commandant George Elliott. Bearss wanted a transfer to shore duty, almost anywhere — he detested sea duty and was more than willing to suffer any pains to get out of it.[39] Elliott, knowing that Hiram and the navy didn't get along, promised him relief soon. It would be when the *Louisiana* arrived at Guantánamo Bay.

In the meantime, Hiram reported two navy officers for their "threatening and overbearing manner toward Marines stationed on duty." One had been heard to mutter something about those "Damn Marines." This Hiram would not allow to pass. He recommended court-martial, which was not done, but Captain Albert G. Winterhalter, USN, assured him that it would not recur. The officers expressed their apologies, settling that problem.

Shortly afterward Winterhalter permitted his Marine orderly to sit outside his door, a situation not permitted by Marine regulations. The rules were that every sentry had to stand for his watch period. Hiram protested the captain's lenience. He was sure that, given the circumstances, the Marine sentries could not help falling asleep. The captain insisted and sure enough, soon afterward a sentry was found asleep on watch. This was a serious offense and the man was placed under arrest and court-martialed. Hiram protested, and because his previous protests had been placed in writing the charges were withdrawn. The Marine was set free with nothing detrimental on his record. This is another example of Hiram going to bat for his nearly blameless subordinate.

As Elliott had promised, when the *Louisiana* reached Guantánamo Bay, Captain Winterhalter sent his orderly to Captain Bearss to present his compliments, and say that he, the captain of the ship, wished to see all Marine officers in his cabin. Bearss became cantankerous and refused to appear. After some hassling, Hiram stated why he refused the invitation. The preferred form, and the one that Hiram would accept, would have to be: "Captain Winterhalter presents his compliments to Captain Bearss

5. Recruiting, Panama, Marriage and Back to the Philippines

and requests that Captain Bearss come to his cabin." With that form, Hiram appeared as directed. He later claimed that it was nothing personal. He was trying to maintain the dignity of the Marines aboard the ship and the entire Corps. Winterhalter was testy, and no wonder, and responded that there was only one naval captain on that ship and it was the ship's captain. Hiram responded that he was a captain of Marines and as such was entitled to the title and dignities invested therein. His job, as he saw it, was to maintain the dignity of the Marine Corps and insist that regulations be consistently carried out. In reality, though they argued this minor point, they were and would remain quite friendly otherwise. It came out that Winterhalter's problem was simple. Previously, on a smaller ship, his Marine detachment was commanded by a sergeant and consequently he had a much easier time getting what he wanted. He was used to being in complete control. He didn't have that with Hiram and it sometimes distressed him. But when it came time for Hiram to leave the ship, Captain Winterhalter honored him by providing him with a steam launch to proceed ashore. (Or, perhaps instead it was for his speedy trip — anywhere else.)

During his time aboard, Hiram had as a subordinate 2d Lt. Bernard L. Smith who was not only a fine Marine officer but also excelled as an engineer. Several times, during Hiram's period aboard the ship, when there were problems down below, Hiram detailed Smith to help out. He managed to solve intricate problems that the ship's engineering officers couldn't. As a result, Hiram facetiously offered his mechanical services at any time the captain required them.[40]

6

Guantánamo and Vera Cruz

On 22 March 1909 Hiram I. Bearss, captain, USMC, arrived at and assumed command of the Marine Barracks at Fisherman's Point, Guantánamo Bay, Cuba. "Gitmo," as it was to be most commonly called, is located near the southeastern end of that island. It was the place at which Major Robert Huntington and his Marine Battalion had landed at 1400 hours, 10 June 1898. In the ensuing days they had conquered and established complete control over the entire surrounding area, proving once and for all that a Marine landing force, properly supported, could take advanced bases for the navy. Later, in 1903, the Navy Department decided to make $100,000 available for development of a base. But six years later Hiram only had 75 or so Marines at any given time with which to defend the base. The buildings and site were completely unsatisfactory if the navy wished to continue it as a permanent base. There never were quite enough men or officers to do the job adequately. When one Marine left another usually took that one's place eventually, and that was the extent of the detachment's quantity. As always, the quality was better than should have been expected. It was Hiram's first separate command and he was determined to make the most of it.

Louise was detained for a minor operation in New York but soon after, she and little Louise arrived. The house assigned to them had been built by the Corps of Engineers and was entirely unsuited for habitation in the tropics. When circumstances necessitated change, Hiram did what he always did — he changed the entire inside by completely gutting what pretended to be a kitchen. He cut out one room and made it into a porch. Once he decided it was livable, he followed regulations. Regulations required that no modifications to any navy houses be made without prior approval of the Navy Department. Hiram knew what to expect from that bureaucratic melange — any request would be denied, or perhaps approved, but only after he had left the base. Consequently, after he'd made the changes, Hiram duly reported them. If any hackles were raised, none could be discerned, since nothing more was said about the matter.

Among other problems he encountered was receiving necessary supplies. One specific problem for him was the delay in shipment of gasoline. He plastered the Navy Department with cablegrams requesting prompt shipment. Their response — "Don't send any more cablegrams." He obeyed save for one brief message — "No gasoline. Can't borrow more. Help!" He also wrote requesting a shipment of citronella to keep down the sand fleas, which were so numerous he couldn't have formations of his troops. This request was denied. But Hiram was always self-reliant. If it couldn't be done one way, find another. So he did. Looking over some medical report from India, he found a word with 17 letters that meant "sand fleas."[1] Because some of his Marines were ill with sore throats and fever from sand flea bites, he cabled for 200 gallons of citronella "to prevent fever in his command caused by this ankhphorahasharat." No one in the Navy Department had any idea what that word meant but no one had the guts to further deny Hiram his citronella. He got it but they had put him through the wringer to do so.

Having alcoholic beverages, including beer, on base was distinctly contrary to regulations. Back home, the Temperance Union was then a political powerhouse and Congress bent to its will. It became the policy of the navy to "not let our 'boys' abroad have beer." However, when the men were on leave they could get whatever they could afford at Baiquiri. It was the nearest place where beverages were sold and wasn't far from the base. Besides beer, which would generally be used (if at all) as a chaser, Baiquiri provided the local vintage, which was much more stimulating, and intoxicating.

Hiram decided to do something, again contrary to regulations, but which would, he believed, remove the need for the "hard stuff." He arbitrarily allowed the men to have beer with their meals on Wednesday and Sunday. It doesn't sound like much now but then it meant something special for the men. He reckoned that there would be no further need to go to town and get drunk. The men greatly appreciated it and, for the most part, played their part well. Unfortunately, there is always the "ten percent" who will always take advantage. Two Marines got rum from the local natives and both were soon falling-down drunk. So drunk, in fact, that it was necessary to impose severe discipline. When ordered before Hiram, they were asked what they had imbibed and where they got it. They told him it was beer, but he could see that the result was far beyond what beer would have engendered. Both were sea lawyers and they believed they had Hiram in a box because he'd broken navy regulations. Their thought was that he would be forced to ignore their indiscretion if they claimed beer as the devil's brew. They didn't know Hiram. Believing they had him over a barrel, they both became quite unmilitary in their behavior and attitude. That lasted a few moments. Hiram's top sergeant, in a voice calculated to wake the dead, told them to keep their hands down and to stand at attention when addressing their superior officer. They were Marine enough, even at this stage, to obey immediately and without question.

Though strongly advised not to—his friends warned him that he was letting himself in for real trouble if he did go forward—Hiram reacted swiftly and with great determination. He concluded that he must court-martial both men, in order to preserve his position within the post. Charges were preferred and both were convicted. The defense, of course, revealed that beer had been allowed and even issued. This did not bode well for Hiram. The secretary of the navy, learning of the trial, called upon Hiram for an explanation. He revealed that he had indeed authorized the issue of beer at mealtimes in order to control the men's drinking after hours. It was his belief that the trial of the two malcontents was absolutely necessary so as not to further expose himself. The secretary agreed fully with him and the matter was then closed. But the secretary suggested that no further beer be issued, to which Hiram agreed. The upshot was that the majority of the enlisted men were for Hiram, mostly because he tried to make beer available for them while taking a great chance with his own career by so doing. We can assume that the two miscreants spent some of their future in the can, possibly counting beer bottle caps.

That year another revolt broke out in Cuba and Hiram was ordered to take his men from Fisherman's Point to quell it. This revolt was by black Cubans who had been as close to slavery as it was still possible to be in the twentieth century Americas. Naturally, Hiram was forced to leave both Louises behind, alone in their house. He became quite alarmed when he learned that there was a band of those Cuban rebels marching directly upon his station. He left a quartermaster sergeant and a Chinese cook stationed in the cupola of his house with a machine gun, rifles and shotguns to repel "boarders." Both men were strategically positioned for an effective defense with instructions to hold out as long as possible. Louise was given a pistol to use should that become necessary.

His first move was to Guantánamo City by boat and by rail. Shortly after, Hiram received orders to take his small expeditionary force to Firmasa to protect the lives and property of Americans located there. He and his men went by boat to Santiago and then by rail to Firmasa. Upon arrival the Marines established themselves at the Firmasa Iron Mining Company, a subsidiary of Bethlehem Steel Corporation of Pennsylvania. As a matter of course and for many years Marines spent abundant hours defending the property of big business in foreign countries. While there, the Marines were housed in an old Spanish fort named Aquadores. One day a volunteer colonel of the Cuban army came to see Hiram. He had a sack containing 100 ears, which he proudly offered to show Hiram. He said he was getting paid for the number of ears he could deliver and he wanted "El Capitan" to verify that he had that number. Captain Bearss told him to exit and make sure he and his cronies left the Americans alone, especially their ears. Shortly after, Hiram and his men were back at Guantánamo safe and sound, all around and so were both his "girls" and their protectors.

Bearss had been raised in circumstances in which the proverbial silver spoon was never far from his mouth. His relations, in addition to being business owners, were quite well to do, with extensive acreage and wealth. They and their ancestors had worked very hard to acquire what they had. Regardless of this, Hiram was usually the worse for wear because his own purse was always empty. This was largely because of his own generosity to friends and those in need. But he was as meticulous with the Corps' money as a good businessman would be.[2]

When he arrived and took responsibility for the base and its financial matters, the canteen fund held all of $14. Two years later, when he was detached, the fund had increased to approximately $10,000. During the period he was there some of his accomplishments included bowling alleys, tennis courts and numerous other recreational facilities built for the welfare of the men. In addition he managed to purchase 13 horses for common use. The fund still had $10,000 remaining when he left.[3]

Hiram tried everything he could think of to please his men. Some times he went overboard and the efforts bounced back on him, such as in the beer incident. One time he appraised the food. It was terrible, and he figured the men must be sick of eating the same thing over and over again. Accordingly he ordered that chicken be prepared three or four times a week. Interspersed were rare roast beef, lamb and other delicacies. After about ten days of this delicious fare a committee of three enlisted men came forward. They had a complaint: They didn't like these fancy spreads and wanted, desperately, to go back to "good old Marine chow." The men, they insisted, wanted "cornwillie" and beans. No doubt that was why they were Marines in the first place; no taste buds, and no sense.

But there were times when the ordinary stomachs of the enlisted men were treated with swell fixins', and Thanksgiving was one of them. Louise and some of the other wives, plus her entire household, busily prepared delights for everyone including these same Marine gourmands. They baked a 30-pound fruit cake for the men. Every few days they doused it with whiskey and brandy. It must have been good. At any rate, the men came forward to thank her and the other ladies for their efforts. In addition, with the regular cooks, she put together 38 three-layer cakes and 17 regulation pies, all for Christmas meals. She even went so far as to bake several hundred small biscuits for the men and was the recipient of the greatest compliments for her cooking. Though biscuits were normally called "sinkers," these were referred to as "feathers" by the men who were possibly trying to make points with the old man's wife. Back in Olongapo, Louise remembered that Smedley Butler's wife, Ethel "Bunny" Conway Butler, often cooked cakes for the men and she had thought that was "wonderfully kind."

Most of the time, the base was relatively quiet, except when the fleet came in. Sometimes it remained as long as three months at a stretch. Then everything was lively and fun prevailed. This was especially true for the officers. There were people to meet, parties in the afternoon, and other exciting diversions to dispel the tedium and boredom for Louise and the other ladies. When the fleet left all was quiet again. But somehow Louise managed to retain her sanity and provide her husband and baby with a relatively happy home. Fortunately, the fleet came in at least twice in a year and when that happened Hiram had an open house.

Something happened in 1910 that made a great deal of difference for the comfort and future of the Marines at Gitmo. That was when the U.S. Army relinquished almost all buildings and other holdings at Fisherman's Point to the Marine Corps. The only exceptions were facilities belonging to the Corps of Engineers. With that exchange came improvements to all quarters — among other important alterations, each was screened, always a necessity in the tropics.

Louise was once again pregnant and the doctor ordered her and little Louise home. On the trip they encountered a terrible storm, possibly a hurricane, which tossed their ship about and caused some delay in their arrival. When she reached New York she immediately made for Ridgeview. There she had a baby boy but, as so often in that era, the baby died at birth. Louise blamed herself. She strongly believed that if she had remained with Hiram the situation would have been altered. It was to be a matter of lifelong regret for Louise. Not long after the tragedy, Louise and little Louise once again set sail for Guantánamo and Hiram. He had suffered nearly as much as his wife at their loss but was naturally happy to see both again.

While Louise had been away, there had been a modicum of activity at Guantánamo. Colonel Littleton W.T. Waller, Hiram's old commander and friend, appeared with a staff and some Marines to land, if necessary, on the territory of our southern neighbor, Mexico. One of the people assigned to Waller's brigade who showed up at about this time was Hiram's old pal Fritz Wise. He mentioned that Hiram "was as broke as ever. So his friends organized an old clothes party. We went over to call on him one evening, each man carrying some ancient part of a uniform. One had a pair of breeches; another a blouse; another a shirt; this one a hat; that one a pair of putees. Hiram was as sore as the devil. But in about fifteen minutes he was better dressed than he had been in a long while."[4]

This condition was of long standing and would continue throughout Hiram's entire career as a Marine. He was sometimes the unhappy target of practical jokes, as in the case described above, but many times he originated the best himself.

There was trouble in Mexico. There always seemed to be trouble in Mexico. Taft was still president and would encourage this latest threat to the sovereign nation just south of our border. This, of course, was what Marines were always waiting for and too infrequently managed to effect— a good, rousing, swift fight with an enemy of substantive size. Nothing serious, mind you, and certainly no hard feelings, but something to alter the boring lack of activity. There had been much turmoil within Mexico for the previous several years. President Madero had been overthrown and with his subsequent murder came merciless bloodshed. Our ambassador to Mexico, Henry Lane Wilson, had been, in effect, lined up with the rebels. He even went so far as to brag about it to the American newspaper men covering the troubles. But Waller and his Marines didn't get into a fight with Mexico; not just yet. They were recalled and sailed to the U.S. shortly thereafter.

It was about this time that the USS *Georgia* appeared in the bay. Aboard was Fritz Wise, a Marine that Hiram was always glad to see. Wise later said,

> He came out to dinner with me on the *Georgia*. Doctor McCullough, the ship's doctor, mixed some cocktails. I wasn't drinking. But Hiram was. Those cocktails were so effective that after dinner Hiram suddenly reached into his pocket, pulled out some money, and paid me seventy-five dollars he had owed me for I don't know how long. I wanted the doctor to make some more [cocktails] so that I could send them around to some other friends.[5]

At the time Louise was about to leave for the United States, the fleet was at Fisherman's Point. Hiram had been rather close to several of the navy chaplains, who were well aware that neither Louise nor Hiram were bound to any specific religion. One of them, a priest of the Roman Catholic faith, talked them into allowing him to baptize little Louise. He must have been very persuasive and insistent and close to both for that to have happened.

When it became known that Hiram's time at Guantánamo was almost up, Louise planned to leave a bit earlier to make efforts to get little Louise into the Wharton Day School in Philadelphia. Arrangements had to be made early. It was a very exclusive school with many applicants for the limited space available. Effective on 22 June 1912, Hiram was ordered detached from Guantánamo to proceed to the Marine Barracks at Norfolk, Virginia. He somehow managed to get approval to leave a bit earlier so as to escort his wife and daughter to the United States. At the same time Captain George Cline, the naval officer commanding the naval base, joined Hiram and his family on their trip to Santiago. There they all entrained for Havana and then caught a civilian ship bound for New York.

At New York, Bearss was temporarily in command of the barracks when, on 15 July 1912, the commanding officer returned. At that point Hiram was transferred to the USS *Utah*. He was on that ship from 4 September to 10 September to observe target practice with the Atlantic Fleet. After his return, on 12 September Hiram was again detached for instruction at the Advance Base School, then at Philadelphia, at which he arrived two days later.[6] The Advance Base unit was a relatively new formation that the Marine Corps was still experimenting with. It was formed to give Marine officers and men practical training in the landing of guns, materiel and men from ship to shore during an emergency. It was a concept that had been several years in the making. Previously it had been a primarily theoretical school, with little hands-on training, unless one could count the experiences at Culebra. The doctrine would continue beyond the Great War before finally settling into what we now know as the Fleet Marine Force (FMF).[7]

Many of Hiram's old pals were there, including Fritz Wise. Smedley Butler would also have been, except instead he was off messing up the Nicaraguans. Life continued happily for at least a year. It wasn't until September 1912 that President Taft became annoyed with the government of Santo Domingo. By 27 September Marines, with Hiram included, had been quickly formed up and embarked aboard the USS *Prairie*. Bearss was in command of Company C of the 2d Provisional Regiment, Col. Franklin J. Moses commanding.[8]

The story of why the Marines, all 750 of them, were about to give the Dominicans what for is beyond the scope of this book. But basically they had been having numerous revolutions, and "our man" wasn't running things. During this same period three ex-presidents were in rebellion against the current holder of that office. As usual, it was a mess. Our State

6. Guantánamo and Vera Cruz

Department employee delivered an ultimatum — their guys accepted it and the Marines went back to where they had come from. But in between this, briefly, is what happened.

Our fleet anchored in the roadstead of the River Ozoma, which flowed through the city of Santo Domingo. Mr. Doyle, the State Department representative, traveled with the fleet. A series of conferences with some rebels took place. Several Marine officers accompanied Doyle in his wanderings, Captain Bearss being one of them. The latter admitted to being somewhat "dazed" at the proposals and counterproposals exchanged between the two sides. After three weeks, Bearss and the other American officers told Doyle to make one and only one more proposal and not accept any changes. It must be accepted within 30 minutes or it meant war. This was done, with accompanying threats, and the proposal was accepted at once. With that, the *Prairie* hauled up its anchor and everyone headed home. The Marines had a good laugh at their success with Doyle. They had all seen the handwriting on the wall. The negotiations would have gone on forever had they not interceded. It was said that even the Dominicans had a good laugh over how it was settled.

The ship reached Philadelphia on 12 December 1912 and Hiram joined his new post in the navy yard that same day. On the trip home, Hiram received a statement from the 1st Battalion commander concerning his "failing" health. It appears that he was tabulated as "Health in General Bad" and incapacitated for duty because he had something called "Bronchitis Catarr. epidem., Antri abscessus." The passed assistant surgeon, Samuel S. Rodman, USN, categorically stated that he was not fit for active field duty. All that Hiram could respond with was, "I have no statement to make." Otherwise, his fitness report for that period, signed by Col. George Barnett, was 3.5 or better, mostly the latter. Barnett added that Hiram was unqualifiedly fit for active service. So much for Doctor Rodman. This sort of thing would dog Hiram for years to come. His health was very poor and he knew it, but Hiram refused to allow that to stop his doing what he still wanted most to do: be a Marine.

Hiram continued at Philadelphia until 18 February 1913 when he was included with a group of Marines shipped out aboard the USS *Meade*. The destination, once again, was Cuba and Guantánamo. They disembarked on 27 February, set up camp and waited for the call, which never came. Once again it was to have been Mexico. Hiram had a company in the 1st Regiment of Marines, 2d Provisional Brigade, Col. George Barnett commanding. It consisted of 72 officers and 2,097 enlisted Marines. The 1st Regiment was under the command of Col. Lincoln Karmany while the 2d Regiment was under the command of Col. Joseph H. Pendleton.[9]

The Republic of Mexico had been having birth pangs for about 100 years, and nothing seemed to ever settle the nation down to a peaceful existence. The previous dozen years had been especially painful. Murders of presidents, especially those duly elected, were commonplace. Turmoil was constant and very upsetting for its near neighbors. During the period of Thomas Woodrow Wilson's tenure as president, the United States constantly probed and poked the Mexicans. Wilson believed, strongly, that it was his task to teach our neighbors "to elect good men." Even though during his presidency he had the U.S. Marines run most of the nations of the Caribbean ragged, he reserved a special place in his heart for Mexico.[10]

The United States is Mexico's nearest neighbor to the north and the hemisphere's most powerful nation. We set the rules and insisted that every other nation jump through our hoops. The Mexicans didn't. They had their own rules and were and still are a very proud people. But ours were usually enforced by the best bang for a buck the nation ever had — the U.S. Marine Corps. Although there were never enough Marines to cover all the hot spots envisioned by State, the Marines did their best, which was always much better than should have been expected.

For some reason by 28 April, the situation had settled down appreciably. The Marines were reembarked and returned to Philadelphia — arriving on 2 May and disembarking that same day. Following this, the only interruption to Hiram's routine was a trip to Indian Head, Maryland, on 29 May to witness what the big naval guns could do. The naval proving grounds allowed the firing of the largest guns down the Potomac to determine accuracy and range. He was back in Philadelphia a few days later and remained there until 3 January 1914. At that time the Advanced Base Force was loaded on transports for shipment to the old favorite, Culebra Island, for more practical training. During this period the training at the school was constantly being interrupted for service abroad. One might say that it was indeed practical training.

Colonel George Barnett had under his command a brigade composed of two regiments of Marines totaling 59 officers and 1,700 enlisted men. Most of the officers had already attended the Advance Base School. Hiram's F Company was a part of Lt. Col. Charles G. "Squeegee" Long's 1st Regiment.[11] The purpose of this unit was to take desirable bases for the U.S. Navy anywhere the navy found a need. With many new ships and an overseas empire needing protection, the navy had plenty of need.

On 3 January 1914, the brigade was shipped aboard both the USS *Prairie* and the *Hancock,* the latter being one of the new transports that the commandant had been requesting for several years. The force was to land against an entrenched opponent. Our Marines were to take the island, establish the fortifications, then place the guns, all within a time limit. The "enemy" had a fleet opposing ours. Everything had been worked out at Philadelphia on a sand-table many times before. Most of the old gang were there, Phil Brown, Logan Feland, Fritz Wise, and Bob Dunlap among many others.[12] Dunlap was already establishing a reputation as a first-class artilleryman. And, of great additional interest, 1st Lt. Bernard L. Smith, now a flyer, was searching overhead for mines or any other dastardly implements the enemy could conjure up. Smith was, if you remember, that young engineering officer whom Hiram had "loaned" to the navy to straighten out some of their mechanical problems on board a ship.

During this rousing event, Hiram continued making a name for himself. He was commended in writing for his fortitude and dashing leadership. The guns were hauled up the hill and positioned, all within eight hours of the first Marines touching the shore. The Marines remained at what they named Camp Roosevelt for about 20 days.[13] It was the first actual expedition launched under this new Advanced Base concept and was considered a rousing success by the chief of the Atlantic Fleet and the Marine commandant.

At its conclusion the invading force was ordered to Pensacola, Florida, where the fleet was to remain for a short time. Payday was held while the fleet was in port and the leave was long enough for the men to spend all of their money. Lucky were the bar owners and madams of those houses of ill repute that were providing untold wonders for the poor benighted heathens. One additional thing happened that undoubtedly made enlisted men, sailors and Marines, very happy. Josephus Daniels, the secretary of the navy, had decided that all enlisted men, regardless of their previous education, had to attend school and study various primary subjects. His idea was very good. There were large numbers of illiterate enlisted men in all services. Many had come into the navy or Marines just to get something to eat, or were foreigners, who could barely understand, let alone speak, the English language. It was Daniels' idea to make the men at least conversant and be able to understand orders from their superiors. The ultimate success of this teaching program isn't obvious now, but we can hope the time taken was worth the time served.

The ships now called upon New Orleans. The city was in the process of rendering a reception for the Roman Catholic cardinal James Gibbons. All Marines and sailors attended this affair, Catholics and Protestants and possibly those of other persuasions. After the parade in Gibbons' honor the Marine officers were welcomed onto the stage. As a gesture of extreme patriotism and respect for their uniform, Gibbons stood and shook the hands of each and every Marine officer. There were many parades and the

Marines had their share of them. The Lenten period lasted five weeks and the fleet remained at New Orleans the whole time. It was considered a good thing, especially for the Roman Catholics, of which there were many in that city and probably also in the navy and Marine Corps.

The Landing at Vera Cruz

As mentioned previously, neither Taft's presidential administration nor Wilson's had gotten on well with the various factions that were running Mexico. General Victoriano Huerta had taken power by the usual method: he seized it. Later, it was evident that he was, at that time, probably the best man for the job. As a last straw, Wilson had tried to entice Huerta into inviting and accepting him as a mediator between the opposing forces. All Mexican factions, Constitutionalists and the provisional government had as much as told Wilson to go soak his head. That response he didn't like; his ego was great. What he did do was wait for an opportunity to soak their heads. That opportunity came by virtue of a simple act by some low-level Mexican officials. It was an act that in reality had little if anything to do with rubbing the nose of the *Yanquis* in dirt, but that was the way it was taken. And, surprisingly, not by anyone in the State Department, but by a sailor, Rear Admiral Henry T. Mayo, USN.[14]

It began on 9 April 1914 at Tampico, Mexico. That seaport city lies midway on the Mexican coast between Vera Cruz to the south and the U.S. border to the north. Sailors from the USS *Dolphin*, anchored offshore, were attempting to obtain gasoline from the normal source ashore. They were arrested, or perhaps just detained, by an overzealous Mexican officer, for some unimportant reason. This was an almost insignificant part of a relatively small American fleet of observation stationed further offshore. A few days before, a U.S. Marine courier had been arrested by Mexican officials but was soon released. Admiral Mayo declined to make an issue of that, but this time he made waves. He demanded, among other things, that the local military apologize in writing and fire a salute to the American flag. The latter they declined to do, for diplomatic reasons. Mayo threatened them with unimaginable horrors if they didn't. They still wouldn't render a salute. His report to his superior, Admiral Frank F. Fletcher, carried the barest details of the incident. Fletcher sent the message to Washington very much as received, with minimal comment, so what the president's staff saw contained no further additional information about what had transpired. All of the officials, including President Wilson, responded that they believed that "Mayo could not have done otherwise."[15]

The American chargé d'affaires in Mexico City, Nelson J. O'Shaughnessy, was instructed to handle the matter with "the utmost earnestness, firmness and frankness, representing to them [Mexican government] its extreme seriousness, etc." In other words, tell them to do what we demand or else. What we demanded, the Mexican officials believed, would have reduced their nation to a subject status so they refused the most unreasonable (to them) points of contention.

There seems not to be any question that the U.S. government had every intention to land troops someplace in Mexico and were just looking for an excuse. Initially, Tampico was the target for any American occupation. By 20 April Col. John A. Lejeune, with a large contingent of Marines, was located just offshore. Mayo believed that he had enough Marines to make the landing and successfully occupy the city. But then it was learned that a German ship, the SS *Ypiranga,* was headed for Vera Cruz with a load of weapons for the Mexican government. In all there were at least 200 machine guns and 15,000,000 rounds of ammunition aboard. No one in his right mind could allow Huerta that increase in armaments, especially with the U.S. planning to land troops. Something had to be done and Vera Cruz was the place to do it.[16]

On 5 March elements of the 2d Marine Regiment, with Lt. Col. Wendell C. Neville in command, set sail from Pensacola, Florida, aboard the USS *Prairie* and arrived at Vera Cruz on 9 March.[17] The unit had 14 officers and 329 men. Initial landings took place on 20 April. Neville's men were the first ashore and they were soon followed by a Marine detachment from Panama. The Marines landed on the principal pier of the port without resistance and promptly occupied the cable station nearby, ensuring contact with the United States. Neville then advanced his men down a street lying between the railroad station and the power plant. The balance of the 2d Regiment, 16 officers and 516 men, remained at Pensacola until 21 April. On that date they embarked aboard the USS *Mississippi* and arrived at Vera Cruz on 24 April. Travel aboard a battleship wasn't common for most Marines, but apparently it was completely adequate for all hands. It wouldn't be the last time it happened.

On 15 April the 1st Marine Regiment, 1st Advance Brigade, Lt. Col. Charles G. Long commanding, boarded the USS *Hancock* at Philadelphia bound for Tampico, Mexico. Included in his force were 24 officers, including Hiram and 810 enlisted Marines. Upon arrival they remained aboard the ship until transferred to Vera Cruz where, on 22 April, they too were landed.[18]

Capt. Bearss led his company ashore and passed through the lines of Neville's men. As they pushed through the town, sniper fire from Mexican forces became extremely severe. The method used by the Marines was to dash within a building and then out and then into another. Soon they came upon a church from which flowed more rifle fire. As Hiram and a few of his men attempted to take out the snipers in the church, other rifle fire came from the surrounding buildings—particularly from the tower of one building located about 600 or 700 yards away.

First they drove out those Mexicans firing from the church; then they went after the snipers in the tower. Bearss directed two of his expert marksmen, McNewland and Trainor, to take prone positions and fire at anyone that moved in the tower. Bearss then looked through his glasses and yelled. He didn't give the order to fire because he saw that the "idiots" in the tower were part of the bluejacket brigade that had also come ashore. They were firing on anything that moved, including Marines. It has been recorded that because these men were so poorly trained in infantry warfare, several Marines paid the ultimate price. Major Albertus Catlin, who was to later command the 6th Marines in France, had just posted a Marine sentry before his headquarters. A navy patrol came down the street and without a word shot the Marine sentry at his post.[19] Fritz Wise's company was pinned down while engaged in searching from door to door for snipers. The snipers pinning them down were bluejackets atop the Hotel Diligencia. As the story went, they had mistaken Marines for Mexicans. Hiram and several other Marine officers made a suggestion that all the bluejackets be returned to their ships. It was a serious recommendation; there were by now enough Marines to handle any situation liable to happen at Vera Cruz. Unfortunately, the proposal was not taken seriously, so nothing was done to relieve the situation and the sailors stayed a few more days. This is not to imply that none of the blue-

Major General John A. Lejeune graduated from the Naval Academy and was commissioned a second lieutenant of Marines in 1890. His service included Cuba, Panama, Philippines, Vera Cruz, and France, where he commanded the 2d Division. Upon his return he was made the thirteenth commandant, leaving office and retiring in 1929. He took office as superintendent of the Virginia Military Institute until 1937.

jacket detachments performed well; many did. It is a truism that some navy officers wanted to lead ashore. The oddity of seamen, with rifles and sometimes machine guns, ashore fighting against infantry, would continue for some years to come.

Bearss and his company were sent to establish an outpost on a sand hill just outside town. He was told to have his men dig trenches and to occupy them, which he did. The sand hill had been created by wind blowing sand as in a desert. The following morning the trenches were filled to the brim with sand. They then brought up bags to fill with sand. These bags helped create the proper environment and protection and the post was entirely satisfactory from then on. Following the creation of this outpost, Hiram took out a patrol to observe the Mexican forces to his front. They were coming in closer and closer — much closer than they had been instructed to do in a negotiated settlement. So, Hiram and some of his men went out and maneuvered behind them. They captured the whole lot and brought them in as prisoners. Admiral Fletcher, who had assumed command of all the forces in the city of Vera Cruz the night before, ordered Hiram to return the Mexicans to where he had picked them up.

On the morning of 22 April, Neville had assumed command of both Marine regiments ashore. But, shortly after noon, Col. John A. Lejeune landed and replaced Neville in command of the entire Marine Brigade. More navy ships, including the big gun battleships, were floating into the Vera Cruz roadway. Most of the Atlantic Fleet had by now arrived. Wilson wanted to impose his will and his strong arm, the naval service, was ready to impose it for him.

More bluejackets were still being landed and moving into their section of the city. That was on the left of the Marines. They were having trouble solidifying their holdings. Mexican snipers were giving them a bad time and they, without solid infantry experience, were not doing well at all. They did have some support from a couple of the smaller ships in the bay. Three, four, and five-inch guns punched holes in buildings in the Naval Brigade's sector — knocking out various snipers' positions and saving the Naval Brigade from further destruction.

On the third day, the 1st and 2d Marine Regiments resumed the advance and cleared the balance of the city. Catlin's 3d Regiment was now absorbed officially into Neville's 2d Regiment. By this time, most all of the actual fighting had already been conducted. Marine commanders were now positioning their men in as much safety and comfort as could be attained.

On the 24th the USS *Mississippi* arrived from Pensacola with a battalion of three batteries of Marine artillery and the balance of the 2d Regiment. By 25 April, Lt. Col. George Reid had another battalion of Marines ashore. These were sent to protect the city's waterworks at El Tejar, about ten miles by rail from Vera Cruz. At this time there were more sailors ashore than Marines. The figures tell us that the naval brigade had 200 officers and approximately 3,760 men, whereas the Marine Brigade now totaled 96 officers and 2,373 enlisted men. There would have been a few more Marines if some of them hadn't gotten in the bluejackets' sights.

For some months before this incident, the U.S. Army had been preparing for an invasion of Mexico. There were a considerable number of army troops along the U.S.-Mexican border and at the seaport of Galveston, Texas; all told, a reinforced brigade was in readiness. Under orders, Brig. Gen. Frederick Funston, USA, embarked with the entire force on 23 April and the following day sailed for Vera Crux. His orders were to relieve the naval forces and to not extend the current limits held by American forces. By the twenty-eighth he had arrived with some soldiers and landed that day. By the thirtieth the entire army force was landed and Funston had assumed overall control ashore. Once again the Marines were serving under U.S. Army command.[20]

The naval forces and Marine detachments from the navy's ships returned to that duty leaving the Marine Brigade of 3,141 officers and men, and the army forces still ashore. On 1 May Colonel Waller arrived and assumed from Colonel Lejeune command of the Marine Brigade. All men ashore now settled down to many boring months of watching and waiting for something that never happened. The Mexican military forces avoided the area.

Several days after the Marines arrived at the waterworks at El Tejar, there came an incident that plagued the Corps and especially one young officer for years to come. In his memoir, Lejeune recounts what he heard and saw. A phone call was received from the El Tejar post excitedly demanding help to "repel a threatened attack ... a Mexican

Brigadier General Albertus W. Catlin was a Naval Academy graduate who was commissioned a second lieutenant of Marines in 1892. He was serving aboard the USS *Maine* when she was sunk the harbor at Havana, Cuba, in 1898. Major Catlin was awarded a Medal of Honor at Vera Cruz in April 1914, and in 1918 he commanded the 6th Marine Regiment in France until wounded at Belleau Wood. He took a disability retirement in December 1919.

force of a thousand men." Colonel James E. Mahoney, who had replaced Lejeune as regimental commander, received instructions from Funston to take all available Marines and go immediately to the aid of their comrades.[21]

The relieving force hurriedly marched out the nine miles or so in the heat of the day, and found, to their intense anger, the following situation when they arrived. One lone Mexican had come into the lines bearing a white flag. Upon reaching the Marines he demanded that they surrender to him and his forces, which, incidentally, were nowhere to be seen. Major John Russell, who commanded and was later to be commandant, had sent the distress call. According to consequent reports, he had threatened to surrender his battalion to this lone Mexican if he didn't receive help soon. Lejeune is quoted as being mad as hell at being dragged out on a nine-mile "goose chase" because one officer lost his nerve.[22] Smedley Butler never forgot the incident and 20 years later made sure that the Senate heard the true story of "The Battle of Russell's Run," as it was called. This was during the hearings to replace Fuller with Russell. At that time, as usual, Lejeune's memory was conveniently lost and he played both sides.

Something of significance did happen that has never been satisfactorily explained. Fletcher and his navy officers were prolific in recommending their comrades for decorations. The only decoration that could be awarded to navy and Marine officers, at that time, was the Medal of Honor.[23] The Marines weren't far behind the navy. They put in the names of every officer who participated in the initial landing and most were awarded the medal, even the Marine commander Neville.

Since the Marines and soldiers would continue to be stationed on Mexican territory for some time to come, they set about making life a bit more comfortable. A Foreign Club was formed and membership was extended to American officers and other non-Mexicans. One new member was Admiral Sir Christopher Cradock, RN, who in a few months would go down with his ship in the Pacific Ocean. There were also some German naval officers who, at least until August, would be friendly with their comrades of the Royal Navy. One member, a German reserve army officer, was a nephew of Bismarck. He was making every effort to make his way back to Germany. Later he traveled aboard the USS *Cyclops* to Philadelphia with some of the Marines.

While in Mexico, Hiram was attacked by an intestinal parasite that nearly felled him. His weight dropped down to less than 130 pounds. As a result, on 4 August 1914 he was detailed to return to Philadelphia for treatment. On 10 August he and his ship arrived at Hampton Roads, Virginia, and by the next train he arrived at the naval hospital at Philadelphia. His doctor labeled it "Enteritis, chronic." It was caused "incident to duty in the tropics." The staff put him on a rigorous regime of proper food, medicine and other curatives. Soon he was given a proper leave of two months, from 2 September, and at once he, and we can assume his two womenfolk, left for Ridgeview. There he languished in what he considered to be perfect comfort. Friends, family and some acquaintances showed up to welcome the wandering hero home. Of course, he was required to tell tales, tall if that made them sound better. And, like those of most Marines, most were tall. His orders allowed him until 2 November, when he once again reported for duty at the Philadelphia naval hospital and was discharged for active service. He went at once to the navy yard where he was fortunate to find that his quarters were secure, since there weren't many Marine officers there at the time. Consequently, Adelaide Louise and little Louise joined him without delay.

The times were slow. On 3 December 1914, Col. George Barnett assigned Hiram to duty with the 1st Marine Brigade. On 16 January 1915 Hiram was reassigned to the barracks detachment at Philadelphia. He continued in this mundane task until 17 May when he was ordered to take his detachment to Westchester, Pennsylvania, to the home of Congressman Thomas S. Butler, the father of Major Smedley D. Butler. Butler was chairman of the House Naval Appropriations Committee, and was a very good friend of the navy and more so of the U.S. Marine Corps.[24]

Hiram and his men marched the distance, to and from, camping in between. They all remained in tents during the period and participated in a couple of reviews. In all, there were at least 2,000 officers and men engaged in this undertaking. After his return he spent another several weeks engaged in a map-making school located at Gettysburg. During his stay he covered the ground thoroughly — examining the contours of the land and road positions and making drawings. Much of this was done by other students upon bicycles, but Hiram chose to walk. On the fifteenth of August he was again detached and ordered to the U.S. Army military school at Fort Leavenworth, Kansas. This was and would continue to be the prime schooling assignment for Marines as well as for army officers.

Arriving on 20 August he immediately reported to General Green, the officer commanding the school. Its reputation for being the finest army school had already been attained. The list of graduates is composed of the most famous names in the military chronicles of the United States. Although he had never been much of a "book soldier" and did not become one at Leavenworth, somehow, after a couple of scrapes, he managed to graduate.[25] On 25 April 1916 Hiram returned to take his examination for major — a rank which he previously had been temporarily advanced to. On 13 May he went before the examining board and on 5 June he received his permanent majority from 16 May 1915. He had been a full-time Marine for 17 years and a captain for nearly 15 of them.

There had been several complaints by the reviewing board. Two complaints were concerning a problem in 1903 and another in 1907, were both for using "stimulants." He was also noted for a poor inspection of the Marine Barracks at Guantánamo in 1911 and his "carelessness ... in management of Post Exchange at ... Guantánamo" in 1913. Otherwise they gave him an overall "General Efficiency" rating of 3.4, which is certainly an acceptable mark. His accompanying medical report showed some interesting details indicative of the numerous debilitating diseases he had suffered, some of which we are familiar with. For many years he had been a victim of gastrointestinal diseases that continued to flare up from time to time. But nothing was noted about his unfortunate fall from a horse while at Leavenworth. Much of the latter part of the program required a ride over several Civil War battlefields. Regardless, nothing could keep him down for any length of time and he was soon back under harness for what lay ahead.

7
Santo Domingo

For many years the island of Hispaniola had been in a state of turmoil. Haiti, a former French colony and now an independent nation, occupied the western portion. Santo Domingo, a former Spanish colony, occupied the eastern part. For many years, since their independence, the two nations had been at loggerheads. Each was sometimes dominant, sometimes subservient to the other. Over the years successive governments of Santo Domingo had begged the northern giant, the United States of America, to take over their country. President Ulysses S. Grant was all for it but everyone else refused to consider it. We pick up the story of Santo Domingo shortly after Hiram put on his oak leaves.

Like Haiti, Santo Domingo had a bad fiscal relationship with other nations, constantly defaulting on her loans, especially those from American banks. The same thing had been going on in Haiti since 1915, and so the Marines had been in the process of subjugating both small nations.[1] The revolution in progress in Santo Domingo at this time was also very serious. Several Marine companies had already been detached from their ships and sent ashore to restore order. Fritz Wise and his 6th Company had been at the city of Santo Domingo since 5 May 1916, as had Capt. Eugene Fortson's 9th Company of artillery. Seven days later Rear Admiral William B. Caperton, USN, delivered the 4th and 5th Marine companies from Haiti and a detachment of the 24th Company from Guantánamo. On 21 May Marine detachments from the USS *New Jersey*, *Rhode Island* and *Louisiana* had sailed for Santo Domingo aboard the *Salem* and *Memphis*. Two days later, Col. Theodore Kane arrived at Santo Domingo City with elements of two more companies plus the headquarters of the 2d Regiment. Kane immediately assumed command ashore of all Marine units in the south.[2] Meanwhile on 1 June, Marines, including a detachment of Marines from the USS *Sacramento*, landed on the north coast at Puerto Plata. Four days later two more companies of Marines landed further west at Monte Cristi.[3] It was obvious to those Marines ashore that many more of their comrades would be required to effectively occupy the entire country and get the rebel Arias. He wasn't "our" man.

Meanwhile, Admiral Caperton requested more Marines. Headquarters ordered "Uncle Joe" Pendleton and his 4th Marines to entrain at San Diego and head for the port at New Orleans. There, a week later, they embarked aboard the USS *Hancock* for passage to Monte Cristi, arriving on 21 June. At that point Pendleton assumed command of all Marines ashore in Santo Domingo.

This intervention would put Hiram right smack into the first major campaign he'd been in since the Philippines, 15 years previous. Here he would make an impressive reputation as a first-class colonial soldier, showing more than just fighting ability and leadership. He would be situated into the same capacity that Waller and Butler were often placed in — Hiram would become a proconsul as well as a conqueror. This was a breed of men who were able to transcend mere command of units. They supplied common-sense values when few existed elsewhere, and made the necessary rules. More often than not they had to think their way out of stupid messes created by civilians, or worse, other military men. Killing badly armed natives was relatively easy but settling difficulties while so doing was more difficult. The real glory is that they succeeded more often than not.

Major General Joseph H. Pendleton graduated from the Naval Academy and accepted a commission as a second lieutenant of Marines in 1884. He chased seal poachers in Alaska and served in Cuba and the Philippines, later as CO of the 1st Marine Brigade. In 1912, he was CO of all Marines in Nicaragua. He was the first CO of the 4th Marines, taking them to Santo Domingo in 1916. He retired in 1924.

On 28 June Hiram sailed from New York aboard the USS *Celtic*, a troop ship bound for Haiti. Having no command as yet he was traveling alone but his orders were to report to his old commanding officer, Colonel Waller, at Port-au-Prince. Haiti had quieted down a trifle but would continue to require Marines for many years to come. So would Santo Domingo, even after it became the Dominican Republic. Although the U.S. State Department believed that the two nations "required" Marines to assist them in solving their own problems, the feelings were not mutual; hence there would continue to be a load of trouble for the Marines in both places.

When the ship stopped at Cape Haitian, Hiram learned of trouble brewing in Santo Domingo. Rushing back aboard the *Celtic*, Hiram sent a wire to the Navy Department and requested a change of orders. A return wire directed him to report to General Joseph Pendleton and his 4th Marines at Monte Cristi.[4] "Uncle Joe" was just about to begin his move into the interior so Hiram was in time. He was directed to replace Maj. Charles B. Hatch, USMC, in command of the Marine battalion at Puerto Plata, about 40 miles down the coast. Pendleton would badly need supplies as he advanced and it would be Hiram's job to see that the 4th Marines would not want for anything. Boarding the USS *New Jersey*, Hiram was transported to Puerto Plata in style. Upon arrival he met with and in short order relieved Hatch.

His new command included the 4th, 9th, and 24th companies and Marine detachments from the *New Jersey* and the *Rhode Island*. The three rifle companies had each been transferred from Haiti to Santo Domingo, and then directed to Puerto Plata.

Hiram immediately set about organizing a supply service for Pendleton. Supplies were to be transported inland 40 miles south by train to meet the general at Santiago City. By nightfall he had the plan organized and ready to go. But there is always a problem and this time was no different. His Marines went looking for a train engine and found one in the rail yards. However, there was no crew around to service it. Looking around in the area Hiram finally located an engineer and his fireman in a local café drinking coffee. He asked them to come get the engine up and ready for a run. They both pretended they didn't understand. Hiram continued in broken Spanish until even they couldn't stand it anymore. Finally, both absolutely refused to work for the *Yanquis*. If Señor Hiram wanted that train with supplies to run, he would have to move it himself.

Hiram was not one to be defeated by two nonentities. The USS *Sacramento* was lying in the harbor with capable navy engineers aboard. To the ship he went and with the permission of her captain obtained six sailors to move the train. Under Bearss' direction, the sailors soon had steam up and were ready to go.[5] He had coal cars and several boxcars with supplies to the rear and two flatcars hooked up before the engine. On the flatcars he posted sand bags to protect his two 3-inch field pieces and machine guns. His locomotive had sandbags placed strategically so as to protect the boilers. Then, taking some Marines as backup, Hiram had his train move southward along the lines to Santiago City to see what he would be running into.

Captain Frederick A. Ramsey's 29th (Signal) Company with a rebel prisoner. They were part of the regiment's advance guard on the way to Santiago.

Hiram was playing it safe. If he had taken a full load of supplies the first trip and run into an ambush, he might have lost it all. Instead, he counted upon reaching Pendleton with at least a few supplies safely delivered. Walking ahead of the engine, Hiram and his men, on both sides and to the rear, kept a weather eye out for hostiles. The skirmishers, in effect, were protecting the train with their bodies. That isn't good duty, for anyone, at any time. Ask any point man.

The ground was very hilly, wooded and tropical. An ambuscade could have caught them almost anywhere along the line. During the first day they ran into a few skirmishers and snipers but suffered no Marine casualties. After a skirmish at Llanos Perez, where shells from a 3-inch dispersed the rebels, the train halted for the night at the village of Lajas. On the twenty-ninth they resumed their forward movement. Hiram learned that a band of 200 insurgents was perched across the rail line at Alta Mira. Arriving at the village about 1500 hours, Hiram and his force fanned out and soon incorporated it into the holdings of the U.S. Marine Corps. They even managed to capture a few of the Dominicans who had been trying to disrupt Pendleton's relatively easy access to the interior. Hiram sent his 4th Company over a mountain trail to outflank the rebel's right flank, while the rest of the command pushed ahead with the train. Fortson's guns banged away on the rebel mountaintop position. The first shot was a trifle short, the second was a little over, the third took off half of a shack overlooking the enemy's trenches and the fourth took away the right side. The fifth hit smack into the middle of what was left of the shack and forced the entire bunch out of their positions. A couple more shots of shrapnel cracking overhead sped them on their way down the hillside. With a combination of both guns, plus frontal and flank attacks, the Marines forced the enemy back to another position just covering a train tunnel. Without doubt, this place, if anywhere, would be where they would probably be ambushed and in serious trouble.[6]

Hiram had his train and men halt about 250 yards before its entrance. Here the track had an upgrade of nearly a dozen degrees, and the intervening hill was some 200 feet high and practically perpendicular. The enemy was dug in on top of that hill. The hills in that area were wooded and stony. Alongside the track on both sides was a precipitous drop of many hundreds of feet straight down. Obviously, Hiram's flanking force was limited in what could be accomplished. Hiram had his artilleryman, Capt. Eugene P. Fortson, unload a gun from the flatcars and swing into action. At Hiram's command Fortson banged away at the hilltop positions while his infantry moved forward. It wasn't too long before the enemy decided that safety was the choice of the day. Down the reverse slope they fled, placing them at the opposite end of the tunnel. Marines could see what looked like smoke coming from about a quarter mile further on beyond the end of the tunnel. There was a bridge which spanned a deep and very hazardous ravine through which the Dagabonica River flowed many hundreds of feet below. If the Dominican rebels destroyed the bridge,

7. Santo Domingo

Captain Fortson's 9th Company Battery in action, possibly near their fight at Alta Mira.

the Marines would be in the soup; another bridge would have to be constructed. Under the existing conditions that would be extremely difficult even if possible. If unsuccessful they would be permanently defeated, at least in that part of the island. If that bridge went down Pendleton's men would be starved for supplies and ammunition. It didn't come to that. Hiram Bearss didn't allow it to happen.

Hiram took a handcar that he had the foresight to have brought along, and pumping the handles, through the tunnel he went. He was closely followed by 60 Marines who charged through the 300-yard-long tunnel. After reaching the other side and finding it clear, he had the train follow him through ever so slowly. The rebels had allowed the Marines to believe that they had already mined the tunnel, and the truth is that they had planned to do so. But Hiram moved faster than they. What Hiram had dreaded actually had happened. The bridge, which was about a half mile from the exit of the tunnel, was afire.

Even though the enemy began putting up a stiffer resistance, the Marines pushed forward with their machine guns and sprinkled them enough that the way was nearly clear. The bridge fire was blazing and they could see some of the rails sliding off into the gorge. Fighting like mad they managed to push the enemy back and reached the bridge in time to extinguish the fire. A brief search located some spare rails on the ground. These were rushed into place and somehow they managed to replace the rails, repair the damaged bridge and push the train across the gorge.

But their troubles didn't end there. In a short time they reached nearly to the town of Navarette, where they found the enemy well entrenched. Hiram moved up front and assumed command. The enemy was once again driven back, and down the tracks the Marines continued on their rail journey. Using artillery as well as rifle and machine gun fire, the town was taken by the end of the day. Losses to the insurgents amounted to an estimated 50 casualties. Marine losses were two wounded. One was 2d Lt. Douglas B. Roben and the other his trumpeter, Pvt. Julius Goldsmith, both of the 4th Company.[7]

Meanwhile, "Uncle Joe" Pendleton and his column were also having troubles. Every few miles or so, they came upon a band of rebels defending ground that the Marines had to assault and take before proceeding forward. Some Marines were falling, and that didn't set well with their comrades. The Marines were using machine guns to their advantage and the natives were in awe. They ran whenever the Marines set them up, but not far enough nor fast enough.

Without further serious problems, on 4 July Colonel Pendleton and his main formation made contact with Hiram and his column at Navarette, where Hiram had been stocking supplies. Hiram had been sending his train back to Puerto Plata once a day to bring back supplies. Each trip required replacing rails and fighting off insurgents who had cut in behind the Marines. In this Hiram was well served by Capt. Douglas C. McDougall, who had joined Hiram during the trip.[8] Hiram had McDougall, who spoke Spanish, pass on the word to the locals that if there were any damage to the rail lines all the houses in the surrounding area would be destroyed. That soon changed everything. The trip back and forth became much easier.[9]

Upon arrival, Pendleton was by now badly in need of supplies, both food and ammunition. His had been a hard running fight, as had Hiram's, but a longer one. The two men had served together before but the differences between them in personality and style made friendship difficult. They were not at odds but they weren't close either. But that was the way it was with Hiram. You were either his friend or an associate. At any rate, they were both professionals and got along, as would be expected. "Uncle Joe" was honest and thoughtful insofar as his men were concerned. He was also just and he was fair. Hiram was an extrovert. He was tough on himself and his men. He was fun to be with and famous for his stories, which entertained officers and men alike. His leadership style was exactly what we

Hiram's Puerto Plata detachment's riflemen crossed the mountains riding his railroad while engaged in delivering supplies to Colonel Pendleton, from the port to Navarette and later to Santiago.

have noted in the introduction — up and at 'em, as evidenced by the rush into the Alta Mira tunnel, and up the cliffs at Sohotón. But, unlike some fire breathers, he was always the first in line.

Some might question why Hiram didn't just go ahead to capture Santiago with his battalion rather than remain at Navarette from 29 June to 4 July waiting for Pendleton. He certainly was able to take the town. Opposition was rapidly declining. His reconnaissance on the thirtieth showed him that he would probably be successful. He had a number of reasons to move forward and a like number not to.

First: He had no authority to move beyond the designated point reached.

Second: He did not wish to go contrary to any plans that General Pendleton had decided upon and which his advance might well upset.

Third: If he and his men had moved forward they would have taken the glory away from Pendleton and their comrades of the 4th Marines.

Those men had fought hard to get where they were, and, he had no wish to provoke annoyance with a fine gentleman like "Uncle Joe." Besides, the whole matter was quite easily settled — getting to Santiago City was attained shortly after their meeting and there was glory enough for everyone. On the following day, 5 July, a peace commission from the city came out to see Pendleton with an offer to surrender. The only condition was that the Dominican general, Arias, be allowed time to disband his men. Pendleton agreed to delay entry but he did take up positions just outside the city, just in case the agreement fell apart. The agreement went off as planned and on 6 July, the hard-fighting 4th Marines marched into Santiago City.

Hiram had a joyous meeting with his old pal Fritz Wise, who was a major in Pendleton's column. He told him all about the tunnel and the bridge and described all the fun he'd had in nearly getting blown up in the former. But Hiram's job was to keep the troops supplied, so on 7 July he on his train headed back north to Puerto Plata. During the following days his battalion repaired the tracks and its bed to keep the lines open; hard work for everyone.

Hiram was running a railroad, and this would be his only opportunity to do so. Therefore he ran it with every bit of energy and ability he could muster. He placed 1st Lt. Howard W. Stone in charge of the repair shops, and Capt. Douglas McDougall in charge of operations. Hiram had a fine group of subordinates, who helped greatly in the overall success. Hiram allowed all kinds of necessary goods to be shipped on "his" railway, including coal. One time he found himself buried under a pile, when a coal car tipped over. He was removed in short order, but he decided that he didn't like it and wouldn't allow it to happen again. Puerto Plata was Hiram's base of operations and he kept a watchful eye open to any and all potential troublemakers—one of whom seemed to be the town governor. Every time Hiram tried to gain his cooperation or assistance, the "gov" managed to throw a monkey wrench into the works. So Hiram figured out how he could solve that difficulty. He had the man hitched up to an old oxcart that gathered refuse throughout the town. That made a difference. Face-saving is every bit as important in Spanish America as it is in Asia. That pompous antagonist lost whatever face he had and his followers quickly dropped him. How it ever happened after that treatment, we'll never know, but the two men became friends and he was a loyal supporter of Hiram thereafter.

Bearss' continued running of the railroad made it more efficient and even profitable. When he turned it over to the natives, they immediately began the standard program of graft. That was something they had all longed for. Without graft the entire economy would fall apart—people would have to get by on their earned wages instead. Almost immediately, the railroad began running into operational problems.

Major Bearss appointed a young American employee of the State

7. Santo Domingo

Marines taking a breather from their exhaustive activities in that very hot Santo Domingo climate.

Department to control income and apply funds toward the debt owed to U.S. banks. The remainder was then turned over to the government of Santo Domingo. That young man advised the local government bank that they would have to turn over enough money to make the first payroll. The management demurred, asking Bearss to get approval from Washington. Hiram recognized that delay would ensue if he did. They threatened to send a cable themselves. Hiram knew that if a cable was sent the State Department would drag their heels and nothing would be done. McDougall was in charge of the communications and Hiram said, "No cables."

The bank finally came across with the money. Hiram and his officers all recognized that there might be trouble if a Marine were selected to handle the money. So, the State Department employee mentioned above was the recipient and handler of all the money, in and out. There were many other instances of corruption and bribery that Hiram and his men straightened out before the problem became too hot to handle. All along the line he got the local businessmen and various government employees to agree to deal honestly—at least until the *Yanquis* went home.

What surprised everyone was that profits went up, as did wages. Yet there were some that were still very unhappy. They were previously privileged individuals, mostly foreigners and including some Americans, who were loud in their denunciation of Bearss and his Marines. They even read a formal proclamation at the railroad station. McDougall sent a Marine gunnery sergeant to settle the matter. He suggested that they disperse and

The 4th Marine Regiment's headquarters in Santiago in 1916.

off they went. Soon after, the problems seemed to die down and nearly everyone was reconciled with the new "management style."

This was tobacco country, and the transport of the nation's most important product took up much railroad time and space. The disturbances had delayed shipment of that product, most of which was exported to the Netherlands and Germany. The latter country was now heavily engaged in a war with the world's most important sea power, Great Britain, so the shipment was, instead, going to a neutral nation.[10] The republic was badly in need of income and tobacco was the product that could accomplish renewal of cash flow most quickly and easily. This would help to reduce the nation's indebtedness to its creditors, so naturally the U.S. State Department was all in favor of returning the rolling stock and rails to facilitate this. Hiram and his Marines made it all possible.

In the meantime Ted Kane was briefly recalled to the States so Hiram was sent to relieve him at Santiago City. His superior, who commanded all forces in the West Indian waters, was Rear Admiral Charles Pond, USN. Life down there was somewhat different. Previously, Hiram had been the boss—absolute authority over all he surveyed. Now he was subjected to rules and orders from superiors. But still, he was able to impress his personality upon the day-to-day running of the city. Once while he was visiting W.W. Russell, the American minister to the Republic, Archbishop Adolpho A. Naul arrived and told Mr. Russell that a revolution would break out that night.[11] Bearss told Russell that the rumor was false and that he had already acted without anyone's knowledge to prevent an outbreak. Naul was furious. Who was this *Yanqui* to question him, who probably knew more about Santo Domingo than this officer would ever know? Shortly after this happened, the archbishop left in a very disgruntled frame of mind.

Brigadier General Theodore P. Kane graduated from the Naval Academy in 1890 and was commissioned a second lieutenant of Marines. Kane saw service in Cuba, and in 1916 was appointed CO of the 1st Brigade of Marines in Haiti, then Santo Domingo. Next was Peking, China, where he commanded the Legation Guard. He retired in 1924.

It seems that Hiram had reacted when he first heard the news—by placing two machine guns in church towers and more on top of well-situated buildings. In addition he had his artillery calculate the range to the homes of prominent politicians and sent a squad of Marines to each. There they advised each male occupant that their orders were to shoot them in the event of a revolution. Somehow this seemed to make a difference. Each politician "on the spot" sent word to their followers to "cool it." Even the archbishop's home had been included. Hiram had two machine guns mounted in his home with a squad of Marines to back them up. Heavy guns were mounted atop Receptoria Hill so as to cover the entire area of the city. Nothing had been left to chance; and, as Hiram had indicated, nothing unpleasant occurred.

Hiram was caricatured in the local newspapers as "Nero" or the "Kaiser" and received a large number of notes foretelling his death. Several proclaimed that his death would be on a certain night. That evening he donned his white dress uniform and strolled about the town plaza, in full sight of everyone who wished him ill. The following day a local told Hiram that he wasn't killed because he wasn't a "damn bit afraid of any of them." The following day the same newspaper editor that had criticized him made the mistake of lambasting President Wilson. The Dominicans had a law that made it unlawful to criticize the head of a "friendly state." Hiram had the editor locked up and tried as fast as he could to move the court. Meanwhile, taking few chances, he had a detachment of his Marines, led by a Spanish-born sergeant, take up positions within the courtroom. In case they were asked, they were to tell the listeners they were there to preserve order and not to interfere with the court proceedings. The editor was convicted before the Supreme Court of Santo Domingo and sentenced to a long, hard term. Later the sentence was greatly commuted and the somewhat chastened editor released.

The same archbishop, while espousing his friendship with the U.S. and its Marines, was continually writing letters to State Department officials complaining about everyone. Hiram was a major target. He knew about this because all the archbishop's mail was being intercepted and read by the Marines. Hiram was well aware of what he was writing and frequently joked with him about the letters. The churchman said how well he had written about Hiram and some of his junior officers, which would bring additional guffaws. The archbishop knew from Hiram's style and language that something was wrong. But he seemed never to learn that his letters went nowhere but to the "dead letter" office in downtown Santiago City.

There were other distractions. The foreign community, which the U.S. Marines were there to protect, often found cause to complain. Sometimes they even went so far as to try devious means directed at the Marines themselves. On one occasion Hiram was invited to make a "personal call" on the wife of the French consul at her home. Hiram had been around and realized that this very beautiful and vivacious woman was up to no good. He accepted, but took two officers with him as his "staff." As expected, she was in a lounging robe in a very seductive setting, stretched out on a chaise lounge. All three Marines remained standing and none were seated when the consul returned, "unexpectedly."

Hiram reckoned that it was a setup. She was to have been only partially clad when her husband returned to find Hiram seated beside her. The created commotion was to have caused Hiram grave embarrassment and forced him to grant certain benefits the foreigners were demanding. The presence of his staff curtailed their clumsy attempts at putting this American proconsul on the spot. The Dominicans weren't too far behind the Europeans in their efforts to nail Hiram because he refused to give in to their demands. They were about as clever and about as successful.

During this period there was the normal Marine program of "rounding up the usual suspects." One who was more than just a suspect was Juan Calcona, a well-known leader of insurgents in the San Pedro de Macoris area who had robbed the customs house at La Romana the previous year. There were numerous American sugar interests in the same area crying for protection from this bandit's depredations. The burden of eliminating this threat fell to Bearss and his command. With a relatively small Marine detachment of three officers and 25 men Hiram went out looking for him. Reports all placed Calcona in the hilly region just east of the town of Higüey, located in the province of La Altagracia, where he was said to have about 1,000 armed men. Accordingly, from Santo Domingo City, Hiram and his men sailed eastward to the port of La Romana where a railroad would take them at least partway toward their objective.

In the meantime, Hiram sent word to Calcona that he wished to meet him someplace convenient for the latter. Calcona responded that he didn't have time to meet with Hiram. That was unfortunate. Hiram always believed that personal meetings could bring about good results. But since Juan wouldn't come to meet Hiram, he would go to meet Juan. Leading his two companies of Marines, Hiram started for Higüey. Most of their 25-mile journey was a horror. The ten miles by train weren't bad but they had 15 more to reach Higüey that consisted of wading or struggling through near quicksand, and all in terrible weather. The rainy season was in full force and the roads were nigh impassable. Some reports claim that the Marines sank in the mud, although those who claimed it was up to their chests may have been exaggerating.

When they arrived, the populace was taken off guard. No one, strangers nor locals, could make the trip in that weather. No one expected Hiram and his Marines. The first thing he did upon arrival was to announce that he was on a horse-buying trip for the U.S. government. Hiram realized that no matter how tied up they might be with Calcona, profits were more important to the natives. So, for the next few days he examined mules and horses. Meanwhile, Hiram's Puerto Rican interpreter, a man named St. Elmo, was able to get information about Calcona, and it seemed that he was someplace nearby. In the meantime, the natives were getting restless. No horses nor mules were being purchased. No gold or American dollars had yet been seen and Hiram and his men were well along the road toward wearing out their welcome. The situation was rapidly going downhill. Then Hiram learned that Calcona was coming to town. He would spend

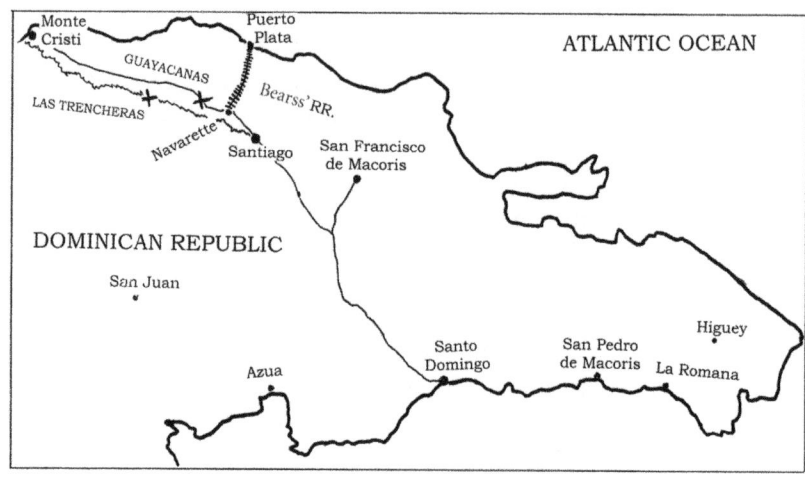

Santo Domingo (now known as the Dominican Republic).

the night in town seemingly without fear when he learned that Hiram had only a few men.[12]

Just after dark on 24 August, Hiram had his two companies pack up and prepare for a quick getaway. With that accomplished he then set out for Calcona's headquarters in the local hotel. Accompanying him were Sergeant Westley, St. Elmo and a few locals. Hiram had already figured that these half dozen or so locals believed in the Golden Rule: he who had the gold made the rules. Hiram had the gold. Under the circumstances, they were as loyal as could be expected. Upon arrival, Hiram stationed Westley and a few of the locals outside with a warning — if they heard any firing, come in shooting. Then he and St. Elmo went inside where they found Calcona sitting at a table. He was surrounded by a few of his men and had several more scattered about the building. The surprise was complete. Coming in unexpectedly like that, Hiram must have seemed like an apparition. And, incredible to them, he had no gun in his holster. Calcona was stunned and for a moment seemed unsure as to what to do. Hiram began a conversation in low tones, suggesting that Calcona come with him to American headquarters to continue their discussion there. This Calcona refused to do. In a twinkling of the eye, Hiram pulled his pistol from under his campaign hat, where he had hidden it, and stuck it into Calcona's ribs. St. Elmo yelled out in Spanish, "Any man moves and Calcona gets it in the belly." The rebels wilted.

Hiram opened the door and in came Westley and several of the locals. They took Calcona outside and mounted him upon a horse, tying his legs

Mounted patrol of Marines searching for "bandits," possibly the regiment's advance body from the 13th Company under First Lieutenant Thomas E. Thrasher.

under the horse's belly so he wouldn't be able to get away in the dark. Calcona begged Hiram not to leave him tied that way. The locals would laugh and ridicule him and he would lose his standing with them. "Tough stuff," or something equally impolite, shouted Hiram. Calcona's embarrassment fit into Hiram's plans nicely. Off they went, traveling all night. The following afternoon they reached La Romana. They then put him in manacles, boarded ship and brought him in to Santiago City for confinement in the Ozama Fortress. Calcona had a fearsome reputation all over the island. Many people were at the dock and along the street leading up into town to witness his degradation. In order to enhance this, Hiram marched him with a thin thread about his neck to the fortress. During the period from July through October, many other rebel leaders were incarcerated in the local hoosegow. Señor Calcona was no longer lonely; he had plenty of company.

Another time, Hiram directed that all natives must turn in all their firearms. He and the governor discussed the matter and after their meeting the governor went right back to a council meeting with the new rules. The council accepted them and proceeded to put them into effect. Marines held an open house and many weapons were brought in by the populace. One of the main reasons for the success of the disarmament plan and rapidity of deliverance was Hiram's threat, which was to search every house and shoot everyone who had weapons. Since his policy was always to do what he threatened, they believed that he wouldn't deviate in any direction. He wasn't really planning on shooting anyone, but the natives didn't know that.

While he was at Santiago City there was still much continuing insurgent activity all over the country, but especially in the eastern tail of the island. Having been made lieutenant colonel in November 1916, in January 1917 Bearss was placed in command of the 3d Provisional Regiment of Marines. He permanently replaced "Tippy" Kane and would hold the command until 20 March 1917. Four months before, when Hiram had been examined for a permanent rank of lieutenant colonel, and he had passed with flying colors. His four signed letters of commendation from Secretary of the Navy Josephus Daniels for services on Hispaniola island plus Sohotón and Samar were well remembered.

Shortly after taking command he sent Major Jay McC. Salladay with a Marine detachment by Coast Guard cutter to operate in the San Pedro de Macoris area. That town is located on the southern coast of the island, so it made more sense to go by boat than by road, of which there weren't many. To back up Salladay, Hiram also sent Captain John Quincey Adams by land with a troop of cavalry. Shortly afterward Adams sent Hiram a wire advising that he was held up at the Macoris River crossing. Somehow he had also learned that Salladay's men couldn't land because the armed insurgents were holding the dock against them. This irritated Hiram. No peasants were going to interfere with the U.S. Marines in the course of their successful completion of their duty.

Hiram took a few men by another cutter to San Pedro. Upon arrival he pushed men into the town using machine guns to clear the way. Adams' troop also rode into town. Hiram left orders to his subordinates on the cutter that when he signaled, they were to shell the town. He sent for all the town officials and ordered them to have all arms turned into him; otherwise, he told them, he was going to flatten the town. They began to turn weapons in that day and by evening the place was reasonably unarmed and fairly quiet. He had also cautioned them not to allow any sniping or he would use the ship's guns on the town.

Hiram now had a sufficient force to do anything he wanted at San Pedro. Soon afterward he managed to occupy all the strategic points with the troops at hand. The situation in Hiram's area of responsibility was just fine. Almost every place was quiet and relatively peaceful. The natives weren't killing each other, nor were the Marines killing them. Everyone should have been most happy. But not everyone was.

In the province of Macoris lived a gentleman named Salustiano Goicoecha with the nickname "Chachá." It isn't clear that he was an expert in that particular dance but he did waltz around the Marines. They began to become very disenchanted with him at about this same period. Somehow Chachá could snap his fingers and the locals would dance around doing his bidding. He even asserted that he could blow a whistle in the middle of a sugar plantation and, "in the twinkling of an eye," several hundred armed subordinates would be assembled around him. He further added that in less than two hours he would have 2,000 armed associates begging to slaughter anyone fool enough to argue with Chachá. This was one tough cookie, if you believed his rhetoric. He was a little guy, but had a lot of personal guts and loads of followers.

They had weapons all right: old Mausers and Krags, a few Winchesters, and the old favorite, sawed-off shotguns. The rebels also had long-barreled revolvers of ancient lineage but with real killing power. So, they were armed, and dangerously so. As the saying goes, "It was his town, and if you didn't like the way he was running it, get out." But instead of getting out, Hiram and his Marines were rushing in.

The standing rule was that all weapons had to be turned in by 29 November 1916, or else. Or else meant that the individual was subject to severe and drastic action. Naturally the bad guys didn't turn in their weapons. They never do and no one expected that they would. Hiram certainly didn't. What happened, though, was that the Marines could whack anyone caught in the act without fear of getting the wrong person. If he was carrying a weapon, he was dead meat. Soon there would be lots of dead meat lying about.

Chachá was a magnet for the rougher elements, especially the criminals. If a person broke the law in Santo Domingo, a serious breach, he would head for Chachá. If the criminal made it to the "sanctuary" he would do the bidding of his protector. There the law was made by Chachá and maintained by his subordinates. The farmers in the surrounding area did what they were told or suffered losses that they could ill afford. He went so far as to offer the locals "protection" for money. No money, no protection. And the protection money was paid to protect them from Chachá.

Hiram had been hearing about this master criminal off and on for some time and decided to move into the territory and nab him. Off he went with 400 Marines to the outskirts of San Pedro, to secure and protect the main mill for grinding sugar cane. This was located on the large plantation known as Consuelo. Chachá and his men were waiting for the Marines. It wasn't quite an ambush and the Marines weren't really hurt, but the firing was heavy from both sides. Captain Adams and his cavalry rode up and were immediately taken under fire. Adams' own horse had the bit shot out of its mouth. At nightfall, when the firing ceased, Hiram laid out his plans for the morrow. At first light off went the Marines towards Consuelo, a mixed command of infantry, artillery and cavalry. As they approached the plantation itself, the firing from Chachá's lines became quite fierce. Bearss ordered Adams to charge the enemy's line, which Adams did in a gallant and fearless manner. The enemy, unused to such tactics, were quickly routed and fled in great disorder.

Completely successful, at least temporarily, Hiram took up residence in the sugar mills to prevent further attempts to destroy them. Though Chachá had been driven back a few miles off the plantation itself, he didn't consider himself defeated. He was anxious to have another go at the Marines. Bearss moved around to the other sugar stations and, leaving a few men here and there, rapidly set up positions everywhere. When necessary, he was able to move them about on the narrow gauge railroad that connected the plantations. This allowed rapid movement without tiring out his men. Hiram was a mover and doer but hesitated to exhaust his fighting men, his most valuable weapon.

Shortly after getting the place in order and the properties well protected, Hiram received orders to report back to San Pedro. Being Hiram Bearss, he just ignored the order, remaining where he was. He well knew that if he had obeyed, the lives of American citizens, their property and the loyal natives would be in jeopardy. Hiram continued his operations from this advanced point. He also received a well-intentioned note from the chief of staff, Lt. Col. Robert H. Dunlap, warning him that he should withdraw. If anything went wrong, Hiram would be left holding the bag and all that he was trying to do would be forgotten. Hiram's response was characteristic — "I don't give a good Goddamn whether I'm court-martialed or not." If he left the Americans out there alone and as potential victims of the bandits, Hiram believed that he should be court-martialed. Instead of going back to San Pedro, Hiram again started after Chachá.

The Marines began whacking Chachá from pillar to post, then back again. They gave him no peace, no rest, no place of sanctuary. No matter where he went the Marines were always right there. Hiram knew he had to move as fast as possible to avoid any further difficulty with the "home office." If he were relieved of command, his replacement would have the good sense to stay where he was told. That would free up Chachá and his followers to do their dirty work.

Chachá began splitting up his columns to get away from the Marine pressure. Hiram did the same. No matter how or where Chachá moved, Hiram followed. The relatively small Marine detachment covered several hundred miles in this cat-and-mouse game. Unfortunately the mouse was really a rat and somehow always seemed to get away. This continued for a month. During that period Hiram figured that all his separate units covered as much as 3,000 miles in all.

Finally, Chachá had had enough. He sent a message through the superintendent at the Consuelo estate that he wanted to talk with Hiram. At their meeting Chachá asked Hiram what were his best terms. Hiram told him, "No deals." If he lived up to the letter of the agreement that would work in his favor at his trial, but no assurances could be given. In a few days Chachá did come in with upwards of 400 men, almost all of his followers. Chachá said he tried to bring as many men as he could and would go out and try to obtain more. He did, with assurances from Hiram that if he didn't return within two days Hiram would personally find and kill him. Hiram convinced Chachá that he meant business. Chachá was back with the rest of his men in the allotted amount of time.

During this period there was a great deal of labor agitation. Union organizers from the United States were heavily engaged behind the scenes in making sure that the rights of laborers were protected. Many were blacks brought in from Jamaica, a British colony in the Caribbean. Although numbers of those same Jamaicans were involved in the various armed bands that the Marines had been fighting, and numbers of them had been killed or wounded, the British consul protested that they were British subjects and were entitled to the rights of British subjects. The matter went back and forth between the British Foreign Office and the U.S. State Department and somehow or other got straightened out. But it didn't bring the dead Jamaicans back to life, which was just fine with the Marines.

Hiram and his Marines were under constant harassment, not only from the natives and the British but even from the Marines appointed over him. During the course of actions on the island, Hiram had issued orders to his officers to get receipts for any goods they obtained during the course of encounters with hostiles. There was a time when Hiram and his officers were being subjected to having their accounts checked by chairborne Marines. Hiram had his adjutant, 1st Lt. Victor Morrison, USMC, obtain a copy of his order which he then took to a meeting with his commanding officer, Rear Adm. Harry S. Knapp. Knapp and a bean-counter named Clemens suggested that Hiram's own accounts be checked. He was madder than hell. How dare they question him? Major Hugh Matthews, temporarily paymaster and trying to temporize, requested that in writing from Knapp. It wasn't put in writing, and the affair went back and forth for some time with nothing ever settled. The final result was that Hiram wasn't audited.

Hiram had been making waves and would continue doing so for years to come. His refusal to retire back to San Pedro as ordered earned some severe criticism at Marine Headquarters. So did some of his laissez-faire attitude at other times. His superiors were especially critical of his allowing Chachá to surrender, then go away perhaps never to return. That Chachá did return made little difference to the micro-managers at Headquarters. One must operate by the book, not by using common sense as Hiram often did. The matter was finally resolved in Hiram's favor. Some-

Patrol of Marines searching a village. This activity went on during Pendleton's entire advance and afterward during most of the occupation period.

one realized that if Hiram hadn't gotten Chachá sooner rather than later, the destruction would have continued and possibly nothing would have been left to protect.

Hiram's superiors were also critical of his using natives as he did to help in the bush against Chachá, so critical that they even refused to pay the salaries he had promised them. The natives were essential in getting Chachá and should have been paid immediately. It was Hiram's creed that "it takes a thief to catch a thief." He raised hell and stood his ground. They were finally paid. But every time he yelled, he added another nail to his coffin. This very controversial Marine had no one at Headquarters to defend him but many to attack him. In a few years a lot of this would come back to haunt him.

Hiram was back in the field but now in the western part of the country. The troublemakers were primarily located in Azua, about 83 miles west of Santo Domingo City and perhaps two miles north of the port. Here another leader had risen. His given name was Vincentico Evangelista (the Evangelist), however, he called himself Jesus Christ and was customarily known by his followers as the Messiah. Somehow he had managed to convince the local natives that he was invincible, that no American bullet could penetrate his hide. Nothing was said about the potential success of non-American bullets. His followers also believed that since he was impenetrable so were they.

Hiram and his Marine detachment were preceded by a small force of natives. They were presumably loyal to the *Yanquis*, which fact no one could prove with certainty. This entire detachment of some 60 men was to disperse some 1,000–3,000 native *insurrectos* led by the self-styled Jesus Christ. If what the Marines had learned was true, these people really believed they would be following and, more importantly, protecting the Messiah. Against such odds Hiram knew, based upon practical experience of many years in jungle warfare, that his small detachment could possibly be captured with their equipment—all arms and ammunition. That would be a disaster.

Hiram prevailed upon Pendleton to allow him to use a Coast Guard cutter to get to the port of Azua, thereby avoiding, at least for that stretch, a potential land ambush. Using the cutter, he and his 67 Marines and 60 natives reached the port in relatively short order. Disembarking, they marched into the town proper. There, they made a hasty survey of what they were up against. In the process of so doing, Hiram quickly learned that the governor of that town was intriguing with troublemakers inland. Hiram immediately fired him from his job and then appointed a man of his own choosing. This kind of appointment was supposed to be made by his superiors back at headquarters but they were usually too busy playing politics to intervene in the business at hand. Hiram was always proactive, never allowing bureaucrats to slow him down. As will be seen later, it just added another layer of bitterness among his contemporaries. All of these controversies were building up against him. Instead of being congratulated for his independent action and ability, Headquarters continually managed to find fault with him.[13] Times were changing. Hiram and those Marines like him, Butler, Wise and quite a few others, had to learn to restrain themselves. Somehow they had to stop being invariably successful.

Soon after arrival Major Bearss and his contingent marched on San Juan, many miles to the north of Azua, to intercept the native contingent and their valuable rifles. Up in the north was a village where lived the daughter of a former president of Santo Domingo. This president was dead —he had been assassinated. The reason given for his assassination was that he murdered, by poisoning, many invited guests at the great dinners he frequently gave. He had been a black man and in Santo Domingo then and possibly now, color of skin was very important. The darker pigmentation were considered inferior and the lighter, as in Haiti, was considered to be superior. The president's daughter, like him, was very black. She was looked down upon by those who were of a lighter hue. But as she was the daughter of a former president Hiram deferred to her and presented his credentials with great decorum. He made it very clear that color meant absolutely nothing to him nor his government. This generated for him her favorable response and through her he obtained considerable advantageous information. For many months she continued to provide needed bits of intelligence that helped him to better control the district.

From her he learned that the village officials were in a league with the insurgents while protesting their loyalty to the American rulers. It seemed that the higher the rank they held, the more they sided with the enemy. Presented with this kind of problem, Hiram took his old course of action. He had the town fathers paint the local garrison. The higher in rank, the lower down on the ladder he had them stand. The lesser lights were higher up. Their careless application of paint splattered the higher ranks below. It might seem to be strange psychology, but it worked. The spectacle of these most honored of townsmen working and having paint splattered on them by subordinates did the trick. Consequently, the higher-ups lost position and influence with those beneath them. This, of course, was exactly what Hiram had intended all along.

One day the president's daughter let Hiram know that most of the military leaders of the insurgents would attend a dinner in San Juan that evening given to honor Hiram. He attended with great gusto. Eulogies for the Americans were on everyone's lips, including three generals whom Hiram wasn't supposed to know were there. He invited them back to his quarters, intending, so he said, to discuss certain matters with them. Upon arrival he had them taken into custody and held until the next morning. That morning Hiram moved against the insurgents with his Marines and native troops. The Messiah and his large number of followers were in a place held holy by the natives. It was a place so sacred that no one usually had the temerity to enter. Hiram, however, had the temerity. In they went against the huge, well-armed and reasonably effective array.

In the meantime Hiram had sent a telegram to 1st Lt. Ellis B. Miller, ordering him to come with his machine guns at once. By traveling all night and obtaining fresh horses every few miles, Miller arrived early in the morning. Upon arrival Hiram set him up on his right flank. He had sent orders for 1st Lt. Samuel L. Harrington and his cavalry detachment to also come posthaste, arriving just a few minutes before 1000 hours. The followers of the Messiah had gathered together too quickly, and Hiram couldn't wait any longer for support. So at 1000 off Hiram and his small unit went. In the beginning Hiram and his lads pushed the insurgents back slowly, from entrenchment to entrenchment. For the first two hours it was slow going, until about noon Miller and his guns got into proper position. From then on the marksmanship of the riflemen and the "sprinkler" guns did great damage to the followers of Evangelista. When the trigger was squeezed, the result was almost always fatal to the target. But as the Marines advanced, any insurgents left alive fired at them as they passed. This meant that all natives had to be shot, especially the wounded. Hiram was up against a dedicated crew of *insurrectos*. It was an extremely bloodthirsty campaign in which many men died; but very few of them were Marines.

Hiram, mounted upon a white horse and moving continually up and down the line, had led the first attack. After that he appeared everywhere astride that horse. It was psychologically effective, it demoralized the enemy and it influenced the native troops Hiram had with him. Hiram's courage was a matter of fact to all who knew of or had served with him. Now it was becoming as well known to the natives, on both sides, who never saw their own leaders up front. Hiram's own men tried to get him to tone it down but that only encouraged him. "At least get off that damn white horse," some of them said. However, he probably was safer on that horse than they were on the ground. He warned them to stay away from him or they might get nailed. Some did, and no one came close to him after that. The natives opposing him must have been terribly superstitious. And perhaps most were afraid to even consider firing on this crazy *Yanqui*. Somehow he managed to escape unscathed even though there were many dead and wounded that day.

Whoever had been planning the insurgent's battle was good.[14] Each time they fell back it was to another equally well prepared position. This went on for ten hours. By the end of the day both sides were exhausted. On the following morning the battle began again. Back the insurgents went — always back — but they continued to fight. Hiram remained on his white horse until he heard one Marine say, "If the old man wouldn't ride that damn horse, we wouldn't have to go so fast." Hiram dismounted immediately and from then on advanced on foot with the rest of his men. At noon they halted and had an improvised mess, after which his adjutant came to him and said, "Colonel, the men would rather that you get back up on that horse. Everyone would rather see you riding because you walk faster than the horse does." Although Hiram and his men had continued the pressure that took the heart out of the resisters, the battle was indecisive. The Evangelistas managed to disappear in the mainly trackless interior. After a night's rest, Hiram and his men were out scouting and patrolling, looking for evidence of which direction the enemy had taken as it fell back. It became clear that they were headed toward the western portion of the island.

Meanwhile, the wounded and prisoners were taken back to San Juan via the road through the Valle de San Juan. It was ranged on both sides by

The 4th Marines in a fire fight with rebels on the road to Santiago.

mountains. San Juan was about 50 miles west of Azua and 30 miles east of Haiti. If the insurgents kept moving in that direction, they would soon run into the Marines in Haiti. As the Marines advanced to the west, Hiram had the property on all sides destroyed. Houses and shacks were burned as were the fields. The peasants were losing much valuable property because of Evangelista and his followers, so many natives came in to make their peace with the *Yanquis*. Hiram reported to Headquarters that his situation was improving rapidly.

Word finally came to Hiram that Evangelista would come to him and surrender if Hiram, with no troops, would meet him alone. That rebel had shown remarkable courage and skills, as had most of his followers. Hiram had suffered some dozen casualties in dead and wounded and to continue fighting, if it was unnecessary, seemed to Hiram an awful waste of human life. His officers were against him going alone but Hiram was convinced that the "Messiah" was a man of his word. The insurgent forces had learned, the hard way, that being sprinkled with holy water was no protection against the Marines' sprinkling lead. Yet, they remained with him even though it must have been apparent that he wasn't going to win. It was Hiram's task to convince those dedicated people that surrender was the best way out of a very bad situation. He felt confident that he could do so.

As agreed, Hiram, two enlisted Marines and one native interpreter rode out about three miles to meet the enemy leader. When they reached the agreed location, no one was to be seen. They had patiently waited some time when all of a sudden the insurgent leader arrived. He and the few men with him had ridden about for several hours looking for a potential trap. Seeing none, they finally came in, all 300 of them. After the conference, in which Evangelista agreed to stop all depredations and the theft of goods from the natives in the countryside, they broke up. Hiram accepted his word and returned with his men to Santo Domingo City by way of San Juan.[15]

On 16 March 1917 Hiram was commissioned lieutenant colonel, effective as of 29 August 1916. Hiram's tour as commander of the 3d Provisional Regiment, 2d Provisional Brigade, technically terminated on 20 March 1917. He remained at Headquarters, Santo Domingo, until he received orders on 10 May 1917 that detached him from the Brigade with orders to report to the Marine Barracks at the Philadelphia navy yard ASAP. It was during this period that the U.S. Congress, at President Wilson's request, had declared war upon imperial Germany. By way of the USS *South Carolina*, Lieutenant Colonel Bearss reached New York City on 21 May, where he was joined by Louise. On 25 May he joined the 1st Regiment of Marines, the Advanced Base Force regiment at Philadelphia. But, shortly after arrival, he received orders detaching him from the 1st Regiment and ordering him to report to the new Marine training base at Quantico, Virginia. There he was to train the new officers entering the Corps. This was a major blow. In ordinary times, training officers would have given Hiram the opportunity to pass along what he had learned in the islands, and he would have been all for it. But these were not ordinary times. What it all meant was that he was to be kept on the west side of the "big pond." It meant that he wouldn't be able to participate in the greatest war that mankind had ever engaged in. It also meant that Hiram would be kept in the States and out of the action. They might even relegate him to the utmost degradation, recruiting duty someplace. Hiram and everyone connected with him were crestfallen. He seethed with rage, as only Hiram could rage. He yelled and screamed and only Adelaide heard.

8

The Great War with the Marines

The Great War had been going on over most of the world since August 1914 but the United States had managed to remain on the sidelines, that is until April 1917. With the Allies and their agents, American as well as foreign born, working like blazes to change that situation, it is surprising that it took so long. There were some American officials, elected and appointed, who did their collective best to get the country involved. By February 1917 Wilson, who had just been reelected because "he kept us out of the war," broke relations with imperial Germany. That was, of course, tantamount to a declaration of war. In April Wilson asked Congress to make it formal. They did, and in we went. The United States wasn't remotely prepared for it, but from there on the United States was knee-deep in the war. And the Marine commandant, Maj. Gen. George Barnett, made sure that the Marines would be fully represented in any force sent to France. Hiram would eventually manage to get into the action, even though things looked very black for him at the moment. The war was destined to be more important to him and the other professionals, army, navy and Marines, than any he or they had been engaged in up till then.[1]

The military record of Hiram Bearss was of the highest order in comparison to his contemporaries. Only a very few other Marines had made the impact that he had. It seemed that those in charge went out of their way to keep many of the fighting Marines out of Europe. Smedley Butler was given a bad time but he forced his way to a command in France.[2] Many of the others were relegated to the backwaters of the Caribbean where the Corps was admittedly heavily engaged all during this period. Only a few of the more senior officers that went to France had been real warriors—such as Logan Feland.[3] Many of the others had been in noncombat positions during most of their careers.

8. The Great War with the Marines

Quantico was a very small village with one secondary dirt track leading to the outside world. Its only other communication with the outside world was via the Potomac River. At this time it was set in an area of about 50,000 acres of jungle. The original spot selected by the board members was rejected by the commandant, Maj. Gen. George Barnett. He must have told his three-man selection board to look again. The next day they went out and found the current site. The land just happened to be the property of the Quantico Company and it is said that Mrs. George Barnett was a major stockholder in the company. Somehow or other, she probably managed to convince someone that her land was just what the U.S. Marine Corps needed.[4] But regardless of who owned it, it was an ideal spot to train Marines.

Meanwhile, Hiram was beside himself with frustration and anger. He was once again stymied and his first reaction was to resign his commission. He went to Philadelphia to see his wife to discuss the problem with her. Louise wouldn't hear of him resigning. She, wiser than her rambunctious husband, told him to cool it. But Hiram had already sent a telegram to Theodore Roosevelt. The former president was engaged in forming a "volunteer" division to go right over to France to represent the United States in Europe. His cut list included Hiram in the number-three slot—a brigade at least. Louise was furious with him. He had also sent Barnett a telegraphed resignation but the commandant had refused to accept it. Instead he ordered Hiram to remain at Quantico and do his assigned job.

Now it was time for Louise to interject herself into what was becoming a major embarrassment. Off to Washington she went. Neither she nor Hiram had ever played politics, a game that neither was philosophically well equipped to engage in. But now she decided that she should go directly to the commandant, something that Marine officers' wives just didn't do. Both George and his wife had socialized at times with Hiram and Adelaide Louise so it wasn't as though she or Hiram was unknown to the Barnetts. In fact, both of them had upbraided her for Hiram's activities on behalf of Tony Waller's candidacy for commandant.

Barnett was adamant: "Hiram has had enough, it's time to give others a chance." He didn't explain how he was measuring "enough." Sure, Barnett admitted, Hiram was highly in demand. Even Brig. Gen. John A. Lejeune, who was himself begging for a chance to serve in France, wanted Hiram to go with him. So did Teddy Roosevelt, but that division of his was entirely pie-in-the sky. Barnett claimed that Hiram had already earned enough glory for several men and anything else would just be "empty honors." That was an easy statement for a noncombatant to make. It just made Hiram more determined to get over to France.

Louise came by some information that promised a possible change in Hiram's status. A senator from California could hold the key to the entire situation, and she learned that he was a great admirer of Bearss. So, after General Barnett's refusal, Louise went directly to the senator. He was smart enough to realize that politics was the game being played, but he thought that it was in the nation's best interest to send qualified men to France. He called upon Barnett, that most political of Marines, and shortly after, some say in moments, Hiram's orders were countermanded. He was ordered to France.

In the meantime he had been training the 5th Regiment's Base Detachment for service in France. It was a 1,200-man unit composed of a machine gun company and four companies of rifles. After Barnett had forced the Marines upon General Pershing and the A.E.F., the rules were changed and the new military formation now required one more company per battalion. While at Quantico, they were intensely trained by Hiram for what he believed they would face in France. Amongst other training, they executed several night problems out in the "boonies." Hiram refused to take any man who had not qualified at least as a marksman. This, presumably, was before the commandant invoked that stipulation. Noncommissioned officers were his especial training targets. Hiram realized that a unit with topnotch noncoms could lose all its officers and still come through any encounter in fighting trim. This would be proven correct time and again in France. Some units with all their officers down were well led by sergeants, sometimes corporals, and more than once by a private. Some of these men were later commissioned, including at least one private.[5]

The officers and men were convinced that this experience was much worse than had been their "boot" training. The rugged training caused a number of the younger officers and many of the men to constantly seek sick call. Sick bay opened at 0930 and during this period some of the officers and enlisted didn't bother to get out of their sacks for early formation. The number of attendees was running about 90 each morning, and one morning it ran up to 99. The officers and men were mostly from Mare Island and it seemed to Hiram that their basic training may not have been as severe as Paris (later Parris) Island had been.

Calling his adjutant, Capt. LeRoy Hunt, to his office, Hiram instructed him to have sick call 15 minutes before reveille each morning.[6] The company commanders were to carefully inspect each sick man and a sergeant would march them to the sick bay. Each man's "skipper" must be there when the man complained to the doctor and was examined. The doctors were instructed to examine each man carefully. If there was anything wrong with the man he should be carefully attended to. Otherwise, Hiram wanted to nail the goldbricks quickly, before their "disease" spread. Next morning only nine Marines showed up for sick call. That was the end of sick bay malingering.

All during this period, Hiram was ably assisted by his second, Maj. Edward S. "Verdie" Greene, who would later do some imposing work with the 3d Battalion, 5th Marines. Hiram personally inspected every meal portioned out to his men, both as to preparation and serving. He was a stickler who tolerated nothing less than the very best in a mess hall. The machine gun company was instructed by the best gunner in the Corps, Maj. Edwin B. Cole.[7] His company of guns was soon as good as or better than anything else in the Corps. They were using Lewis guns but after arrival in France would lose them for the heavy but reliable French Hotchkiss machine guns.

The battalion's time terminated at Quantico and they would soon be on their way to France. It had been only two weeks since Hiram had assumed command but the officers and men must have felt the time to be that many months. But, unlike before, they would now be real Marines and capable of doing what they would be called upon to do. With Hiram in command, they left for France in July.

They left in a long troop train for Philadelphia. Detraining, the battalion marched through the streets of the navy yard and on 31 July 1917 boarded the transport USS *Henderson*. As usual, it was hurry up and wait. It wouldn't be until 5 August that the *HendyMaru*, as it would later become known, weighed anchor when its convoy was ready. Five miserable days sitting on a ship tied up to a dock near a major city did not do much for the morale of the officers and men. Hiram got right to work. He had the men doing drills of all kinds. *Abandon ship* was one of the most important, which, fortunately, they never had to utilize.

Finally the ship got under way. More drills. Hiram even set his men to scraping and chipping paint — allowing no "down time" for idle hands. Under his personal direction he also had Major Greene conduct classes for the young officers. Hiram had noticed that most of the younger men thought that just wearing the Sam Browne belt constituted being on duty. That attitude had to change. He quickly became aware that in class most of the officers asked questions of him and Greene, not so much to learn but to have both senior men do the actual work. One morning Hiram silently entered the room while class was in session. He yelled out, "Attention!" All rose and stood straight. He issued oral instructions, later reduced to paper, to the effect that unless lessons were learned properly school would be held beginning at 0400. He made sure they all knew what "properly" meant. Answers to questions would be forthcoming from the class promptly. The class would answer, not the instructors. Otherwise, 0400 for the entire length of the voyage. Thereafter, the lessons were well prepared by the class and their beginning time modified to five hours later, which helped the sleep-oriented.

The enlisted men were also subjected to schooling. As the instructing French officers called it, theirs was "The School of the Platoon." Between those Frenchmen traveling with them and Hiram's discipline — particularly his insistence upon them knowing their weapons — when they landed at St. Nazaire they beat French troops at their own game. They were put through their paces and the judges, French as well as American army officers, were of a unanimous opinion on that matter. Hiram's adage to his men was, "Know your weapon; it may save your life and properly used will kill your foe." His men paid close attention. They knew that Hiram wasn't a blowhard — he'd been there and done that, himself.

The voyage over was much the same as all the others from the United States to France. Besides schooling, the enlisted men were on constant watches topside to spot subs before they spotted the ship. The Marines stood most of those watches and they were all outside. There usually was one sailor in the crow's nest with binoculars. Just below that place was a platform where two Marines stood watch continually — observing every spot of the ocean, looking for a periscope or perhaps even smoke from another vessel. Their period was just one hour out of four, but it was an agonizing hour. Peering continually can tire anyone, so the time was limited. The relief would climb the ladder and begin their watch. Three hours later the first two Marines would ascend again and replace those then on duty. The identical routine was observed at the after mast. Some enlisted Marines were assigned to assist in the mess hall below decks. Their own allocation and quality of food may have surpassed most of the other Marines on board. The more experienced Marines always tried for that duty.

On 20 August the ship reached St. Nazaire but the men remained aboard until the twenty-second. Hiram even had that worked out — all men were trained to be at certain positions, by squads. They would then be called by their number assigned, and then were to race down the gangplank onto the dock where they would form up once again. By the numbers, everything by the numbers. There was no confusion and as mentioned above, they were acclaimed to be superbly trained.

Bearss was appointed to the command of the camp to which his men were assigned, just outside the city. At this time, a labor battalion composed entirely of black Americans had reluctantly continued what they considered to be degrading work. The native French had accepted them as

Americans and exhibited no prejudice toward them socially. Hiram's Marines were set to work alongside them with him in overall command. Although the attitudes of Americans in general were not as liberal as the French, Hiram ensured that the rules were the same for all. He carefully instructed all as to their duties and courtesy to each other. Until Hiram's arrival their command had been very lax and discipline was nearly nil. Hiram changed all that but at first it was difficult for the soldiers to accept.

Hiram was nothing if not a strict disciplinarian. Upon arrival, he set certain restrictions in place. The first problem was the extinguishing of lights in the buildings at a certain time. The soldiers had been turning them out whenever they felt like it. Hiram issued orders for the lights to be turned out at 2230. A Marine corporal of the guard, of rather small stature, went into the barracks and called upon the men to extinguish the lights and quiet down at taps. The hubbub continued. The soldiers completely ignored the corporal. They shouldn't have. He now yelled to them, "Extinguish the God damn lights and shut up." That did it. One man grabbed his rifle, leaped from his bunk and started for the Marine corporal while two others followed his lead. There were at least 150 soldiers in that bunk room, and they all were furious with that corporal. The Marine corporal ordered the man to halt and when he didn't he pulled his .45 and drilled the advancing soldier dead. That seemed sufficient for the moment, and stopped the other two soldiers in their tracks. The corporal stepped to the door and called for the sergeant of the guard. There was no more insubordination. The extreme quiet and calm that followed were overwhelming. No noise, not a peep from anyone.

In order to protect the corporal, Hiram instantly preferred charges against him. A court-martial was convened as soon as possible. Identification of the body, a man who had been living with his comrades for some time, was nearly impossible. No one there wanted to admit being on the scene. It finally came out that the man's name was Lesley Jones. Some men said that they had heard that Jones had been killed but they hadn't been there when it happened. The stories were, of course, implausible. All the soldiers had to be in their barracks at that hour — there was no other place for them to go. It appears that the corporal and his .45 had scared the hell out of all of them. Finally, in order to complete the inquiry, Hiram had to intervene. He asked one witness, "Lesley Jones is dead, isn't he?" He received the reply, "Yes, Sir!" Which proved that there indeed was a Private Lesley Jones, after all. The court acquitted the corporal as the testimony showed that he had fired in self defense and in the performance of his duty. There was very little trouble after that.

It was at about this time that Bearss' machine gun company had their

Lewis guns and wheeled carts removed. It isn't clear what was done with the carts, but the guns were to be used on airplanes. The Marines received French Hotchkiss machine guns as a replacement. Each monster weighed in at 54 pounds and its tripod at another 54 pounds—not very movable and at first not very popular with the Americans. But later, when the Germans were coming directly at one, they were considered better than nothing, much better. They accounted for a lot of the enemy dead.

After being at St. Nazaire a short time, the Base Detachment was transferred south to Bordeaux to establish an American base there. Here Hiram found himself the most junior American officer and already in a crazy mixed-up mess not of his making. No one seemed in command, and no one seemed to know what to do. Hiram decided how to solve his problems. He signed every order after his signature, "By Order of General Pershing." That got everyone's attention. He, by taking action, took over the management of the city's general policing. The French authorities accepted his terms whereby his Marines would police the city. Through their vigorous efforts they drove out all the criminals usually found in a port city. Most went south to Spain to continue their "business" activities and for the moment, none were immediately available to create trouble for the Marines.

Hiram first made an appointment and then went to pay his respects to the mayor of the city. He was kept in an anteroom while the mayor was in a conference. Hiram soon learned that the conference was really with newspapermen. Hiram raised hell. He wasn't about to be kept waiting for his appointment. As far as he was concerned, the appointment had been kept and he was going. The mayor suddenly appeared out of nowhere; the newspapermen had been dismissed. He made sure that the mayor understood that he was representing the United States and his manners were based upon that and not personal pique. Perhaps it was partly true.

One problem that occurred almost as soon as Hiram arrived at Bordeaux involved the allotted docking space for U.S. supply ships. His space was between the site for the French army and another for the French navy. This forced him to move everything over one or the other. That didn't make any sense to him but apparently it did to the French authorities. He had sense enough to take with him 1st Lt. Albert Alphonse Le Bouf, a young Marine officer who claimed relationship with a famous French general of that name.[8] The conference was getting nowhere when Hiram asked them if he might take one or the other spaces to avoid the confusion. They replied, "Oui." They well knew that an agreement like that had to be approved in Paris and permission would most likely take longer to obtain than the war would last. No real decision was made and their tail coats were still clean.

Hiram left behind the French-speaking Le Bouf to keep the French busy in conversation while he went over to the docks and made the changes he wanted. No one there questioned him, since he told everybody that "headquarters has approved it." He was soon informed that the French Mission was furious with him for what he had done.[9] His response was that he was not very good at understanding French and assumed that they had told him that it was all right to make those changes. He had hurried to enact them so as not to offend them by delay. The French Mission accepted that answer because it was a *fait accompli*. After that they must have counted their fingers when shaking hands with Hiram. At least, for now, there was some badly needed movement of supplies to the AEF.

Hiram realized that men being what they are, liable to frequent houses of ill repute, he needed to set up a system in this port city to protect the men and "girls." He selected those houses that seemed to be well run and designated all others off-limits. His system required close watch and records kept so as to be able to monitor each night and day. He went so far as to have U.S. military doctors on hand to do the inspecting. His orders also stipulated that any American seen on the streets with a woman of questionable character be arrested on sight. That slowed down the street traffic.

One of the doctors was from Delphi, Indiana. He and a few other doctors decided to play a prank on Hiram involving that order. Hiram had proclaimed that no woman had ever accosted him and he didn't believe that would happen to anyone that didn't encourage it. They managed to get two notorious French prostitutes to accost him on the street. It was just after he had left a restaurant following dinner with his Indiana doctor friend. Hiram had proceeded but a few feet when two women came up to him and both took an arm. He managed to shake them both, but it was several years before he learned that he had been set up by his pal from back home. Fortunately he wasn't picked up by the MP's while so engaged.

He also issued orders that no doctors nor nurses from Base Hospital No. 5, which came under his jurisdiction, come to Bordeaux together for recreation or entertainment, even though he said, "I'm sure there isn't any hanky-panky. His object, he proclaimed, was to defer a possible breakdown in discipline and integrity between superiors and subordinates. That undoubtedly made him popular with both groups. The local army commander at Bordeaux was so please with Hiram's activities that he personally recommended him to Pershing, which didn't hurt his future reputation with the U.S. Army.

When Col. Charles Doyen was promoted to brigadier general as of 30 October, and handed command of the newly created 4th Marine Brigade,

Hiram got command of the 5th Marines. Actually, for a brief period, while Doyen commanded the 2d Division, Hiram commanded the 4th Brigade, from 9 November to 8 December 1917. He would revert to command the regiment and continue in the post until Col. Wendell Neville arrived and replaced him on 1 January 1918. We already know about the Base Detachment sent over in July to support the 5th Regiment of Marines. It, ostensibly, was formed to quickly provide trained replacements for anticipated casualties to that Marine regiment. By the time Pershing and his nascent staff sorted out where they were going, it had been decided to create larger units than previously planned for. The extra units and men of the Base Detachment were quickly utilized in the expanded regiment or as guards at various AEF stations in France.[10]

Soon after getting the AEF to accept a regiment of Marines, the commandant once again managed to bypass Pershing and got easy acceptance for a second regiment of Marines. Then Barnett pulled a machine gun battalion out of his hat in order to create a full brigade. The 6th Marines would begin showing up in late fall of 1917 and by early 1918 the makings of a brigade would be in place in France. Hiram was on the scene but he wasn't the most senior Marine in Europe. Naturally, all the others who were aggressive and career minded wanted a Marine command in France. Neville was a full colonel and, while in command of the Marine detachment at Peking, China, had requested duty in France. They shipped him back to the States and then overseas to command the 5th Marines; hence Hiram had to suffer the indignity of being relieved of the regiment.

But we are getting ahead of ourselves. Hiram was temporarily the new regimental commander and as such had a great impact on the regiment before it ever got near a battle line. He was at first assigned to command of the 3rd Battalion, 5th Marines and told to "clean up the bad situation that had developed there." What caused that admonition isn't clear, but it suggests that problems might have been caused by keeping 3/5 in the backwaters for a longer period than the other battalions. The fact that they were not trained as a battalion until much later than the rest of the regiment might also have had something to do with the problem. Later, beginning in March 1918, they had a considerable turnover of leadership, which also indicates that there were problem areas.

Hiram always did something ornery. A large gathering was awaiting his arrival and there had been much agonizing about their new commander. "Hiking Hiram" was well known as one tough SOB whom no one had ever been able to put anything past in 18 years. So, they planned to butter him up. A big welcoming party was just the thing.

Unfortunately, Hiram did not arrive where they expected him. He came into the area from the rear and immediately went into the enlisted men's mess hall. During the course of his inspection he met an old-timer well known to him whom he asked, "What in hell is the matter with this battalion?" Sergeant Alfred B. Collins answered, "The colonel knows." Hiram repeated his question and got the same response. The answer, of course, was in what Hiram had already inspected. No officer was present and the food preparation was not properly inspected. It was also obvious that little attention was paid to procurement of food.[11]

Leaving the mess hall, Hiram went to the other locations he wanted to see. Then he headed for battalion headquarters, arriving very late that afternoon. The party had been held in abeyance and everyone was still waiting for him. Salutes, heel-clicking and all the obsequiousness that goes from juniors to seniors

Brigadier General Charles Augustus Doyen graduated from the Naval Academy and was commissioned as a second lieutenant of Marines in 1883. He commanded the 5th Marines in France and later was the CO of the 4th Marine Brigade. He was also the first CO of the U.S. Army's 2d Division, making him the first Marine to command any division. In the spring of 1918 he was sent home as physically incapable and died of influenza in October 1918.

greeted him. Then came the drinks and salutations by carefully selected officers. Hiram responded by stating that he expressed all of the happy sentiments in return. Then he let them have it. He had been at the mess hall at the noon meal and none of them had been there to make sure the men were fed properly. Food was served that was "far below Marine Corps standards." And he added, "I won't tolerate that any longer." His "suggestion" was that the officers give up their classy digs in town and come out to the camp for accommodations. The same with their food. No more special messes in town. "We will all eat with the enlisted men." As he well knew, that was sure to improve the food quality. Hiram had a partition constructed that separated officers and men, but their food was served from the same kitchen. He had a roster made up assigning at least one officer as inspector at each and every mess formation. One more thing—

short arm inspections had been ignored. Every morning, each man was to be inspected by a medical officer.¹² Hiram was nothing if not tough and by the book when necessary.

Shortly after this encounter he became Doyen's replacement as colonel of the 5th Marines.¹³ He evidently found the other two battalions in good order — at least nothing untoward happened after his arrival, unless you could consider the following situation as abnormal for Bearss.

While inspecting his pal Wise's outfit, 2/5, at Damblain he went into a recreation center that was under the direction of the unit chaplain. There were members of the various auxiliary organizations within — such as the Red Cross, YMCA, YMHA, and Salvation Army. Hiram noted that the interior was dirty, and when he asked why he was told, "The detail of Marines has not arrived to clean it up." As Hiram later said, "They were all able-bodied and living the life of Riley" compared to his Marines, so he ordered brooms brought in. Then he ordered those living Riley's life to man the brooms and clean the place up — and "keep it clean in the future" without the aid of fighting Marines. He and they exchanged verbs, nouns and adjectives. But they kept the place clean after that.¹⁴

He soon learned that no time had been spent on weapons practice, or at least not for quite a while. Hiram located a spot he thought would make a splendid range. There was one problem though: a stream had to be diverted. His subordinate officers told him it could not be accomplished. He said it could. Hiram had the stream diverted, and during the diversion his officers stood, with him, in the water with the enlisted men as they diverted it.

Then the shooting began. The French residents were soon up in arms about the noise. Hiram ignored them. Instead, he was, as they should have been, concerned about the Germans. Then his men began training with the French but he soon vetoed that. Their techniques were opposite what Pershing, and Hiram, considered to be most important. He and old "Black Jack" believed in that holiest of things borne by Marines—his rifle. It was their firm belief that Americans would fight much better in the American way and not as the Europeans had been. Open warfare, rather than trench warfare, was the way to go.¹⁵

During the very short period that the French soldiers were training Marines, Hiram paid for feeding them. The reason was simple: Rather than having their allies go back and forth to their mess halls and to the training fields, he agreed to pick up the tab. Soon after, Omar Bundy assumed command of the 2d Division, and one of his queries of Hiram was, "Why did you feed the French?" He added that Hiram did not have the authority to do so. Hiram explained his rationale and added that he was trying to shield Bundy so that no one could hold him responsible for what Hiram did. That satisfied Bundy and no more was heard along that line. Bundy even went so far as to recommend Hiram for a full colonelcy in the National Army.[16]

It was during this period that Col. Wendell Neville arrived with orders to assume command of the 5th Marines. Hiram, until 26 February 1918, reverted to second in command of the regiment. The U.S. Army leadership knew a good thing when they saw it. Effective 27 February, he was transferred to the command of the 3d Battalion, 9th Infantry, which was also a part of the 2d Division.[17] The 9th Infantry had once been a first-class U.S. Army regiment with a long, honorable lineage, and had service association with Marines on several battle fronts. But this wasn't the 9th Infantry of old. It was consisted largely of drafted men badly in need of discipline and training. As the "boots" soon learned, Hiram was just the man to do both.

Major General Wendell C. Neville graduated from the Naval Academy and was commissioned a second lieutenant in 1892. His services included Cuba, China, Nicaragua, the Philippines, Hawaii, and Vera Cruz. He was chosen to command the Peking Legation Guard and was CO of the 5th Regiment, the 4th Brigade, and the 2d Division. He became the fourteenth commandant, dying in office on 8 July 1930. He was awarded a Medal of Honor at Vera Cruz and a Brevet Medal for Cuba.

9th Infantry Verdun Sector

Hiram wasn't the only Marine serving in command of an army unit. Major Harry G. Bartlett, USMC, was in command of the 1st Battalion, 9th Infantry, and would soon take command of the 3d Battalion, 7th Infantry, 3d Division. There were others, just as there were junior U.S. Army officers commanding companies of Marines in the 4th Brigade. It was that kind of an American Expeditionary Force.

Bearss had to do something about his command. The men hadn't been taught discipline nor required to obey their superiors immediately, if not sooner. They were good stock and later would prove themselves, but just now the men were unruly and discipline was very bad. Upon assuming the leadership his first command was to put the battalion under arms and move them out into the field. Officers that didn't meet Hiram's very strict standards were relieved posthaste. Some of them were regulars and didn't take kindly to a Marine removing them from their command. Word was sent up the line to General Bundy that he might very well have a mutiny on his hands if he didn't look closely into what was happening to 3/9.

Bundy went to see Hiram and they discussed the problems. The major complaint was that Hiram had reversed the training schedule. Instead of training during the day, he trained them at night. Hiram explained to Bundy that the problem, as he saw it, was that when they went into the lines, the Germans would do to them what they had been doing all along the line. They would come into the lines, raiding where newly arrived Americans were located.[18] This had previously been especially effective with green troops, nighttime being the worst possible time for commanders because of the lack of control over their men. To Hiram, preparation for the probability of attacks at night by German stormtroopers was the most important training he could give his men. He was eventually proven right and highly commended for his foresight.

So, for weeks he trained the battalion to absorb the enemy's hit and then throw him back out of the trench. It couldn't be repeated too often. He also formed raiding parties to better prepare the men. "Raiders" were repelled and "enemy prisoners" taken. Hiram's objective was to lose no men as prisoners, few to enemy fire, and to capture as many raiders as possible. His battalion tightened up. The remaining officers and replacements were soon sharp, as were the men. Hiram had arrived none too soon. The 9th Infantry, along with the balance of the division, entered the lines near Verdun in mid-March 1918.

At that point, significant contention no longer existed between the Marines and the army men. Hiram still didn't let down his or their guard. Training and instruction, even in the trenches, continued, reminding all of them what they had learned. He wanted his men ready for any eventuality.

He had his patrols out each night and the Germans began shelling the Americans every day and night. German intelligence soon learned that a new American unit was opposite them. The Germans prepared to pay a call on the newcomers. One afternoon the shelling pattern changed. That night, Hiram knew, they would have some uninvited guests. Intelligence was passed down the line — anyone wearing a French uniform was in reality a German, so be ready. Hiram worked overtime to ensure that his officers knew what to expect and that they in turn would make the enlisted men aware. He also ensured that all their French advisors stayed below ground so as not to make them targets of the "green" Yanks.

The shelling intensified, thousands of shells falling and demolishing trenches. Then came the rolling barrage behind which the heinies would come looking for the Yankees. They found them and found much to dislike about them, too. Bitter hand-to-hand fighting in and out of the trenches proved that Americans could take it and hand it out. Bayonets, hand grenades and rifle butts were the common tool for both sides. Americans also used a cute toy that would be very common in Chicago in a few years. Sawed-off shotguns claimed their victims and boy, did the Germans squeal about them. The raid failed and 3/9 assisted the Germans back to their own digs. Three more tries and fighting continued until daylight. However, the Germans finally gave it up as a bad deal. French officers highly recommended that Hiram now retreat. He refused. That wasn't his style. He'd lost men to hold those trenches and he was damned if he was going to give them up now.

Hiram had lost a doctor (Lieutenant Gordon), five men killed and a substantial number of enlisted men captured. He quickly decided to balance the ticket and launched a counterattack. Official records show that the numbers were 11 German prisoners captured and 67 German dead. As he expected, his men managed to hold the line. Hiram's rigid discipline had formed a unit that could be very proud of itself. This was probably the first time American soldiers had been so engaged in a German trench raid by shock troops.[19] The regimental history puts the 3/9 loss at "five killed and eleven missing." During this engagement one of his French liaison officers, named D'Orsay, burst into laughter when a German shell explosion cut Hiram's cigar in half. Hiram was a confirmed cigar smoker who at all times had one lit or even unlit in his mouth. But the laugh was on the Frenchman. He didn't realize it, but the same shell cut a piece from his coat. D'Orsay had planned a trip to Paris to visit a lady friend. But now his coat was ruined and this wrecked his forthcoming trip.

Hiram had notified his supply officer in the middle of the night that he wanted food for his men in the morning. Roast beef, boiled potatoes, coffee and bread, and Hot! It was to be ready at six that morning and brought up for the men who had been fighting all night. Word came back from the mess officer that a bridge had been blown and they wouldn't be able to get across that stream with the hot food. Hiram told them, "I don't give a God Damn if the bridge is blown, the men need hot food and God Damn it get it to them, and by six o'clock." The food arrived safely, hot, and edible and was devoured immediately.[20]

Two of his companies, I and L, were especially noted in several citations, notably one by Maj. Gen. Omar Bundy on 14 April 1918. The regimental commander, Col. Lewis S. Upton, in his report to Gen. Bundy proclaimed that he thought the people in the U.S. should be apprised of what happened to "let them know how good are [sic] men are."[21] Recognition of the spectacular services rendered descended from Chaumont, and Hiram was one of five mentioned in dispatches.

> General Headquarters American Expeditionary Forces
> Office of the Inspector General
> France
>
> 29 April 18
>
> Memorandum for Personnel Officer, A.G.O.
>
> The following officers and soldiers who took part in the defense of their trenches against the German raid on the night of April 13–14 are worthy of commendation:
> ... 5. Lieut. Col. Hiram I. Bearss, 5th Regiment Marines, commands the Third Battalion, 9th Regiment Infantry. When he was placed in command of this Battalion its discipline was at a very low ebb. His division, brigade and regimental commanders all unite in saying that had it not been for the efforts of this officer who has brought about a state of discipline and training in his battalion, the affair of the night of April 13–14 would have been a failure instead of a great success; That these troops in the condition they were when he took command could not possibly have stood off an assault. I recommend that if it be within the provisions of the law that this officer be promoted to the colonelcy in the National Army, and that a commendatory letter be written through the Secretary of War to the Secretary of the Navy in his case.
>
> A.W. Brewster
> Major General, I.G., AEF[22]

Years later, Maj. Gen. Omar Bundy described how he came to make Hiram available to the 9th Infantry. It seems that the regiment was in dire need of majors to command their battalions. The Marine Corps had a surfeit of higher ranks, so Bundy asked Colonel Doyen to send one to the 9th Infantry for duty. Bearss arrived and "at once entered upon his new duties with his characteristic energy and skill." Literally in hours there was a "great improvement in the discipline and training of the battalion ... the new leader had won the respect and confidence of the officers and men." His statement continued with laudatory comments about how well Bearss performed at Verdun: "The prompt action and good leadership of Colonel Bearss had saved the day." Nothing more was said about the potential mutiny.[23]

Interestingly, James Harbord, then Pershing's chief of staff at Chaumont, sent a memo dated 2 May 1918 in which he lauded Hiram's actions. He added, "In view of my *probable* assignment to command the 4th Brigade … it gives me particular pride and pleasure to be the writer of the above letter" (emphasis added).[24]

Sometime during this period, in April, Hiram was assigned temporary command of the entire 9th Infantry Regiment. The division was to be withdrawn from the line but one regiment was required to remain behind. Hiram made sure it was the 9th Infantry. To his officers and men he simply said, "They are calling for some regiment to stay in the line and relieve the 5th Regiment of Marines. You, together with your officers and men, all wish to volunteer, do you not?" The voice, sort of like a bolt of lightening followed by a thunderclap resounded and the responses were a meek, "Yes, sir."

The 5th Marines had held the left of the line. When Hiram and his lads were going in, the following exchange was heard. "Hey Bo," said one of the Marines, "who's your commanding officer now?" Someone yelled back, "Go to hell, you bastard, you had him first."

The loneliness of the 9th Infantry only lasted a few days. They too were soon relieved and went into a rest area. Hiram scattered the battalions into three or four towns and arranged for training—what else? But, while he was having so much fun, he came down with a severe case of pneumonia and was transported to a hospital in Paris. When the ambulance arrived at the first hospital, Hiram was told there was no room for him. He had a raging temperature and was taken to another hospital with the same result. Finally, at the third he moved in and took a room. It was set aside for the officer of the day. Bearss told them he'd shoot the hell out of anyone that tried to move him. He removed his clothes and jumped into bed. Later, the OD showed up and was told the same story. He learned that Hiram was just back from the front and that they believed that he must be demented. Hiram stayed in that hospital for two weeks and then he declared himself recovered. This was contrary to the opinion of the staff doctor, but that didn't seem to matter much to Hiram; he dressed and made for the Hotel Crillion bar. As he walked through the afternoon tea and coffee room officers and their ladies rose and almost in unison declared, "We thought you were dead."

The medical authorities at the hospital had decided that not only was he barely recovered from pneumonia, he was also suffering from other internal difficulties. Worse yet, he had hiked too many miles and his feet were troubling him. It was determined that his lung troubles, on top of the pneumonia, his internal problems and the terrible condition of his feet all pointed to a disability retirement.

In May, Hiram had been relieved in command of 3/9 by Major Alfred C. Arnold, USA, and Hiram returned to the 4th Brigade. Arnold would take good care of the battalion. He would be the recipient of a DSC and several Silver Star citations plus three *Croix de guerre*, most in October at Blanc Mont. Meanwhile, there was a very active move afoot to medically survey Hiram back to the States. The medical establishment was trying to do what the heinies had been unable to accomplish — get Bearss out of Europe. But, the Germans went about it the wrong way. They launched a massive assault along the Chemins des Dames, smack into the French forces holding that line. That led to a scream for American troops and Hiram was an American troop.

The advent of the fierce 2d Division (Regulars) into the quarrel in the Aisne-Marne region is too well known to be recounted in any detail, but suffice to say it brought the Marine Brigade into its most famous action at Belleau Wood.[25] It also eventually brought Hiram Bearss back home to the Marines. As was usual in Hiram's travels, the road was twisted. He was resting in the Paris hospital waiting for the inevitable deportation back to the United States when a propitious situation occurred. One of Hiram's army friends, a Colonel Grant, who had just obtained permission to join the 2d Division, stopped by to see Hiram one last time. Hiram was ecstatic. He got Grant to meet him in his automobile just beyond the hospital at a certain street corner. Hiram packed his trench bag and his personal weapon and then slipped out of sight. Within minutes at the agreed-upon rendezvous, he slid into Grant's car and away they went.[26]

It was at the city of Meux that they caught up with the division headquarters. Hiram met with Maj. Gen. Omar Bundy, who just then was a very busy man. He told Bundy what he'd done — gone AWOL from the hospital, "damned doctors" about to get him — and that he needed a job. Bundy needed him. He was initially assigned again to the 9th Infantry and a few days later was reassigned to command the division military police. Here his task was to keep the lines open to the rear so that the supplies could get through. One sweet American woman from Baltimore named Lainader had driven out from Paris with two cans of prepared coffee for the troops. It was Hiram's job to assure her of everyone's heartfelt thanks but please get the hell out of the way. There would soon be 27,000 American troops in this area and no way to feed them all from her two cans of coffee. She soon realized that a great event was unfolding and went back to Paris.

But supplies were in demand so Bundy sent Hiram back to obtain what he could from any source that was available. He hurried off in a car to Paris where he contacted the head of the Red Cross. The RC men were very courteous and responsive. He needed victuals for his 9,000 man infantry brigade so they offered him what seemed reasonable to them — five cases of canned fruit. Recognizing that he was dealing with people whose hearts were in the right place but whose knowledge wasn't, he thanked them and asked them for a general requisition "for anything he could carry." He noted that he had a spare seat that could hold some goods. They readily gave him the permission, in writing, and he set out for the navy headquarters in Paris. There he obtained approximately one dozen large trucks and drivers. He also went to the army, and they let him have more trucks. Across town they raced to the warehouse in which the Red Cross maintained their supplies. There he produced his papers and with his usual command presence easily got all the trucks loaded to the gunnels.

With that, the wagons headed for the Château Thierry area via the Paris-Metz road. Division was thrilled. He'd done so well that Bundy wanted him out and again on the move as soon as possible. Hiram suggested that another appearance by him might bring down the gods from Valhalla. General Bundy concurred and instead assigned Hiram to an inspection of the lines occupied by the 4th Brigade.

For the next few weeks Hiram was assigned to duty with the 4th Marine Brigade as an extra officer. As a lieutenant colonel, he was a higher grade than what was needed in the 4th Brigade. His rank meant

Major General Logan Feland accepted a direct appointment as a first lieutenant in 1899. He served in the Philippines, China, Cuba, Vera Cruz, Haiti, Santo Domingo, and France with the 5th Marines, then as its CO. After the war he served in Santo Domingo and then Nicaragua as CO of the 2d Brigade. He was one general considered as a replacement for the deceased commandant Major General Wendell C. Neville. Feland retired in 1933.

assistant regimental commander or above. Wendell Neville commanded the 5th Marines and was ably assisted by Lt. Col. Logan Feland.[27] Albertus Catlin commanded the 6th Marines and was assisted by Lt. Col. Harry Lee, who, as luck would have it, was four numbers in grade above Hiram. Hiram couldn't command a Marine regiment and his rank exceeded that to command a battalion, so what was he to do? If he hadn't been any good, considering the physical shape he was in they would have somehow managed to get him shipped home. Instead he was shipped about the division for a few days. Then something happened that caused a major change for the Marine Brigade.

On 6 June the entire 4th Brigade was smashed to pieces, with the loss of many officers and men, but all of lower rank, all but one. He was the colonel commanding the 6th Marines, Col. Albertus Catlin — wounded in action and removed from the lists that same day. Now Hiram had a job. He was appointed assistant to Harry Lee, who was moved up to command. A curse on those four numbers![28]

6th Marines Belleau Wood

The two assistant regimental commanders Feland and Bearss kept their regiment well apprised as to what was going on in the world. During the month of June both men were constantly exposed to all the horror of what was going on around them. Up and down the lines they went, subjected constantly to enemy fire from mortars, artillery, machine guns and heavy gas contamination. During his tours Hiram was known to often have a handful of cigars, and for the enlisted Marines he came across in his wanderings, a cheery "Hello boys, have a cigar," was a common greeting. Another was "Where are you from?" If he should happen to hear "Indiana," the war went to hell. "Where from?" "Know anyone there?" Indiana was and would continue to be the most important place on earth, at least on Hiram's earth.

The Marine Brigade continued bleeding until mid-month when the 7th U.S. Infantry was sent in to relieve an already badly overworked remnant of men. The Marines were given minimal rest. They were being touted, by the French, as the saviors of Paris. (Many in the know agree with that assessment.) But what a price they paid to do that. Both Marine regiments, 5th and 6th, were well worked. That also includes their support, the 6th Machine Gun Battalion and their buddies of the 2d Engineers, who were with them all the way. That is not to denigrate the great infantrymen of the 9th and 23rd nor the artillery of the 12th, 15th and 17th Regiments, all of whom did, and would continue to, play their part. But it was the Marine Brigade that was active for three weeks, and so much less the infantry. It had been planned that way. One brigade to fight while one remained as a solid reserve. That decision had already been made by Bundy and his chief of staff, Col. Preston Brown.

After less than a week of rest, the Marines were summoned to return. The 7th Infantry had tried but they weren't trained nor, as yet, adequately led; consequently they lost some of the ground previously gained by the Marine Brigade. It made the Marines work harder when they had to go back in and retake lost ground. It also made many of them very angry; angry with the poor infantry rather than those who led them into a no-win situation. The Marines had suffered heavy casualties, well over 4,000, and nothing but a premier regiment could have been their replacement. The 7th Infantry wasn't a premier regiment at this point in time. Later in the war they did respectable work elsewhere.

Back in went both Marine regiments. The fighting was heaviest in the wood, as it had been before the relief. It was still the 5th Marines doing the heaviest lifting. The 6th maintained defensive positions in all directions but it was another week of offensive fighting for the old 5th. Finally, on 26 June, 3/5, which had suffered heavily earlier in the month, could proudly proclaim, "Woods now Marine Corps entirely." The Germans hadn't just run away. They were all about but not now in the woods, except the dead. They were in Torcy, Bussaires and Belleau, the town. They were still first-class fighting men. Hiram assumed the task of reconnaissance for the brigade. While others were making tracks for unknown parts, he was leading small detachments in probes in the German lines. A large group of soldiers and Marines left for Paris and the 4th of July parade. Hiram stayed and minded the store. On the night of 4/5 July he led a sizeable detachment of one officer and 25 men of the 67th Company, 1st Battalion, 5th Marines out into the German lines at Torcy and brought home some "bacon." Two prisoners were taken and two of the enemy were killed but all his men were back undamaged. As they came back toward their own lines the area was being heavily shelled. Hiram had both live prisoners by the nape of the neck. He yelled to his subordinate, "If I am killed or wounded, pay no attention to me, but grab these bastards. Don't let either one of them get away."

There was an explanation for a lieutenant colonel of Marines leading a small patrol as he did. Harbord and Bundy desperately needed to know what the Germans were doing and promised a week's leave for any officer who could bring in a prisoner who survived and provided solid information to headquarters. Hiram needed internal work badly. He was sick but didn't want to just go anywhere. He realized that would be his finish. So he cooked this up with Bundy and Harbord in order to get a week's leave and go to friendly navy doctors who would take care of him. The order was issued that day with the words, "The division commander authorizes me to inform you that your application for leave of seven days will be approved." On 27 August 1918, Harbord, then directing services of supply, wrote to the assistant secretary of the navy, Franklin Delano Roosevelt, explaining the above action:

> My Dear Mr. Secretary
>
> After our meeting at Bordeaux, it came to my ears that you had been making some inquiry as to individual exploits of officers of the Marine Corps. One among many that I could recall occurs to me as being particularly worthy of being brought to your attention. Lt. Col. H.I. Bearss was without command, being the lt. col. on duty with the 6th Regiment. He was particularly keen to get a chance to show his activity. Our patrols had been unsuccessful for a number of nights in getting any identifications by capture of prisoners. I concluded to give Bearss a chance and told him to pick a patrol, and although it was not supposed to be done by officers of the rank of lt. col. [I told him] I would give him a chance to take it into the German lines that night; that I wanted some prisoners for identification purposes, and if successful would hold his patrol up as an example to all others. He took twenty-five men and went into the German lines, personally leading the patrol, killed three or four Germans, and brought back two prisoners, establishing the identity of a new division in that part of the front, the presence of which had not been previously known. There is no doubt that the fine personal courage of Colonel Bearss carried the patrol through to a success.
>
> The record of individual exploits of officers of the Marine Corps, while under my command, is the most stirring chronicle that man ever read. I suggest that you call officially for the recommendation for awards of the Distinguished Service Cross and citations in orders for the months of June and July from the Fourth Brigade, and promise you that you will not be able to read them without tears coming to your eyes in your pride in the gallantry of your countrymen.
>
> Sincerely Yours,
>
> J.G. Harbord
>
> Hon. Franklin D. Roosevelt
> Assistant Secretary of the Navy
> Washington, D.C.[29]

Hiram arrived back in Paris late on 5 July, riding in a motorcycle sidecar. His back was killing him. But he knew how to fight and he also knew how to have fun even when he felt like hell. Being on leave was always a great joy to him. His close friends looked forward to seeing him, always at the top of his form, no matter how badly he hurt. He had already communicated with some friends to let them know that he would soon be amongst them once again. Yes, this was the man whose innards were in tough shape. Although he had been dressed to the hilt, and his uniform was spattered with mud from the road, he had another carefully prepared dress uniform waiting in his locker at the Grand Hotel.

When he arrived at the hotel, he leaped from the sidecar and headed toward the bar. He was quite an apparition. His clothing was badly soiled and his face was covered with mud. A young army captain just happened to be standing where Hiram was racing. Halting Hiram in his mad dash the captain, obviously just off the boat from the States, demanded to know what this wretch was doing in such a dilapidated costume. What right had he to be in the lobby of this grand hotel, which was off-limits to enlisted men? Several of Hiram's friends saw what was occurring but at his signal they let well enough alone. This young man, possibly with upwards of 90 days' service, was getting right into his full annoyance at this old reprobate: "What are you doing here in the first place? These areas are restricted to officers. Look at you, mud and filth all over you, and you without the courtesy to salute a superior officer."

Hiram, with much apparent shame and chagrin, responded to the young man's query by telling him that he was well over draft age and would the captain please not turn him over to the military police. Hiram was unduly meek—his humility though faked was of the highest order. This was when Hiram was at his most dangerous. After considerable upbraiding, the captain allowed him to pass but with the proviso that he clean himself up before he allowed himself to be seen in public again. The captain then proceeded in the opposite direction.

Not many paces later Hiram yelled "HALT!" It has been written that an entire brigade would come to a halt upon hearing that word from Lt. Col. Hiram I. Bearss. When he called the captain to attention, the lad was visibly trembling. Somehow or another he had blown it and he realized this was not an old enlisted man. Hiram swung around and stood directly in front of the young captain: "Let your eyes hit the deck forty paces forward! Pull in your chin! Throw out your chest! Bring your belly in! Keep your heels at a 45° angle! Let your hands hang naturally at your sides!"[30]

Hiram gave his directions to the captain very carefully and in a modulated voice that didn't allow the young man to escape one nuance. He warned him that he should be extremely careful, in the future, as to how he addressed any "poor enlisted men." Then he let him go. With that, the onlookers claim, that captain made careful use of his feet and legs as he rushed out and away from his tormentor. Then Hiram made for the showers—cleaned himself up and in his sparkling uniform sped to the bar.

Everyone who had been in attendance, soldiers, sailors and Marines plus their ladies, joined in the merrymaking. The poor captain was the object of much amusement for many people for the balance of that day. A few hours later he returned to the scene of his crime and the local area general called him to task. "Captain," said the general, "I understand you had a little run in earlier today with a buck private." The captain responded, "No sir, no buck private ever said 'Halt!' like that. When I heard him give the command, I knew he was no private."

Hiram enjoyed his libation but he also found time to spend with several navy doctor friends concerning his spine. They, of course, wouldn't turn him in, perhaps even had he been on the point of death. So, he had a great time in Paris. But it wasn't to last. A few days later the word quickly spread throughout Paris that the Germans had launched another major attack along the Marne, just east of Château Thierry, where a couple of infantry regiments let them have it. They were the solid 30th Infantry and the extraordinary 38th which now and forever will be known as the "Rock of the Marne." Between the fifteenth and eighteenth of July the Germans did their worst, but to no avail. They got across the river but they didn't stay there. The lads of both American regiments saw to that.

Meanwhile, in the north, up nearer to the old provincial town of Soissons, the 1st and 2d Divisions (Regular) and the 1st French Colonial Division launched an attack that would be referred to as the beginning of the end for the Germans. On 18 July all three divisions punched eastward to cut the Château Thierry–Soissons road. The 1st Division was at the north end, the 2d Division in the south, with the Colonials in between them both. The 2d Division's first day was agony for the 5th Marines and their comrades of the 9th and 23rd infantries. The Marines had a very bad time getting to their jump-off position and barely made it on time. The three regiments were badly handled but at the end of the first day were well on their way to accomplishing their task. The following day was to be the turn of the 6th Marines, but all by themselves.

In the meantime, Hiram was still enjoying Paris, but he heard what was going on and managed to get transport to Soissons. He landed in the area at the end of the first day after the fighting had ceased. As always seemed to be the case, Hiram had no command even though he was trying desperately to assemble something. The following day, 19 July, was the day of the 6th Marines and Hiram was only an observer, having no part in their destruction other than being a witness.

Through no fault of their own, the 6th advanced late, after their artillery support had long since passed them by. Unlike the previous day, the Germans were ready. And now there was only the one regiment on line where on the eighteenth there had been three. The Germans shot the hell out of them. The regiment lost over 50 percent of its manpower in a couple of hours. The 2d Division, all of which had paid a horrendous price, would remember those two days forever. It was a prime example of man's inhumanity to man. The French were running things and didn't seem to care what sufferings the Americans might have undergone. They had proven beyond a doubt that fact with their own people. After this, Hiram was appointed once again to command a battalion of the 9th Infantry. But, still experiencing terrible pain from his spine, he was again sent to a hospital at Paris.

One night, no detailed explanation given, the patients were being moved south. Hiram had recently purchased a brand new, expensive uniform and boots, which he demanded to take with him. The adjutant told him that the "uniform will be packed up and sent." Hiram replied, "No! I'm too damn old in the game for that kind of story." He insisted upon the uniform and the adjutant was just as insistent that it would come "later." He added, "You are a patient here and under our command. You will go, with or without your uniform." Hiram drew his pistol and said, "Get my uniform and boots or I don't move." They were found without undue delay and Hiram then agreed to be moved.

The train moved down south — about 120 miles to Nevers — but this was also to be temporary. When they arrived, one of the first problems Hiram noted was a very badly wounded black American officer in extreme pain. Hiram demanded that the officer be put right but everyone seemed to ignore the man. Hiram yelled out, "God Damn it, this man needs help — it doesn't make one bit of difference what his color is, help him." With that a doctor jumped to and soon the officer was resting more comfortably. Bearss was undoubtedly prejudiced, as were most other Americans of his time, but not so as to be unable to separate right from wrong. At any other time, Hiram would probably have completely ignored the man or worse, been condescending toward him. But this is an example of the times. His basic decency transcended his other faults.

Hiram and the other patients were moved to another hospital. At about 1300 he and many other officers, of all ranks and some badly wounded, were in a large room. In addition there were numerous enlisted men mixed amongst them. Hiram went to sleep as best he could. The next morning a hospital attendant woke him and presented a tray, saying, "Here is your breakfast." Hiram asked instead for a pan of warm water to wash his face and clean his teeth. The response was to stick the plate of bacon and eggs in his face and proclaim, "Eat!" Hiram pushed the plate in the attendant's face as he jumped out of bed. A major came to see him and Hiram demanded that the conditions change greatly. He wanted quarters commensurate with his rank and food equal to the amount for which he and the other officers were being charged. Hiram also wanted the young officers, those badly wounded, to be given better accommodations and to have more rest and quiet. He wanted the enlisted men not to be mixed with the officers, not because of bias regarding rank, but to give them as much freedom from officers as it was possible to do. Suffering from wounds was bad enough without having to tolerate nearby officers.

Another vexing matter was the coffee. It was creamed and sugared no matter what the man wanted to drink. Most officers and enlisted men had gotten used to drinking strong black coffee and any "coloring" or sweetening was detested. Hiram was one of the loudest to complain about this. That problem was fixed nearly at once but other problems weren't quite so easy to disassemble.

This hospital, like most others brought to France by the Americans, was primarily a university teaching hospital uprooted and transferred nearly intact. No one was a military officer in more than name. Most were professional physicians when they had been scooped up by the army. Actually, the words "freshly caught" were in common usage when discussing a young officer who was in for the duration, medical or line. They did the best they could but no one could satisfactorily address all the issues that prompted complaints, so those continued for the duration of the war.

Hiram somehow managed to be transferred once more — this time back to a hospital in Paris. The doctor in command was Joseph Blake, then a famous surgeon. Blake, the hospital director, urged an immediate operation on Hiram's spine to try to repair the extensive damage. Naturally Hiram could envisage himself a cripple for life if he allowed the "quacks" to operate. This was the most dangerous situation that Hiram ever found himself in. The doctors were convinced that Hiram had given his all for his country and must now be sent back home as a disabled hero. Hiram had to somehow arrange his bleak future but he wanted to do better than that. He had miles to go and things to do before he would cash in his chips. X-rays were done of Bearss' spine, while another officer was having his head and chest gone over. Somehow the x-rays got mixed up. The other man had Hiram's spine and he the head and chest of the other. The latter officer was shipped home with head spinning swiftness. Hiram, the genuine object of the planned transfer, remained in France. Meanwhile, Hiram began to purr like a cat. Everything Blake and his associates mentioned, Hiram responded to with enthusiasm and good will. Blake was peering through rose tinted glasses if he believed Hiram was agreeable, but he didn't know Hiram all that well. Navy doctors would have immediately recognized that he was now at his most dangerous. But Blake didn't know what he was up against and went merrily about his business. If Blake had his way, Hiram would be on the next boat.

Blake was amazed at what a changed patient he was. So cooperative, so congenial, and so obedient. Hiram made a simple request which was readily granted. He asked to be allowed to move to a nearby hospital commanded by an old friend, one Colonel Lloyd. Lloyd was well aware of Hiram's back problems but also of his capacity. The transfer took place. Hiram immediately requested an interview with Lloyd, a family friend who was only too willing to allow him any latitude that he could. Somehow Hiram's powers of persuasion were such that his rating was changed from "disability" to "active combat service." Hiram talked swiftly and was able to accomplish that change in no more than 15 minutes. He had retained the photographs of "his" chest and head injuries and convinced Lloyd they were his and that he was really all right. Hiram also managed to obtain clearance papers that ensured that he was truly discharged from medical care and fit for duty, someplace. With that he hustled himself out of the way of the medics and grabbed a passing sidecar that took him to AEF Headquarters in Chaumont. The following day he was assigned to the 26th "YD"—the "Yankee" Division—to take command of the 102d Infantry of the 51st Brigade.

With the "YD" St. Mihiel

The 26th "Yankee" Division was the first national guard unit federalized after war was declared. It appeared in such good overall condition that it was shipped to France in the fall of 1917. Major General Clarence Edwards, the commanding general and West Point regular, was possibly the most popular division-commanding general in the AEF — popular with his officers and men, but not with General John Pershing, with whom he was out of favor. This fact would harm the division on several occasions, when Pershing faulted the officers and men because of his personal attitude toward Edwards. The division had been in action in February 1918 and, regardless of what Old Black Jack said, they had done good work. At least they had been highly commended by the French forces under whom they spent a period in the trenches north of Soissons. Subsequently, they relieved the 1st Division in April in the Ansauville sector.[31] At the end of June 1918 the division was transferred to the Château Thierry–Belleau Wood sector, relieving the 2d Division. Between 14 and 28 July the division participated as part of the overall Franco-American push in the Aisne-

Marne operation. There they helped to successfully push back the German units lying before them. As it was with all national guard divisions, the "YD" was loaded with political appointments. Pershing and his staff were intent on getting rid of the political appointments (whether good or bad) and it took some time before the higher ranks were expunged. Hiram's arrival was part of this.

His regiment, the 102d Infantry, was formed from the blending together of the 1st and 2d Connecticut infantries plus some smaller units from Vermont. Each of the subunits had a long and noble history, going back to the early days on the Eastern frontier. When Hiram arrived the 102d was mainly composed of Connecticut men. His arrival coincided with their encampment at the Châtillon-sur-Seine area, where they were resting up. This was on 24 August 1918. They would leave this area four days later in transit toward the western face of the St. Mihiel salient. That same day, Hiram was temporarily promoted to colonel to date from 1 July 1918. Between 8 and 12 September they would occupy the Rupt sector in Lorraine. Then they entered into the cauldron of the reduction of the St. Mihiel salient.

Upon arrival Hiram immediately reported to Major General Edwards. Evidently Edwards didn't know Hiram nor his background. He launched into an exhaustive verbal examination as to Hiram's experience. It appears as though Edwards may not have been thrilled at having a Marine officer replace one of his own. At first Hiram seemed to be as testy as he thought Edwards was being toward him. When the general asked what his experience was, he replied that he had "little." It didn't take long, after his description of service in the Philippines and command of a mixed brigade in Santo Domingo, for Edwards to accept his new officer without further qualifications. Hiram knew, of course, that his experience far exceeded that of any other officers in the division, including Edwards, so he wasn't too terribly concerned. This is another example of Hiram's intransigence. Instead of trying to win over Edwards with good will he chose the opposite tack. This was a constant factor in the interaction of Bearss with nearly everyone else. What seems most odd is that he made many friends, army, navy and Marines, in spite of his troublesome mannerisms.

The first commanding officer of the 102d, Col. Ernest L. Isbell, had brought the unit to France but was soon a victim of the regular and national guard rivalries then existing throughout the AEF. The 102d was rumored to be a "sick" regiment. Isbell's replacement, regular Col. John H. "Machine Gun" Parker, USA, did a good job in his training of the regiment, especially around Château Thierry. But then, for some reason, he too was relieved and transferred to AEF Headquarters at Chaumont. It was at about this time that Hiram arrived. Later, when the history of the regiment was being written, it was a common saying that "Isbell trained it; Parker inspired it; and Bearss fought it."

What his reception at regimental headquarters was like isn't clear, but we can assume that he was received with due courtesy. After all, he was a colonel of Marines with a reputation as a fighting man that transcended both services. He was well known to old army buddies from back in the Philippines, including "Black Jack" Pershing. Many of them knew that Hiram was a real character. The officers and men quickly learned that he was widely known as "Hiking Hiram" Bearss to the Marines. It wouldn't be long before they too would get a taste of his favorite exercise, and begin calling him by the same or a similar sobriquet.[32] Somewhere along the line he picked up a "batman," Private Frank J. Cummings, who was loyal and true to Hiram. Wherever Hiram was, so was Frank, and usually with Hiram's box of cigars. Frank Cummings, from Headquarters Company, 102d Infantry, eventually made sergeant. He was originally from New Haven, the home of Yale University, but it was unlikely that he was a graduate. In his first operation with his new regiment Hiram delighted all, rank and file, and made them all proud to be led by one so full of audacity that he made the regulars blanch when they heard his name.

Not too long after he arrived, AEF Inspector General Brewster came to see him. In the course of their discussion Brewster told him he was expected to shape up this not-very-highly-thought-of regiment. But, he told Hiram, he would give him time. Hiram responded that he thought that one week would do it. Brewster was shocked, and later admitted he thought that Hiram was a real "blowhard." He didn't know Hiram. After his arrival, Hiram found that much important equipment was missing. In particular there were no Chauchats in the unit and most of the other equipment was not of the best.[33] He set to work and soon decent materiel and weapons were working their way into the regiment. No matter how good a unit might have been, Hiram would have to impress it with his own attitude and personality. There were also some disciplinary requirements, but those he took care of in very short order. Hiram turned the regiment around soon after taking command and shortly had earned full support from his officers and men. He noted a surfeit of political discussions in the officers mess—"When we get back home we'll do so and so." Hiram told them, "Forget about going home. You are all going over the top and many won't survive so just think about that. Think about Berlin not Hartford or New Haven precincts." Or words similar enough to scare the living hell out of many of them.

Not long afterward they were on their way to the Rupt sector. Here they would be in position for the massive attack by which Pershing's staff planned to reduce the St. Mihiel salient. Most of the American divisions engaged would be on the southeast face. The 26th was the only American division on the northwest face. As their support, they were surrounded by several French divisions. Pershing's plan was simply that the attack would be primarily from the south face, northward. Any attacks from the north would be mainly diversions and the anvil to the hammer blows. The French were concerned that the Americans would not be able to pull this trick off, so they wanted their troops nearby to stop any further German counter advance if it came to that.

At just after midnight on 12 September, hundreds of millions of dollars worth of shells went off toward the German-infested salient. The bombardment persisted until 0800 the following morning. It was devastating, it was gigantic, and it convinced the Germans of what they had suspected for several days past: The "French" were making a grand move to retake the St. Mihiel salient. At first the Germans seemed not to have realized that this was primarily an American show. Their high command, like the French and British, didn't believe the Americans were capable of planning and launching a masterful attack such as this. Lieutenant Colonel George C. Marshall, USA, was the man who primarily pulled the whole thing together. The salient had been in the possession of the Germans since September 1914. It was a sore that had festered in the French subconscious, and Pershing had early on made his mind up — this would be the earliest AEF target. Though there were diversions when the AEF divisions were plugging holes elsewhere, this was the campaign Pershing always came back to.

On the southeastern flank the Americans were on the move following the cessation of the barrage. The divisions engaged, including the 2d Division with its Marine Brigade, were having a relatively easy time of it. But back north where the 26th Division was located, all was different. The advance of the Americans and the several French divisions through forests along the northwest face was a bit slower than on the opposite side. There the Germans seemed to have been better prepared and were able to stop the French 26th Division and to slow up the "Yankee" 26th Division.

Initially, the 102d Infantry was in division reserve. You can well imagine Hiram's reaction to this sad state of affairs. The other three regiments went forward, as best they could. The ground before them was an old, badly chewed up battlefield with all the impedimenta expected — wire, trenches, dugouts and the like — all of which helped to slow down the attacking forces. The 101st Infantry was leading the 51st Brigade. They were covering a half-mile wide swath on both sides of La Grande Tranchee. At noon the 102d Infantry moved ahead of the leading 101st toward the junction of La Grande Tranchee and the Vaux–St. Remy road, and off went Hiram I. Bearss leading his 102d. Needless to state, he had been anxiously awaiting this opportunity to lead.

Hiram, now astride a horse he had found someplace, was everywhere riding directly into the German positions, somehow managing to avoid receiving any lead for his pains. "On! Forward!" Hiram exhorted his men. It was only when they had advanced a short distance that he found the division engineers valiantly trying to put together some destroyed roads and bridges. He soon learned that passage forward was impossible even on a horse. The Tranchee was heavily overgrown and almost obliterated as a place of transit at this point. Orders from division headquarters kept pouring in, directing the 102d to obey orders and "occupy the junction of Vaux–St. Remy and Tranchee." It was impossible to obey. A support unit from the 101st Infantry had not occupied its position and had left the flank of the 102d in the air. Hiram never liked being placed in this embarrassing position and we can imagine that he must have rent the air with his "mild" curses.

Meanwhile, other observers mentioned a "sight to behold." That was Hiram, yelling for everyone to keep his head down while he sailed across the fire-littered battleground. It inspired his subordinates—here was their colonel riding a horse, hellbent for glory. The spectacle was invigorating, especially since no one had ever expected their regimental commander to be so far forward. About 20 years later A.G. Nelson, a Connecticut man who was there, told of what he saw: "It took place on 12 September 1918 on the Grande Tranchee Road that runs into the little town of Vigneulles les Haddonchatel, being the axis of our drive to cut off the enemy. Why Colonel Bearss didn't get picked off, horse and all, I don't know. He certainly was way out front and easily spotted by the enemy."[34]

The chief of staff of the division finally got into the act and pressed the 101st to get to its position so the rest of the line could continue forward. Five hours were lost during this embarrassing situation. Within five minutes of the advance Company K of the 102d had turned in 40 prisoners and were "progressing rapidly." One private, James B. Carty, went in and took an entire German company prisoner. For that he was awarded a Distinguished Service Cross. The 102d reached that day's objective and somewhat later the balance of the division arrived at its objective by 2200 hours on 12 September.

Vigneulles

That night a plan was put forward by Corps that would make this more than just a common vulgar brawl. It was directed that the 1st Division (Regular) should advance from their positions on the southeastern face to the center of the salient and meet the 26th Division coming in from the northwest. There, in the pocket closed off, both would seal off a further retreat of any German forces still within. The village or town selected for the meeting was Vigneulles, which is located just a mile or so south of Hattonchatel. The latter had been the residence of a bishop who many years before had built a roadway for his king. It was called La Grande Tranchee de Calonne and it ran directly into Hattonchatel from Verdun. It was very narrow and was paved with grass and had rich flower bushes on both sides for its entire 15-mile length. As we have seen, at this time it was closer to being a jungle, barely wide enough for a few men marching abreast. But for Hiram's purposes it would do very nicely.

To begin with, the 51st Brigade, of which the 102d Infantry was a part, was located on each side of the Tranchee de Calonne. When Hiram found out what plans were afoot at division headquarters, he volunteered his 102d Infantry to make the advance. It was soon agreed that Hiking Hiram and his infantry, which were in reserve, might just as well be given the "opportunity" to meet the 1st Division. Besides, no one else seemed overly interested in making a night march straight through the unbroken German lines. It would be a genuine, old-fashioned Hiram I. Bearss maneuver, straight out of his everyday Marine life.

The orders were quite straightforward. Beginning at 2100 hours the 102d was to march down La Grande Tranchee de Calonne, all nine kilometers of it. Serious thought was given to fighting the Germans along the way but Hiram would have none of that. If the men were to make it to their objective, ahead of the regulars, they couldn't be expected to do any fighting along the way. His plan was to go right straight down the neck of the bottle and ignore the Germans on both sides of him. Naturally, not too many of his officers were with him at first. But the men sensed a bit of excitement and were willing to give anything to beat those "God damn regulars." The 1st Division was noted to be Pershing's pets and because of it were denounced throughout the AEF. On the 26th's right flank, the French 2d Cavalry Division was to keep abreast if they could so as to ward off any German attack. But there wouldn't be anyone else making the trip to Vigneulles.

Bearss has been given credit for coming up with the plan for the march along the Grande Tranchee. It is more likely that someone at division head-

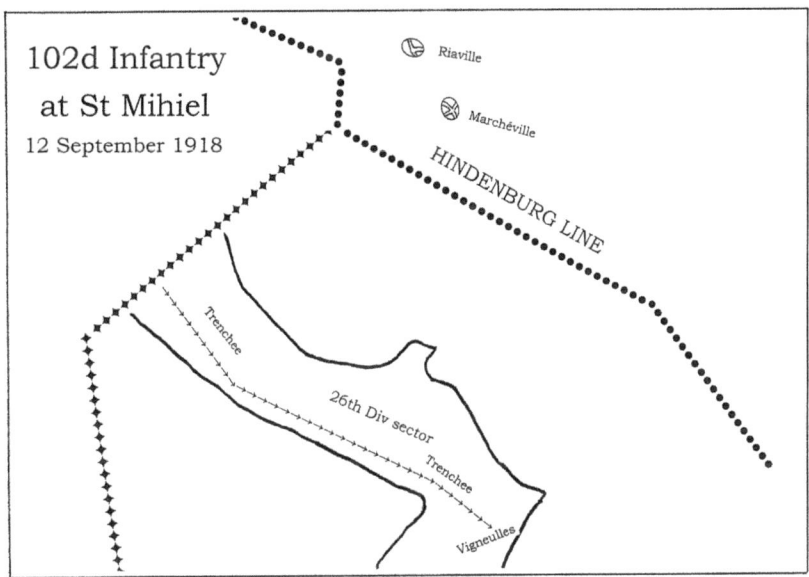

The 102d Infantry at St. Mihiel, 12 September 1918.

quarters said, "We gotta get to Vigneulles first," and Hiram, who had volunteered his regiment, saw how "easy it would all be." Straight down the line they would go. No fighting — just bayonets fixed, in case some stupid German got in the way. And that was how they did it. Hiram ensured that there would be no cartridges in the rifle chambers, even going so far as to inspect the rifles himself. No sound, no words, no firing and no giving the plan away. Hiram moved fast. He was fearful that somebody from headquarters would come up with another plan, or find some way to interfere with his fun. It wasn't only Hiram whose adrenaline was worked up; his officers and men also began to feel the excitement. He rode up and down the lines to impart his plan and to ensure that they recognized that the "glory and majesty of the great state of Connecticut was at stake." It was shameful hyperbole, of course, but that was what was needed at the time.

Hiram plus his staff and his bat-boy, cigar carrier, bodyguard and general factotum and friend, Frank Cummings, lurched out ahead of everyone else on their way to glory. Included in his staff was Hiram's intelligence man, another veritable tiger, Captain A. Frederick Oberlin. Down the road they went. The balance of the 102d Infantry following at a discreet distance behind. Hiram and Oberlin were first with Frank Cummings slightly to the rear, but not too far back. After all, he had the cigars.

They had walked a short distance when the inevitable happened. The

French cavalry interrupted their march shortly after it had begun. No Frenchman could understand what in hell these crazy Americans were up to. Fortunately the Germans' imagination was just as limited. Hiram gave the French what for and they soon stood aside.

Back into motion they went. The column moved ever forward but not in any recognizable formation. It wasn't necessary; they had Hiram up front and bayonets fixed on every Springfield .03. Down the trail they continued. It was learned later that the Germans on each side of the wall along the pathway could hear some kind of noise but none could or wanted to break through the hedge to learn what was passing them. Their attitude seemed to be "let well enough alone." Hiram was happy because no one, not even headquarters, tried to stop them. So he just kept right on going until they arrived at their destination.

At the break of dawn, Hiram, Oberlin and Cummings were way ahead of the rest of the regiment. Hiram could still hike and much earlier he had made up his mind that he, even if not his regiment, would get where he was going long before the 1st Division. His audacity was well known in the Corps but not quite so much among his newfound friends of the army. They knew they had a tiger by the tail but none was quite aware of just how far Hiram would go to get into a fight. They found out and, more importantly, he hadn't misjudged his men. They were right with him all the way. As we shall see, the 102d made an enviable reputation while under Hiram's direction and guidance.

Down into the valley in which the little town of Vigneulles rests they strode. Then into the main street Hiram, Oberlin and Cummings marched. There they were confronted with a large body of German soldiers on the move. The Germans seemed quite surprised, even more so when Hiram yelled "Surrender!" to them in a voice calculated to wake the dead. They faltered and came to a stop. Like that poor captain back at the Paris hotel, they knew when they heard a command from that man, it was serious and that they should obey. Hiram yelled to Sergeant Johnson, one of his staff members, to "run like hell and get the 102d up here, double time."

Hiram then noted a suspicious movement by a German soldier in the ranks. It appeared as though he was pulling a "potato-masher" from his sleeve to hurl it toward Hiram and his staff. Hiram ran to the man and smacked him in his face, knocking him flat. That ended that threat. When Hiram yelled "Achtung!" the Germans snapped to attention. The entire column put up their hands in self protection.[35]

Hearing a rumbling sound coming toward them, Oberlin ran toward a wagon which had just come around a corner, with his .45 drawn and firing. The Germans discreetly pulled up and raised their hands to this fighting man because there might have been many more where he came from.

With the Germans in good shape and in a formation he could control, Hiram gave orders that coffee and breakfast should be prepared for his men who would be showing up any minute. Being an old campaigner himself, Hiram knew the way to a fighting man's heart was through a full stomach, especially when he wasn't sure where his next meal would be coming from. He also had the Germans break out their band instruments, and when his regiment showed up, at his direction they played *"Hail the Conquering Hero Comes."*

As his men marched into town, they grinned when they saw the colonel and the Germans cooking up a mess of food on the main street. This was good old Hiking Hiram at his best. The officers and men lapped up the soup and coffee and now were ready to continue the fun already begun. Taking prisoners was loads of fun so they all began rounding up any Germans they could find anywhere in the area. They heard of Germans in Heudicourt, located just about two miles south, and at 0500 a couple of companies headed down there to take more prisoners. They returned by 0630, completely successful. That sort of thing continued for several hours. At about 0900 Hiram was notified that elements of the 1st Division were waiting for artillery support before trying to make an entrance into the town. Hiram had a message sent to the doughboy commander explaining that all was well in Vigneulles and no artillery on the town was necessary. By noon more American forces made their way into town but the honor of being there first belonged to the tried and true 102d Infantry, National Guard. How that must have grated the regulars! And, how happy that made the guardsmen. Fun may be fun but in truth the regulars had had open ground to cover against German delaying forces whereas Hiram's men had plunged through a veritable jungle.

No matter who they were, the Americans were received like conquering heroes by the freed French peasants, who had been captives for four long years. Food and wine that had been buried to hide it from the enemy was now broken out. The tricolor of France, which had been forbidden for the same period, was now broken out and displayed all over the freed zone. There were even a few American flags. If it wasn't for the war continuing, it might have been a very festive occasion.

Somehow or other Hiram managed to "conquer" another horse. He clambered on its back and rode everywhere in great style. Crisp orders were given for dispersion and maintenance of prisoners that included every exigency. Information about the Germans flowed from the French peasants. Locations cited as places in which the Germans were holed up were immediately gone to by companies from the 102d. All the while Hiram had the German band play patriotic French and American war songs to entertain everyone, and, perhaps, even the Germans.

The soldiers continued coming in with prisoners and war equipment from the surrounding towns. Much of it had been easy to find. The Americans had open fires to warm themselves and the coming light made it easy to locate German soldiers moving around. Many additional Germans were taken, as was much war materiel including many machine guns. Well after daybreak, Hiram ordered that all thousand or more German prisoners be gathered together in the village square. There they could be counted and prepared for transport back of the lines. The German officer that Hiram had first encountered that morning was greatly perturbed. He desired to keep the respect of his own men and asked Hiram if he could have permission to lead his men into captivity. The response was as follows: "Yes, if you will give me your word of honor as a Prussian officer and a gentleman that you will march them back without attempting to put anything over on me. No escape attempt, no fermenting of trouble among your own ranks."[36]

The officer responded that he would keep that promise. He also conceded that if he had known how few troops Hiram had with him that morning, he wouldn't have surrendered so quickly. Hiram responded, "Had you unlimbered but one gun, my regiment might have passed into history, but such is fate caused by the fog of war." With that, the German presented his Luger and pocket watch to Hiram. Hiram asked, "What is this for?" The German responded, "That is what you wish?" "Certainly not," replied Hiram. "Your weapons yes, nothing else." The satisfied German then told Hiram that his watch was a family heirloom and he was much gratified at not losing it.

Hiram then gave the orders for the prisoner return and placed the German officer directly in command of his own machine gun company, sans the guns of course. At the parting the officer told Hiram that he was a gentleman and would never be forgotten as such. Hiram responded in kind and allowed the German the further honor of being lightly guarded on the return trip.

The great advance and satisfactory closure of the trap at Vigneulles elicited many justified paeans of praise for Hiram and the 102d Infantry. Hiram himself addressed kind words to his battalion commanders:

> The Division Commander visited Vigneulles yesterday to congratulate the officers and men of this regiment. We beat the 1st Division in the race across the salient for Vigneulles.
> The Regimental Commander takes great pleasure in announcing the

> Commanding General's approval of this recent operation and feels assured that the spirit and high morale of this command will continue to be in the future, what it has been in the past.³⁷

Hiram was the recipient of a letter from Brig. Gen. George H. Shelton, his brigade commander, which was lengthy and laudatory. Portions are extracted:

> The march of the 102d Infantry ... was of such unique and important character and was performed in such efficient and spirited manner that I desire to place immediately on record my personal appreciation of this accomplishment.
> ... To have attempted to push forward a line covering our whole sector would have meant, in view of the woods and difficulties of the terrain, to fail in the accomplishment of our mission. The only alternative was to push boldly forward on the only existing road, through unknown hostile country, losing for the time being liaison with the elements of our forces on our right and left, and exposing the brigade in part to the possibility of being cut off and surrounded by the enemy.
> ... I congratulate you and your regiment upon this success and upon the boldness and fine spirit manifest throughout its accomplishment.³⁸

There were many more congratulations. Some were addressed directly to Bearss, and he was written up in General Orders, No. 19, but there were many others to the division from the AEF and the French High Command. There was just one additional thing left to do to create the end of a perfect campaign, and that was to keep "Fritzy" moving eastward. In fact, Pershing and his staff had planned a fitting end to St. Mihiel by pushing the German army directly back to Metz. Unfortunately, Marshal Foch and his staff, ably assisted by Field Marshal Haig, had already precluded the AEF from doing so. Pershing had already received orders to be ready for a big push in the Argonne to begin in late September. No further advance on Metz was to be allowed.

We will not get into the controversy that was engendered by Pershing's plan here.³⁹ But suffice to state, the Americans were all for it. Hiram was furious when he learned that his regiment wouldn't be taking the iron mines in the Metz district. But there was little he or anyone else in the division could do to change it. Pershing was forced to accede to plans already made by Foch and Haig to utilize the American divisions. The resultant change set the stage for the AEF's heavy losses in the Argonne during September and October 1918.⁴⁰

Troyon Sector

The St. Mihiel campaign was terminated and by direction of Marshal Foch, most of the American divisions were being transferred north to the Argonne Forest. One division that wasn't going to the new fray was the 26th. This, of course, precluded the 102d Infantry from immersion in what was to become the final and bloodiest battle of the war. Instead the division was assigned to fight the German army opposite where the St. Mihiel salient had once been. Basically, the division was a continued danger to the Germans—a perceived threat that they planned to continue going eastward toward Metz and the all-important railway that supplied the German army. Everyone on the Allied side knew that was a dead issue, but Pershing hoped the Germans wouldn't realize it. For some time they didn't. They realized that they would have grave difficulties had the AEF continued eastward. Consequently, they made contingency plans to thwart any move by the 26th Division. It helped tie up several important divisions on both sides.

So, Hiram was once again shunted to a backwater. In reality there would be enough fighting in this area to satisfy even Hiram. Within a few days his regimental boundaries had been expanded so that now a part of his responsibility was located behind German lines. This meant that the 102d would have to be very aggressive so the colonel could fulfill his responsibilities. After nightfall on 17 September the general positions on the front were altered. The 102d Regiment had the 3d Battalion on line, the 1st in support and the 2d in reserve. On the 20th their boundaries increased again. They would now include St. Hilaire (still held by the Germans) to Montpelier and Wadonville. Hiram established his headquarters in an old German first aid station built into a hill, just southwest of Hentenville. He then set his men to digging entrenchments, installing barbed wire and doing anything else that would strengthen the northern slope near the hilltop. Previous entrenchments were either in bad shape or too well known by the Germans for continued usage. The enemy had withdrawn some distance and much of the work could only be completed safely at night. Enemy camouflage was used in different locations so that should the Germans return they would be terribly confused.

During this period the Germans threw over many artillery shells and a great deal of gas upon the regiment. Even though the infantry was very exposed, casualty rates were modest. Orders to Hiram from on high stipulated "no raids or other provocations," which of course was contrary to his style of conducting a war. This vexed him considerably. The idea of a non-fighting war did not appeal but for once he obeyed and waited.

Without permission and to gain some activity, Hiram organized raids upon the Germans, but in his reports they were called "patrols." There had been no orders from on high that prohibited patrols so Hiram was using his own best judgment to get around the rules. Someone must have wondered what was going on when his reports began coming in with a lengthy listing of German prisoners together with exhaustive and important information about who and what was in front of the 102d Infantry. Still, no questions were raised at headquarters about these "patrols." They were Hiram's pride and joy. They were constant and very productive. He not only supervised them but also led some of them. It was rather an imprudent move for any colonel to make, but that was Hiram. The information obtained was consistent and helpful, not only to their front but also for the offensive now brewing in the Argonne. Information on the numbers of men and officers in each German unit plus their morale and physical condition were more than helpful in making important decisions. Knowledge of well-constructed trenches and deep shelter dugouts was of prime importance, and only raids conducted against them could provide that information. Factual data produced included the designation of three German divisions to their front. The 3d, 10th and 77th reserve divisions were the current occupants and recently the 88th had been moved someplace else.

This kind of information was of great significance, as was the fact that no enemy offensive seemed in the planning stages. Hiram's intelligence established simply that the enemy was to hold the line against the Americans, nothing more. They still considered that the next American movement to be made was the all-important thrust toward Metz, but Foch and Haig seemed blind to that potential. Propaganda leaflets in German were dropped by planes all over the area to reinforce what the Germans already expected. "We'll be in Metz by 26 September," they proclaimed, and the Germans were convinced that was what would happen. Obviously any attack by the "YD" would be resisted by the Germans with every ounce of strength they could muster.

Hiram's information went far toward providing the division intelligence office with data needed to plan real raids. These were set for the period between 23 and 29 September and were to keep the enemy off balance and bring in more prisoners. But in the meantime, on the nights of 18 and 19 September, two raids were organized by Hiram. He gave over the command of the St. Hilaire raid to Captain Oberlin, his comrade from Vigneulles. The other, directed and led by Capt. Alexander W. Dillard, went to the Bois de Warville.

Artillery support for the raids was systematically organized. Firing was to be centered upon certain locations, interposed by quiet, then move on to another target. Then the fire was to be centered here and there by "box barrages" of definite duration. Following this were to be the raids. The raiders were formed by two platoons, one in advance and the other to be the covering party. Both raids were set up the same way.

As a result 16 prisoners were taken. They were a mixed bag, mainly from the 64th and 51st Austro-Hungarian regiments of the 35th Division which had recently been transferred from the Eastern Front to aid Germany on the Western Front. Unfortunately the raid upon St. Hilaire was considered, by headquarters, to be unsuccessful because no prisoners were taken whereas Dillard got his share. The artillery support from the 101st and 103d field artillery was considered excellent. As the brigade commander wrote, "The credit for the conception and for the execution of these raids, is due entirely to Colonel Hiram I. Bearss, who personally supervised the operations from his advance post at Wadonville." Among the individuals named was one Private Frank J. Cummings, Colonel Bearss' favorite orderly, general handyman and cigar box carrier — who was also a fighting fool of the first chop.

It was one of Hiram's favorite exercises, when possible, to utilize enemy supplies and equipment. His watchword was always, "Save Uncle Sam's money, expend the enemy's." With that he directed Sergeant James J. Tracy to go forward and drag back whatever enemy guns he could find and any shells that remained unfired.[41] Regardless of his activity, the war was passing the 26th by and not many of the officers and men were too thrilled with being sidelined. But something came up that altered everything.

On the 26th of September an order was sent down to the troops to launch another raid. This one gave Hiram the opportunity of selecting who was to lead and, as you might expect, he selected himself for that honor. Of course, like most raids a colonel had no right to be even remotely engaged in what promised to be a rough and tumble brawl.

This raid was to be launched against Riaville and Marcheville. It was going to be a real fight. For Marcheville two companies of the 1st Battalion, 102d Infantry, were selected as were two from the 102d Machine Gun Battalion, a mortar platoon and two platoons of engineers to add dignity to what might ordinarily be just a roughhouse brawl. For the attack upon Riaville the 1st Battalion, 103d Infantry was selected plus a machine gun company from the 103d Machine Gun Battalion.

Their job was to take both towns and the trenches that connected the two. Then, for some reason, by the morning of the twenty-seventh the entire body was to fall back to their old locations. It was just to upset the

Germans into thinking a "real attack" was coming.⁴² Hiram had no time to make his subordinates aware in detail of what they were doing, let alone give them a description of the terrain. But he managed to give them a brief and hurried go-through of what they were to do. In that he described the inherent dangers and what to do or not to do should they or their men be captured. The closeness of the enemy and their activity greatly lent itself to that possibility. In fact, as we will later see, Hiram must have had a premonition of being captured himself. But he was adamant. "There is no conceivable set of circumstances, which would justify an American officer to allow himself to be taken by the enemy." And for Hiram, that meant him too. No exceptions.

Bearss established his "headquarters" at Saulx, which was near where they were to begin the raid. With a few selected men and officers for liaison work he led them through the old interconnecting German trenches until they were almost at the edge of Marcheville. There they found an enemy machine gun nest, which they promptly destroyed. According to the newspaper reporter Frank P. Sibley, "Colonel Bearss ... in command of the whole operation, had headquarters in Saulx, but did not stay there. Instead, he went out with his advancing lines and into Marcheville itself, and established a command post right in the town. In some accounts he is said to have been the first man to enter Marcheville."⁴³

The attack on Riaville was directed by a Major Hanson. He had his headquarters back at Champion and, according to records, there he remained. That attack went nowhere.⁴⁴ The one led by Hiram plowed ahead and after he entered Marcheville, he established his forward headquarters. One officer from the 103d Infantry, 1st Lt. Charles E.H. Bates, and his company were liaison between the 103d and 102d. Bearss came across him in a trench and asked who "in blue blazes" he was. Bates told him and Bearss responded that Bates should rejoin his outfit. That he did but not long after that Hiram came upon him again, and since it was the hour to attack Hiram told him to "go ahead and take the town ... you can do it." With that Bates took his men and went right into that town, knocking off several machine guns on the way in. Hiram had a way about him when it came to leadership.⁴⁵

Meanwhile, most of Hanson's unit remained pretty much where they were all day, at least 700 meters distant from Riaville, their target. There was some activity and several prisoners captured but generally the German artillery fire kept them from doing to Riaville what the 102d did to Marcheville. Other divisions in the vicinity managed to advance and take a few prisoners and then retire by noon. By that hour Hiram's unit was right smack in the middle of Marcheville and in the process of "cleaning

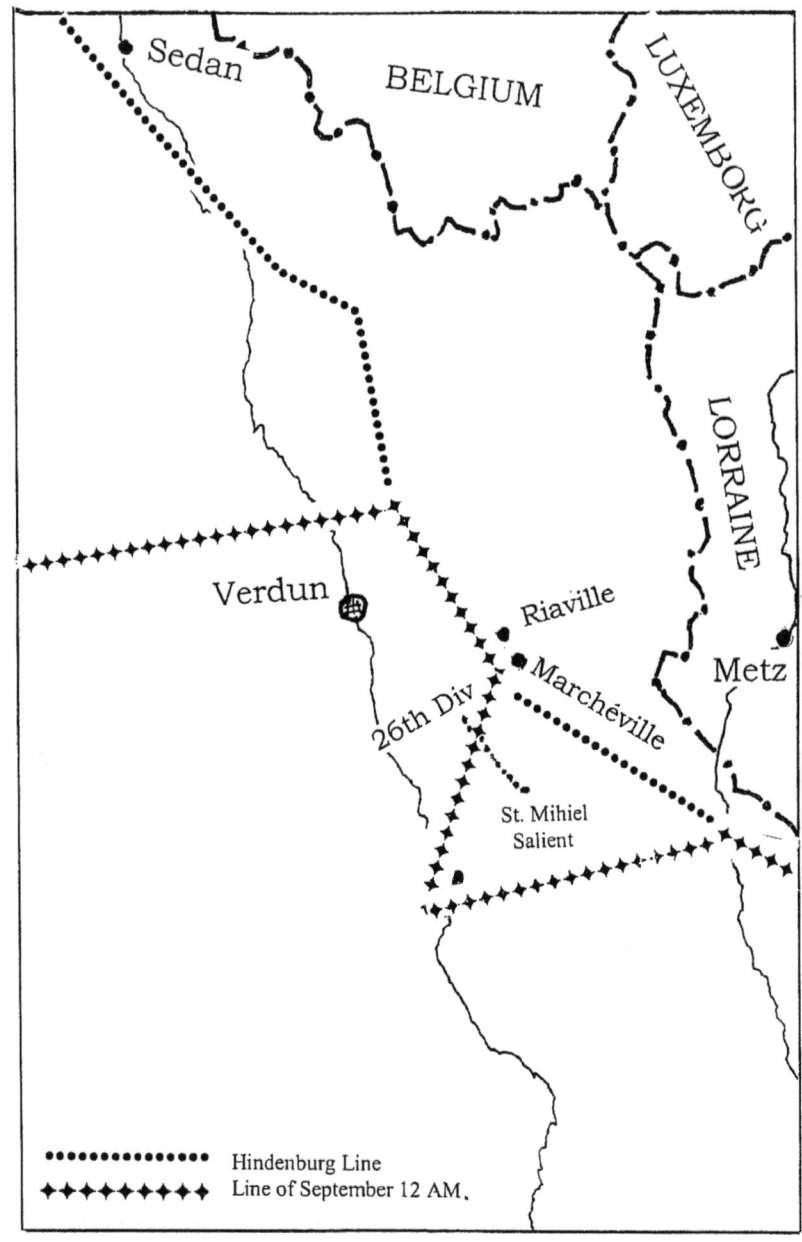

The 26th Division in eastern France.

up the town." Enemy artillery and infantry found they had little to worry about except from Marcheville so that was where they concentrated much of their fire all day. Shells were landing directly on Hiram's men in the advanced trenches, the location of which were well known to the Germans. Troops on the right of the town lost so heavily that they had to fall back to the southern edge.

At 1300 the enemy launched a counterattack from St. Hilaire and Harville, having no difficulty entering Riaville since no American troops were there to hinder them. The enemy and the few Americans on hand were fighting desperately in the various interconnecting trenches. In this the enemy initially took more punishment than the defending doughboys. However, many of the latter found themselves trapped like the proverbial rats and were forced to surrender to avoid extermination. This was also a very dangerous time for Hiram and his staff. They happened to be located in the northwestern edge of the village and were subjected to the heaviest concentration of enemy artillery. Their position in a concrete shelter was soon completely surrounded by the German attacking troops. Hiram's troops had been driven back at least 200 yards leaving him and his staff quite isolated, behind German lines. It was at this time that Hiram believed that he might have overreached himself just a bit. He even went so far as to tell Cummings, "Give me my box of cigars, Frank, I'll be damned if I'm going to go into Germany without some smokes." Things must have looked bad at that moment for Hiram to make such an observation. Just then an officer said, "Colonel, I think the Germans are forming a counterattack over in that field." His reply was, "Gentlemen, we can lick the whole German army. Have a cigar." And he then picked out a box of cigars that Frank was carrying and passed them around.[46]

Wild rumors reached the rear concerning the capture of Colonel Bearss and the annihilation of his battalion. But now he was truly in a mess of his own devising. The German officers and men poured into the shelter from above and could plainly see Hiram in the light through an opening. Hiram called in his huge voice to his aide, "Tell them to surrender." Great laughter erupted from the Germans, some of whom understood English. They recognized Hiram's rank and told the aide, "Tell the old man it is his time to surrender." And the Germans continued laughing at the preposterousness of Hiram's demand. One even went so far as to slap his knee heartily with great merriment. It was the last thing he did on earth. Hiram pulled his pistol and let him have it. He then quickly sized up the situation and gathered his remaining forces about him. The shelter was in the shape of a "U" and both entrances were loaded with Germans. One man had a Chauchat, others had pistols. They gathered themselves into a circle and fought like tigers.

Individual Germans came in from both sides of the shelter and they and some of the Americans died in hand-to-hand fighting. Hiram, with the few men still available, including the walking wounded, though fired upon and heavily hit by "potato-mashers," somehow fought their way out of the shelter. They then moved through the trenches toward the rear, fighting all the way. Shortly after making this breakthrough they successfully rejoined their own troops. Safety was being located behind a good stout stone wall at the southern limit of the Château grounds. There was a hole in that wall large enough for one man at a time to get through. Each of the party made the trip under heavy enemy machine gun fire. Somehow, all of the surviving Americans from the "U" made it with no further casualties. They had ceased to be prisoners, if they ever really were. Later both sides sent patrols back into the town. Some German prisoners were captured but no further attempt was made by either side to "cleanse" the town, or to reoccupy the advance positions.

One young officer named Linton took a patrol out and in an attempt to destroy a machine gun nest was mortally wounded. The final withdrawal was delayed in order to go out and get Linton and his subordinates. Otherwise, the attempt to hold what had been gained was abandoned when Hiram realized that it was only he and his men who were trying to hold the towns. That was given up as a bad deal and at midnight back to Saulx they went. There is no question that if Hiram had led the 103d Infantry instead of his own 102d he might have taken and held Riaville. According to an account of the 26th Division, Hanson's group was precluded from advancing any further than they did because of severe artillery fire. It is true that they suffered many casualties during the raid, but certainly nowhere near the quantity suffered by Bearss' group.[47]

The raid had been to assure the enemy that an assault upon Metz and its environs was still a serious consideration. The Germans put everything they had into stopping it before it could begin. In effect, the raid was successful since the Germans were convinced that it was at least the beginning of that attack they had long expected. But it was just a diversion and a large number of "YD" men paid a fearful price. Since there seemed not to be a reason for the attack, this added to what was already a serious morale problem. The junior officers and men were convinced that Pershing was just using them up. They believed that the 26th was the "goat" division. It was well known that Pershing had made disparaging comments about the 26th and its commander, Clarence Edwards. He had once threatened to court-martial a number of officers for perceived errors at Seicheprey in April. And he was furious when following the fight the French decorated a large number of the officers and men without his permission.[48] The Germans had a high regard for the "YD" and in one recorded conversation a German officer captured at Marcheville asked, "How many Yankee Divisions are there? Is there more than one? I have heard of this division of New England men on every front. We look upon it as a shock division." That could have been "butter" being spread thickly for the benefit of the listeners but a look at the YD's record would convince most anyone that they did have a busy time in France.

For the next several days the division continued holding the line amidst heavy mustard gas shelling. The men deduced that it was in retaliation for their working over of the enemy lines. The Germans were of the opinion that an advance against Metz was still in the cards. Leaves among the men of the 26th were asked for but few were granted. The morale of the division's complement since Marcheville was notoriously low. Casualties had been very heavy in the 102d and nearly as heavy in the 103d regiment. In the meantime the French were still very impressed by the fighting qualities of the YD. General Orders No. 89 from General Blondlat, commanding the 2d Colonial Corps, recommended a citation for the 1st Battalion, 102d Infantry. Part of the citation read:

> The dimension and duration of the raid executed by the 26th Division certainly deceived the enemy as to our intentions; the losses suffered by the troops taking part in this operation were fairly severe, but there is no doubt that those suffered by the Germans were much more serious.[49]

A further statement from Blondlat did Hiram partial justice:

> Picked troops who, trained by Colonel Hiram J. [sic] Bearss who led the attack in the first line, carried out brilliantly and with splendid energy, a particularly delicate operation; engaged [in] battle with a superb dash; won a victory after a violent combat over an enemy who was both stubborn and superior in numbers, entrenched in concreted shelters, strongly supported by numerous machine guns and powerful artillery, and who made use of, in the course of the action, infamous methods of warfare; heroically carried out their mission in capturing in heavy fighting a village where they maintained themselves all day in spite of four counterattacks, and thus furnished the finest example of courage, abnegation and self-sacrifice.[50]

Bearss would soon get his. For his leadership skills at Marcheville, he was to receive, among other decorations, the Distinguished Service Cross. (see appendices). For the next few weeks the division would continue to support the French along the line facing towards Metz. In early October it was transferred to a position nearer to Verdun. There, Hiram passed along to his regiment a communication from the division chief of staff. In addition he highlighted the importance of the ground they were now responsible for:

> Under no circumstances must a foot of the line taken over from the 18th [French] Division be lost. This is vital. A foot of ground in this sector is worth one kilometer of ground in the Troyon sector lately occupied by this division. Our mission will be an active defensive, etc. Any ground lost must be taken immediately by counterattack.
>
> By order: Colonel Bearss, USMC[51]

While in this new location the men finally got four days to themselves in order to clean and bathe their bodies and their weapons, both being worn out. With all the replacements coming in there were new acquaintances to make, but hardly any old-timers left to welcome them. The division was in a bad way. Their morale and nerves, for the most part, were all shot. The situation wasn't much better across the way. German prisoners admitted that they were barely holding on and every day they were expecting a massive American attack towards Metz. But both sides were composed of men who wouldn't just give up, no matter how bad things were. Brave men always pay the highest price.

The new ground had little to offer the men of the 26th. The trenches and dugouts had all been prepared by the Germans when they controlled the ground and were all facing the wrong way. Enemy artillery had long since plotted every inch of the ground and that left very little protection for the Americans. The situation wasn't all that good in the Argonne, either. Pershing had to stop what forward movement there was to give the battered American divisions some time to regroup and to bring in fresh troops. Our old friends of the 2d Division, after busting the Germans at Blanc Mont while fighting for the French, had been brought in to help in the new phase to begin on 1 November. Pershing was bringing in the heavies for the tough work ahead.

Meanwhile, fraternization became a serious problem for the Yankee Division. Their lines were extremely close to the enemy now and there were attempts by the Germans to sort of "slow things down a bit." They realized the war was nearly over, and they had already lost it, so why die? Before the trenches of the 102d, approximately 100 yards east, lay the trenches occupied by the Saxon Landwehr.[52] On 20 October some of them came out of their trenches toward the 102d and made friendly gestures to the Americans to come over and visit. The Yankees refused but indicated that they would welcome the Germans if they came over. But that the Germans were afraid to do. They too had rules that said "no fraternization." Sergeant Major Julius Y. Wax, of Headquarters, 26th Division, and a mechanic named Josef Rechen, Jr., of Company K., both of whom spoke German fluently, jumped out of their trench and made their way across No-Man's-Land for the German trenches.

When they got to the other line, the two Americans demanded to know what it was the Germans wanted. A German lieutenant replied, "For you to stop shooting at us. We are Saxons here and we know the war is over. We don't want to kill unnecessarily." He might have added, "nor to be killed either." Wax told them to come on over and surrender. "No, we can't do that either, we would be sent deeply into France and it would be a long time before we were sent home." The conversation continued with a mixture of friendship for Americans and loyalty to their oath. It ended pretty much on the note that the Saxons would not fire on the Americans if the Americans treated them likewise. Wax told them to consider surrender and to make their decision by "tomorrow or else."

When the two reported what happened the message went up the line—directly to Hiram, because he was now in command of the 51st Brigade, Shelton being in the hospital with the flu. Bearss spoke to Wax and Rechen and agreed that they should try to obtain the surrender of the Saxons. Next day he would go with them in the uniform of an enlisted man. His plan was to tell the Germans that if they didn't surrender at that moment a heavy artillery fire would be laid upon their trenches immediately. He figured that they wouldn't immediately surrender and the fire would last two hours making them more willing on the following day. The next day they would ask for another conference and if the Germans still refused to surrender they would be threatened with being gassed continuously while they were on the line. It looked good, and even sounded good. But as the plan went up the line it dead ended and was disapproved at Division Headquarters. It was not the best of times for Hiram. He and his plan were fiercely criticized as being "utterly impossible and entirely against orders."[53]

No action was taken against Hiram, nor against Lt. Col. Evan E. Lewis, Hiram's replacement in command of the 102d Infantry.[54] Brigadier General Cole of the 52d Brigade had issued special orders that no one in his brigade was to enter into any fraternization with the enemy, under any guise. But he was the man relieved because of fraternization.[55] Cole was eventually reinstated because he had records that showed that he had given orders of "no fraternization"; consequently, he wasn't responsible for what his men did contrary to those orders.[56]

It was also during this period that Maj. Gen. Clarence Edwards was relieved of command of the division he had helped to form upon federalization in 1917. He had also successfully led it in every battle fought since then. It was the AEF Headquarters' worst possible offence against the officers and men of the 26th Division. Pershing finally had his way. The official reason put forward was a new policy to transfer experienced generals home to "train new divisions." Edwards was the very first person selected for the "honor." This was made official on 24 October 1918. No one at division seemed to be privy to what actually happened.[57]

Regardless of what was about to happen to him, and his shock upon learning of the death of his daughter, Edwards went back to work planning the attack for 25 October. When Hiram learned what had happened he prepared a missive of his own. Runners took copies to every platoon. It said, "Every officer, noncommissioned officer and man, is depended upon to uphold the glorious traditions of the Twenty-sixth Division. All Hell's flying artillery cannot stop this brigade when it has once gone into action."[58]

Edwards was prevailed upon by his staff to stay with his division while the attack was proceeding. He did and following the attack had the following citation sent to the attacking 51st Brigade:

> 1. The Division command extends to the commanding officer, 51st Infantry Brigade [Bearss], and the officers and men of the following organizations, his hearty congratulations on their great success in the operations of this date for the capture of the heights of the Meuse in the region of Le Houppy Bois and Belieu Bois....
> 2. The attack as planned was difficult of execution, and only to be attempted by trained troops. You carried it out like the veterans you are, and with a dash and valor worthy of the best traditions of the Twenty-sixth Division.
>
> C.R. Edwards, Major General Commanding.[59]

The attack mentioned above was assigned to the 51st Brigade. Hiram's regiment, the 102d, made it to the top of Hill 360 in Belieu Bois, several times. This was a crucial point in the enemy's defensive system and they whacked the hell out of the 102d troops who had taken it and tried to remain there. Hiram's lads were not being fully supported by the 101st and were finally forced to fall back off Hill 360 and the Belieu Bois. They were "blown off it and back to the original line." At 1152 on 27 October Hiram sent the following message to 1st Lt. Gregory P. Connolly, commanding Company H, 3d Battalion:

> [Maj. Harry B.] Bissell ordered to drive through between you and [Capt. A. W.] Dillard. Directed to reach your normal objective. *You must drive enemy from Hill 360 if it takes every man* [emphasis added].[60]

And another message to Connolly at 1300 hours:

8. The Great War with the Marines   197

> Put in immediately every bit of force and energy you have. Spare nobody or any efforts. *You must take Hill 360, without further delay in order to do your full part in this fight* [emphasis added].[61]

Connolly had his say. Ten minutes later he asked for artillery "on 100 yards rear of Boche line ... fifteen minutes of it." One hour later he was still sending the same message. By 1501 he was told that both the 101st and 2d Battalion, 102d, had done their "stuff"; what about Connolly? At 1543 Bearss sent another prodding message, which emphasized that "all reaching objectives so far, now up to you to come across. You must go forward."[62]

One might get the impression from the foregoing that Hiram was working that young lieutenant over more than necessary. Not so. He was busy, but took some time out to nurture Connolly who probably was new and needed help. Later Hiram made many complimentary comments about his lieutenant and during the course of the fight sent him a message which said, "Tell Connolly to go to it, rap on wood, and God Bless Him." It has been estimated that on that day at least 10,000 shells landed on Hill 360. By the end of the overall campaign, on 29 October, sergeants were commanding companies and platoons. One private was made "1st Sergt." of what was left of another company. These weren't unusual happenings, either. Corporal Timothy Ahearn of New Haven sent Hiram a message:

> To: Commanding Officer, 102d Inf.
> From: "C" Co. Commander.
> Subject: Reorganization of Co.
> Time: 11:20
>
>> Have made two skelton [sic] platoons of four squads apiece.
>> Pvt. Keeney, is made Act. 1st Sgt.
>> Am ready for any duty that I am called upon to perform.
>> Am ready for replacements.
>
>> T. Ahearn,
>
>> Cpl. C Co. 102d U.S. Inf.[63]

Note how his regiment was no longer a national guard regiment but "U.S. Inf." There were lots of those kinds of "Yankees" still in the regiment. At the end the 1st Battalion, 102d Infantry's four company commanders were three sergeants and, as we have seen above, a corporal. Third Battalion was down from 1000 rifles to 145 men. Captain Dillard, who commanded 1/102, sent a message to Bearss in which he told him among other things that "The N.C.O.'s in charge of companies all state they cannot hold their men under fire in their present nervous and exhausted condition." On 29 October Hiram sent a memo to his subordinates that read:

> 1. You must commence immediately the reorganization of your commands. This means practically a complete reorganization. You must be ready without delay for any duty that you may be called upon to perform. I hope to receive replacement troops for your command, and your reorganization must also be based upon this idea, in order that replacements may be quickly assimilated.
>
> 2. Make report to these headquarters by 16 o'clock tomorrow of what you have done.
>
> H.I. Bearss
>
> Colonel, USMC, Commanding.[64]

On 30 October, from his hospital bed, George Shelton sent his brigade a message congratulating and thanking them for what they had accomplished during the week of fighting.

Edwards left his division and the sorrow was felt by everyone who came in contact with him on his last day. His relief, Brigadier General Bamford, USA, had just shown up. It must have been a very trying time for him since it was obvious that his predecessor was going to be sorely missed. Bamford was just in time to be responsible for the relief of several regimental commanders. Although this was already predetermined before he showed up, he was the Judas Goat.[65]

One officer, Colonel H.P. Hobbs, commanding the 101st Infantry, had been acting in the capacity of division inspector. As such he had previously rattled Shelton's cage with charges that the morale of the 51st Brigade was at an absolute low. Shelton was furious, as he had every right to be. One factor which seemed to have had some important bearing upon the morale was the unofficial recognition that an armistice was in the offing. There had been some interchanges between the fighting men on both sides—it was called "fraternization with the enemy." Strict orders had been issued against this activity. To learn that the war might soon be over would weaken the will and break down the morale of any unit. Not many officers and men wanted to be scapegoats at this stage of the war.

On 8 November Shelton, who had been sick, returned to the division and assumed command of the 52d Brigade while Hiram continued in command of the 51st. Shelton's predecessor, Brigadier General Cole, had been relieved because elements of his 104th Infantry had fraternized with the enemy.[66] Other changes also affected the morale of officers and men. Colonel Grant of the Staff of the First Army charged the 51st Brigade with a low morale factor brought about by constant action and destruction. Shelton was furious and while trying to respond failed, because no one was listening. Hiram remained in command only until relieved on 23 November when Brig. Gen. Lucius L. Durfee arrived and assumed command of the brigade. In early December Shelton returned and Durfee left the division. That was the way it was just following the end of the war.

In mid- to late October, following the Marcheville attack, several cablegrams were sent to the War Department in Washington attesting to Hiram's superb handling of the 102d Infantry in battle. One was from General John J. Pershing and another was from Major General Clarence Edwards. Both recommended that Hiram be promoted to brigadier general, in the U.S. Army if necessary. Unfortunately, nothing worked. Hiram remained a colonel.[67]

9

Paris and Home

The war was over and there was no longer any need for Hiram to remain in France. He was due for hospitalization. His insides were on fire, or at least smoldering. His legs and feet were in tough shape. He had serious discomfort with his spinal column. Hiram was a wreck. A doctor named Colonel Blake had him in tow, but had somehow misplaced him along the line. Well, it was time to go back and pay the piper. Just after the armistice, Hiram requested release from the Yankee Division, which was immediately granted. Pershing's attempts to have him promoted were not heeded. It really wasn't because of Hiram; it was national policy. After the armistice no one in the AEF, army or Marines, was promoted to general officer. That just happened to be Hiram's luck.[1]

So Hiram returned to Gay Paree. He knew he was due in some hospital but by now he couldn't remember which, nor what they wanted to do to him. Something the matter with his spine? He guessed that if his backbone needed straightening now was the time to do it. His farewell to his men of the 102d was short and sweet. He did it in a formal communication and avoided personal contact, possibly because he had become terribly attached to these men whom he had led through some tough battles during the past few months. Perhaps he spent some time with Frank Cummings and maybe Lewis, who now commanded what was left of the great 102d Infantry. Unfortunately Oberlin, still a POW in Germany, was not available. Otherwise, Hiram made his escape through the back door. He didn't want to be anywhere near the front. The war was over.

When he did reach Paris his first stop was the Hotel Crillion to see his friends and get drunk. It wouldn't be until after the celebration that he'd allow the doctors to work their will upon his spine. When he did turn himself in, the first directive he received from the staff was "get thee to the U.S."

Rear Admiral Henry T. Mayo, number two in the naval listing, was

9. Paris and Home

an old friend of Hiram's—for many years since they had first clashed.² Admiral Mayo rode the USS *Pennsylvania* and offered Hiram a ride back to the States, which of course he accepted. Just riding a huge battleship would be pleasure enough for any man but to be the honored guest of an admiral was quite another level of gratification. You can be quite sure that Mayo and his guest were given the run of the ship by its captain.³ They left Europe on 14 December and the calm ride plus the beautiful sea breezes, even in midwinter, must have nearly made a new man of Bearss. Everyone aboard enjoyed Christmas Day and there was much great food plus frivolous entertainment for officers and men.

A chaplain, Father Rainey, whom we have met before, was master of ceremonies in the ward room on Christmas Eve. There he read everyone's horoscope, predicting what was going to happen them in the near future. Hiram, whose daughter he had helped baptize a Roman Catholic many years before, he predicted would become governor of Indiana.⁴ Father Gleason, the priest who had actually baptized little Louise, was also a chaplain aboard.⁵ It was his task to say early Mass on Christmas morning, but he didn't expect many officers and men to show up. What a surprise he had when, lo and behold, a long file of men recruited and headed by Bearss jammed the cabin in which services were to be held. Gleason was flabbergasted because he knew there were not that many Catholic men aboard. Tears didn't come easily to any chaplain—they had to be somewhat "hard"—but they did pour out of Gleason's eyes that morning. He found out later that Hiram had rounded the decks and gathered up anyone he found who wasn't busy, and perhaps some who were.

Hiram later bragged that he should take Gleason's role since he could make men attend religious services and the priest could die safely in bat-

Colonel Bearrs posed in a clean and neat uniform sometime following the Armistice. He is wearing his prized Distinguished Service Cross plus one Croix de Guerre with Palm. He was forty-three years of age.

tle with no sin on his soul. Gleason explained that force on the battlefield was OK but it had to be persuasion in religion. So, he concluded, each had better retain their respective positions. Hiram agreed and for the future ceased all his effort towards holy orders.

Home Again

On 27 December 1918 the USS *Pennsylvania* steamed into New York City with full colors flying, bands playing and the ship's Marine Detachment at attention. Hiram didn't expect the attention he was going to receive. It was his intent to slip in and out of the city with no fanfare but that was not to be. There on the pier he could see Louise and a not-so-little Louise. The newspapers were full of articles about this storied gent. *The Evening Telegram* gave him the first three columns of page four with the heading *Heroic Commander of Marines, Who Fought in the War's Fiercest Battles, Lauds Americans' Courage and Skill*. And those were columns 21 inches long by 2¼ inches wide. The lurid tales told included the following passage:

> Let Colonel Hiram I. Bearss of the U.S. Marines tell you about it. He has just returned on board the dreadnought Pennsylvania. Colonel Bearss has a right to speak on the subject with authority, for he was at Chateau Thierry. He was in that glorious conflict of the giants there at the Marne, where our men, our own splendid Americans, turned back the Prussian eagle, just as he was preparing to seize Paris *in his unclean talons.*[6]

Purple prose perhaps, but much of it was rather good and told plenty of what Hiram had accomplished in France. Quoted in the article, Hiram paid high compliments to his old commander Clarence Edwards and the men of his regiment and brigade. He also added some nice phrases about old "Black Jack," whom Hiram always seemed to have gotten along well with. Not every officer of army, navy or Marines could say that. He also added that he was in favor of "universal military training ... [which] should be two years instead of one." He was also complimentary about the French army, officers and men "who are experts in all that pertains to war." He didn't say that when he refused to accept their training methods for his Marines. They even printed the story of his smacking the German soldier at Vigneulles but changed the man from enlisted to captain. That version of the story persisted for many years. His portrait, with the inevitable cigar, appeared, two columns wide and seven inches in length. There were many other articles, all of the same genre. He must have been quite famous to have received those plaudits. They certainly didn't make so much of every colonel who returned from France.

One interesting newspaper article which appeared much later was headlined, "Col. Bearss to return home soon. Leader of 102d Recovers from his Wounds." The story goes on to describe his adventures and exploits such as:

> He had many narrow escapes from death while in France and at times it appeared that he couldn't die.... His closest escape was when he walked out of a front line dugout one night with a lighted cigar in his mouth. A German sniper detected the light and the cigar was shot out of his mouth. He was an inveterate cigar smoker and was never seen without one.

It further gives an explanation of his injuries:

> In October, while leading his regiment in the *Argonne* [sic], Colonel Bearss received severe internal injuries when a shell burst near him and hurled him to the ground, shaking him up badly and causing injury to his *spine* [emphasis added].[7]

That article appeared three months after he had arrived back in the U.S. Possibly it was included for the many friends and members of the "YD" in the Boston area. That story of his injury from a shell burst does not seem to have appeared anywhere else. The article also listed his birthplace as Vermont.

Hiram wanted desperately to go to Ridgeview. He and young Louise plus his brother-in-law, O.G. Muhlfeld, left by train the following day for his Nirvana. Poor Adelaide Louise was sick with the flu and was forced to remain in New York.

Hiram expected a reception at Ridgeview, but nothing like he received. Besides the Peru town band, most of the important and not so important residents were on hand to greet their returning hero. To most of them he was, after all, their greatest soldier of the age. That night he made a speech in an overflowing opera house. But his visit with his family, especially his aged father, was over all too soon. Orders came for him to report to his new command, the Marine Barracks at Philadelphia, at which he arrived sometime in January 1919. For a few weeks he was allowed some leave and several trips to physicians concerning his back problems. They were very serious and he was beginning to admit it, even to himself.

His reception in Philadelphia surprised even him. New York perhaps, Ridgeview of course, but Philly was an old Marine town. Many Marines had passed through, over so many years, but he was well known to many Philadelphians as well as to most of the more senior Marines at the barracks. He found himself the subject of great acclaim.

Trouble at Philadelphia

When Hiram arrived at Philadelphia to take command in January 1919, he found conditions at the base not to his liking.[8] He had several occasions to complain to his subordinate officers about the condition of the "police of their barracks." That included the sick bay and several of the mess halls as well. Complaints did little good. He tried several tricks of the trade but none seemed to do very much to change what he perceived as a "dirty duty station." This situation and his complaints went on for several weeks. Finally, he tried something altogether different, probably something that he'd done or had done to him in the past. Hiram was a noted disciplinarian, both in the Corps and in the U.S. Army. Several of his commanding officers, notably Major General Omar Bundy and Brigadier General Shelton referred to how he "cleaned up a real mess" for them. Both mentioned his being a stern disciplinarian and how that was necessary for the job he had at hand. His view of what he acquired at Philadelphia must have been along the same lines. If the responses in the hearing records are accurate, he had one hell of a mess to contend with.

First, when his orders were virtually ignored, he restricted ten Marine officers and one Navy officer to the base for three days, eleven officers in all. Many, probably as many as seven, of those lived off base in town and were somewhat inconvenienced. The restriction was imposed on 25 March 1919. Then he had his officers drilled on the parade ground, ostensibly to teach them the new regulations governing the sabre, rather than sword, at which they weren't at all practiced. Because the drilling was done on the public parade ground, a couple of the officers later complained that it was "humiliating to be drilled before the enlisted men." Hiram was also accused of berating his officers by "swearing at them before the men." Last was the accusation that he was "drunk on duty." Being drunk on duty and swearing in public were sufficiently serious for a hearing. The real question is, were they genuine or "developed" for the occasion?

Charges and Hearing

Obviously one or several of the 11 officers wrote and complained to the commandant. Colonel Albert S. McLemore, assistant adjutant inspector, was assigned to hold a hearing to determine whether the matter was as described and if it would be apropos to court-martial the colonel. Hiram tells us that McLemore, whom he knew, showed up one morning unannounced. Bearss said, "I didn't know you were coming down. I'll tell the sergeant to turn out the guard." McLemore's unpleasant response was, "You are under arrest, Bearss, don't leave this room." No charges were yet preferred and Hiram was puzzled. His flag was hauled down and he sent for his sword and sidearms to present to his confining officer. He wasn't allowed to communicate with anyone, but his sergeant major overheard the words and quickly figured out the situation. A quick phone call to Louise got action.

When the charges were presented to Hiram, the same sergeant major got a copy to Louise. She, with a presence of mind, called several of Hiram's navy friends of high rank and then caught a train to Washington. Regardless of his many clashes with members of that branch, they seemed to be his staunchest friends. When the going got tough, they were the people who came to his aid. They were waiting for her at the railroad station in Washington when she arrived and spirited her away to a local restaurant where they planned their campaign. Somehow a meeting had been arranged with Joseph Tumlty, secretary to President Wilson. It seems that the editor of *New York World*, Frank Cobb, who was a great admirer of Hiram, had made all the arrangements which would include, if need be, an interview with Wilson himself.

The group agreed that the commandant was behind this effort to "bag" Hiram. Although Barnett was out of town and most of the paper work was signed by Col. Charles G. "Squeege" Long, they all agreed that Long wouldn't have pulled this one out of his hat. By coincidence, Long arrived at that same restaurant for lunch. When he saw the gathering, as indicated by the expression on his face, he knew at once what was going on. According to one witness, Long knew that "hell was to pay." He got up from his table and walked out of the restaurant. Unfortunately, no record of Louise's trip has survived, but she and the navy appear to have been unsuccessful.

Meanwhile, back in Philadelphia, McLemore wasted no time. Upon arrival he commenced the hearings, in which he allowed Bearss to sit at each interrogation and cross-question the witness if he desired. The officers called before the hearing, in addition to the restricted 11, were Lt. Col. Frank Evans, CO, guard detachment, naval station; Lt. Col. John A. Hughes, CO, barracks detachment, Marine Barracks, Philadelphia; Major James J. Meade, CO Signal Bn.; Maj. Arthur B. Owens, post adjutant; Maj. Albert R. Sutherland, duties unknown; Captain Thomas B. Wood, attached to 147th Co., Signal Bn.; 2d Lt. Thomas J. Kilcourse, assistant post adjutant; 2d Lt. Stanley Klos, duties unknown; 2d Lt. Hoxsie W. Lillibridge, duties unknown; QM Clerk Wilfred L. Kent, in charge, construction and steam engineering.[9]

The restricted 11 were:
Major Charles A.E. King, Barracks commander, Barracks Three.
Major John F.S. Norris, duties unknown.[10]
Captain William O. Corbin, duties unknown.*
Captain William L. Crabbe, CO, 2d Signal Detachment.*
Captain William Merrill, CO, 147th Company.
Captain Francis E. Pierce, acting CO, Field Signal Battalion.
Captain Clate C. Snyder, CO, 87th Company.
Captain Arthur J. Trask, in charge, Mining Property.
Captain Donald Curtis, CO, 162d Company.
Second Lieutenant Charles Wald, CO, mess hall.
Second Lieutenant James E. Doran, officer of the navy yard guard.
Lieutenant Junior Grade J. James Cancelmo, USN, medical corps.
*both combat veterans of the 4th Brigade.

Hiram hired Mr. Cornelius Haggerty, a local attorney, to counsel him. He was on hand for the second day of hearings. After one day of receiving testimony, Colonel McLemore made official the following remark:

> In the opinion of the Investigating Officer, there is already testimony of record which is not controverted, except perhaps in a negative manner, to support allegations as follows:[11]

McLemore then lists the five points of contention. This appears to indicate that after just one day of hearing testimony, McLemore had already made up his mind about the outcome. However, Hiram's counsel had not yet had an opportunity to question anyone. Hughes had not yet been heard from. He was, admittedly, Hiram's strongest supporter. Both had served in the 6th Marines, and in other places at other times. Both were from the fighting element of the Corps so it is natural that they would think alike. Hughes testified that he had written up four of the 11 officers who were placed on restriction. One of them was described by John Hughes at the hearing thus:

> One officer, Captain Trask, volunteered orally that he had never been on report since he had been in the Marine Corps and had never been corrected, which statement I know to be false from my personal knowledge.

Hughes added:

> Frequently, I relieved him [Trask] from all military duty with the barracks detachment and I sent him to his quarters to shave, wash and clean the spots of grease on his clothes. I reported him to the Commanding Officer as being unfit to hold a commissioned rank in the Marine Corps; in fact I

said he was unfit to be a noncommissioned officer. Not once but many times have I reported him to the Commanding Officer.[12]

It seems obvious that Johnny "the Hard" Hughes didn't respect Trask, and he was equally pointed regarding some of the other officers at Philadelphia. Hughes was a very hard man, hence the nickname, but he was, I believe, a fair man. Apparently, from language of the hearing, Hughes' statements were contrary to what McLemore wanted to hear. Hughes had nothing to lose since in July of 1919 he would retire.

Hughes had an occasion to be directly cross-examined about conditions at the barracks when he arrived, "about a month after Colonel Bearss arrived here." He was asked, "Will you tell in your own words just the condition of the post at that time, and the change that took place in regard to the morale of the men, and the cleanliness of the Yard, since Colonel Bearss has had command?" He replied,

> Well, when I came here I found conditions in the organizations, which I took over, Barracks Detachments and Casuals, at that time about twelve or thirteen hundred men–I found it in a very, very bad condition. From what I discovered from working in the office, I found it had been much worse shortly before that. There was a routine here which had never been followed out. Men who had not attended Roll Call in months. The Barracks were pig stys.
>
> I interrogated my men, as I always do when I join a post, about the mess [food service], and they told me that the mess was perfect, or very good, rather. And that prior to the arrival of Colonel Bearss as Commanding Officer, they claim that they had been practically starved to death. I believe they are exactly the words that most of them used.
>
> I know a great deal about the improvement made here, because, until a few days ago I was Colonel Bearss's second in command, and acted as his assistant. The drills were a farce, and the Guard Duty was performed in a slovenly, inefficient, and in fact, disgraceful manner. The men were dirty, and a large number of the officers nearly as bad. In the two months that I have been here, I saw things improve daily, due principally to the exertions of Colonel Bearss, and somewhat to myself, acting under his orders. The personnel that Colonel Bearss had to deal with were *as poor as any I have ever seen in the 19 years [of my] service* [emphasis added]. A fair proportion of the officers were, and are, unfit to be corporals. The noncommissioned officers, a large majority of them, were absolutely inefficient, ignorant, and lacking any semblance of force. The Casual Detachments were in a most disgraceful state, the paper work stacked up; Roll Calls all wrong; men not paid, and this has been remedied to a great extent, entirely, or almost altogether, by the exertions of Colonel Bearss as Commanding Officer.[13]

McLemore then asked who Hughes had spoken with and was told, "My officers, noncommissioned officers and men." McLemore's own biases come out quite clearly with his sarcastic rejoinder:

> By interrogating these officers, who are unfit to be corporals, and these noncommissioned officers who are absolutely inefficient and ignorant?

Hughes replied,

> No sir. I gained it from the officers who are fit to be officers, and the noncommissioned officers who are good noncommissioned officers. There are some.[14]

Obviously, Hughes wasn't awed by the representative from the "home office." He had much more to add later in a separate hearing about the overall condition of the mess halls when he took them over. It caused much anguish in Washington and forced the commandant to request written confirmation or rejection of his charges from his predecessors. This is outside our study of Hiram and will remain there.

Hiram received a poor rating from McLemore. It was his contention that the five charges were easily proved in the results of his interrogations. He recommended that court-martial proceedings go forward, based upon the evidence he had collected.[15] The charge that Bearss swore at his subordinates was based upon his use in anguish of the rather common term "God Dammit" when he was trying to get the officers to properly perform their maneuvers on the parade ground. There were only two major complaints of his using that phrase. In addition, two senior men said that they had heard Hiram use words like that on occasion. But when asked whether "God damn you" was used against anyone, the answer was no.

The other specious charge was being drunk or "inebriated" on duty or in public. No one being interrogated could charge him with the latter. But Captain Trask claimed he was "lying on his desk, obviously under the weather." When Hiram's attorney asked him to be more specific Trask said that he had his head on his folded arms on his desk. In other words, Hiram wasn't lying on the desk; he was resting his head after a very long night "on the town." It was before duty hours and Hiram went out and got himself back together again within two hours, and he then had returned to his command. We mustn't forget the "humiliation" of the parade ground and the unbearable period of three-day restrictions imposed. These, it appears, were the main causes for the upset and rebellion rather than the specious charges used.

Fortunately for Hiram, he had people working overtime for him: his brother-in-law, O.G. Mulhfeld, president of Stone-Webster of New York City and more importantly his friend Franklin D. Roosevelt, assistant secretary of the navy. When Mulhfeld learned from Hiram that he was being court-martialed he reacted immediately. He learned that Roosevelt was traveling westward aboard a train. FDR was then acting as secretary because Josephus Daniels was traveling in Europe at this time. This is what saved Hiram. Daniels was a teetotaler whose level of approval for booze and boozers was a few degrees lower than nil. Had he been in charge, Muhlfeld could have done nothing to save Hiram from the charges of being drunk on duty.[16]

Muhlfeld found that FDR's train was going to stop briefly at a certain junction and he made himself available when it did. He boarded and entered FDR's compartment shortly after 0200 and found FDR sound asleep. They knew each other extremely well, socially moving in the same crowd. According to Smith the conversation went something like this:

> The Assistant Secretary of the Navy uttered "Why Hiram, why he is the greatest Marine in the world." Muhlfeld explained that no matter how good Hiram was, "they are after him. He is under court-martial, which conviction would lead to dishonorable expulsion." Both men agreed that there were jealousy and factual abuse [lying] in the Marine Corps and Hiram's court martial was a result of this.[17]

Smith adds that the men worked out a satisfactory agreement between them. According to the story, they got Hiram's father to "work on Hiram" to encourage him to accept the plan. The conclusion was that he would apply for a physical discharge. None of this seems to be completely accurate. That FDR knew Bearss personally is not doubted. He was a very well known character at that time. After all, by this time Roosevelt had been assistant secretary of the navy for quite a few years and his responsibility was the Marine Corps. In fact, he was quoted several times as saying, "We Marines." At any rate, he came through for Bearss when he was needed.

On 14 May Roosevelt addressed a lengthy letter to the major general commandant on the subject of the "Special Investigation into conduct of Colonel Hiram I. Bearss, USMC, Commanding Marine Barracks, Navy Yard, Philadelphia." In it he clearly comes down on the side of the victim. Using legal terminology, FDR disputes the so-called evidence and concludes:

> I must, therefore, hold that the evidence produced by the investigation is insufficient to warrant court-martial proceedings against Colonel Bearss. In view of this, I must further hold that a letter of reprimand shall not be placed on Colonel Bearss' record.[18]

On that same day he wrote Bearss telling him he was "free." He also told him in no uncertain words that he knew that Hiram was guilty of "using profane language." The intimation of the letter was that he shouldn't do it again during the balance of his services in the Marine Corps. If Hiram had already made a "deal" that he would retire, Roosevelt wouldn't have used the language that he did.

Shortly after this episode closed, Hiram was, at the instigation of Barnett, transferred from Philadelphia to Quantico. One reason may well have been that Hiram had written to Barnett requesting an increase in personnel at Philadelphia. He cogently describes in a report dated 31 March 1919 how the enlisted men were engaged in activities all over the place; how just 118 men were available for "the next guard"; and how, under the circumstances "it will soon be impossible to furnish the required guard details." Barnett added a postscript dated 7 April 1919 that said that he was of the opinion that the Marines at the station were not overworked and "possibly a change in Commanding Officers might help to solve the difficulties." At Quantico, Bearss would also be easier to observe from Washington, D.C. Not many official records concerning Hiram are available after the hearing until he applied for a disability discharge later that same year.

But meanwhile, next on Hiram's agenda was being promoted to brigadier general. As we have already seen, several letters from high personages had been sent to the secretary of war and passed on to Marine Headquarters recommending Hiram for promotion to that rank. The armistice had seen the cancellation of all promotions in the AEF but not in the balance of the army, or for that matter in the U.S. Marine Corps.[19]

The story goes that while still at Philadelphia (in actuality sometime in mid-March), Hiram received a telephone call from a friend assigned to Marine Headquarters advising him that vacancies for promotion to brigadier general were about to be filled.[20] He was told to "get busy, his record was short"—meaning that it lacked "meat" for reviewers to make a conclusion based upon his real merit. His faithful wife Louise reacted at once. She had been a Marine wife long enough to know how to move and do in the Corps for her husband. South on the train she went. In the process she made notes of all his postings, decorations, achievements, heroic undertakings, official and unofficial letters of commendation and recommendation, his medals and awards, of which there were a multitude from this latest war, and of course the recommendation for the Medal of Honor. But this wasn't the first time his record "was short."[21]

That he had served for several months, in January to late May 1918, with the 9th U.S. Infantry and again in August through November with the 102d Infantry and the 51st Brigade, both of the 26th Division, should have been well known. But perhaps, for reasons unknown, it was not so well known at Headquarters, USMC in 1919. So, Hiram sent an "Index of

Orders and Letters Submitted" to the commandant's office. This listing of 15 items included letters from officers of substance in the AEF, but all were U.S. Army, no Marines, including the one from Harbord when he commanded the 4th Brigade at Belleau Wood. But, after all, Bearss had been bypassed in the Brigade except for the period he served with the 6th Marines during June 1918. We can only imagine why his superior, Col. Harry Lee, wasn't called upon for comment—or was he? The 5th Marines were in great shape when Neville took command on 1 January 1918, due mainly to his predecessors, Charles Doyen and Hiram Bearss. But no letter from Neville thanking or supporting Hiram is found in the official records.

Shortly after her arrival, Louise visited with Mr. Tumlty, who gave her no help, and then with the secretary of the navy, Josephus Daniels. The latter received her with due courtesy, but when she explained the purpose of her visit he replied, "It is all arranged—there is nothing I can do now." He told her that all selections had been made; that the outcome was final and nothing could alter that fact. He also told her that the four applicants' paperwork was on his desk and that Hiram was one of the four. She asked if she might look at them and he answered yes, then pushed the papers toward her. She immediately spotted why Hiram wasn't the finalist nor even second. The other three were at least three full, single-spaced sheets outlining their qualifications, while that for Hiram was less than a full page. She pointed out to Daniels the errors and handed over her own compilation of his activities since 1898. They added up to many more pages of details than any of the other three candidates. Daniels looked them over and seemed genuinely surprised at the difference in what was there as opposed to what was contained in the records from the commandant's office. He told her that he was very sorry at what had transpired but regardless of the obvious mistake, nothing could now alter the finality of the selection. Daniels advised her that of course Hiram could make an issue of it but that "we are one hour too late."

In a letter to Barnett dated 20 March, Hiram had requested various documents, which is what Long's letter was all about. On 31 March 1919 Col. Charles G. Long sent a letter from the commandant to the adjutant general of the army, requesting that "[Clarence] Edwards be asked to forward copies of endorsements on all official reports." It seems that Headquarters, USMC, was belatedly trying to do something to aid Bearss. But a problem arose. General Edwards, now commanding the Northeastern Department, wrote a letter dated 10 May 1919 in which contradicted his earlier letter of support. The wording of this was as follows:

> After I was relieved of the command on the 24th of October, Colonel Bearss was put in temporary command of the 51st Infantry Brigade. *From information that comes to me in the exercise of that command, I feel it my duty to withdraw my recommendation.*[22]

Just a few months before, Edwards had recommended Hiram with these words:

> I unqualifiedly and earnestly recommend Colonel Bearss for that vacancy [the Doyen vacancy]. I do not believe any officer in the Marine Corps has seen more field service and he has particularly and peculiarly distinguished himself in battle while under my command. I urge this promotion."[23]

Regardless of what transactions occurred between interested players, it appears that Logan Feland may have had the inside track, so all of this maneuvering was just that. Effective as of 9 March 1919 Feland was promoted to brigadier general. He would have a distinguished career in the Corps until he retired after being bypassed for the office of the commandant ten or more years later.[24]

Retirement

We have already seen that Hiram's days at Philadelphia were numbered. He was detached on 14 May 1919 and on 19 May began his new duties at Quantico. This was shortly after his clearance from the charges preferred by Colonel McLemore. Apparently Hiram had finally come to realize that his days and career options in the Marine Corps were greatly limited by the hearing and the close call with a court-martial. He was discouraged and depressed by his fallen stature and his bad health. What he had believed would be a passport to higher rank and even a chance at the "brass ring," eventually being selected as the commandant, was now obviously a forlorn dream that would never be fulfilled. Some of his old pals were being shipped south to the islands of Haiti and Santo Domingo. His health forbade his participation in anything like active service, especially in the tropics, and he would never fit in at Headquarters as an administrative officer.

His poor health convinced Louise, his father, and some other members of his family that he should retire. He had more diseases than most men could tolerate. His poor physical condition wasn't just based upon his back problems. He had been carrying an internal parasite for many years. It was picked up in some backwater, probably the Philippines or maybe Panama, and flared up now and again as it had in Mexico and later

9. Paris and Home

in France. His medical records indicated that he had many of these kinds of illnesses floating in his system. They weren't going to go away no matter what treatment he received.

Although the letter applying for retirement doesn't seem to be in any available official file it most probably was submitted sometime in late summer. In Hiram's files there is a letter dated 17 July 1919 that notified Col. Theodore P. Kane, USMC, that he was appointed to and made president of the Marine Retirement Board. In August, Col. Louis J. Magill replaced Col. Charles S. "Jumbo" Hill on that same board. To indicate what a fouled up mess the whole thing was: the day before Kane was designated, Brig. Gen. Eli K. Cole was appointed president of the board. His orders were to convene the board at Philadelphia as soon as was possible.

In mid-month Hiram's official Department of the Navy medical record, which included the U.S. Army hospital reports, were made part of his record. There it showed, as early as 23 July 1918, complaints about his back. Two days later he was admitted to Base Hospital #20 because he had a "simple fracture, 2d vertebrae, Origin duty." He said that the fracture happened at Ft. Leavenworth in March 1916. He fell off a horse at which time it was "diagnosed as a sprain of the muscle."

Shortly after Hiram arrived at Philadelphia, on 23 January 1919, his annual physical report shows: "Physical defects none. Is physically fit to perform the active duties of his grade." So much for serious physicals at Philadelphia in 1919. Later, on 16 September 1919, the U.S. Naval Hospital at Philadelphia provided an entirely different conclusion:

> Diagnosis—Sprain (sacroiliac)
> Origin—in the line of duty. Disability is not the result of his own misconduct. Facts are as follows:—Patient was injured by a fall from a horse at Fort Leavenworth, Kansas, in 1916, injuring right sacroiliac joint. He had very little trouble until August 1917, in France, at that time he began to have pain over right sacroiliac joint and inability to walk any distance, any motion causing considerable pain. Condition has gradually grown worse. XRay shows sacrolized transverse process of fifth lumbar vertebra. There is also some sacroiliac relaxation.
> Present condition—Unfit for service.
> Probable future duration—Permanent.
> Recommendation—That he be ordered to appear before a U.S. Marine Retirement Board for disposition.
> Reference should be made to the Health Record.
> W.C. Braisted[25]

The following month Col. Harry Lee was appointed to the retirement board and on the same day Hiram's record was made part of the board's files. On 24 September the major general commandant's office sent to the judge advocate, U.S. Navy's office, requesting that "all papers on file ... in the case of Colonel Hiram I. Bearss, USMC, for retirement, be furnished this office." Within six days pertinent documents plus all recommendations for promotion and awards were forwarded to Colonel Kane, at Philadelphia. Included were three pages related to Bearss' service with the U.S. Army in France. The rather nasty investigation regarding affairs at the Marine Barracks in Philadelphia was excluded. On 2 October he received orders at the naval hospital in Philadelphia to report to Kane on 24 October and "when discharged by the board, you will return to the Naval Hospital, and resume treatment at that place." In the meantime an old friend, Maj. Gen. L.W.T. Waller, was ordered to take the position of president of the retirement board, "by virtue of rank," Harry Lee being relieved.

The board hearing was on 16 October, with Waller, Kane, Magill, two naval doctors and one Marine captain as recorder, sitting. In a report submitted by Lieut. Comdr. D.C. Walton, USN, Hiram's physical condition was recorded: eyesight 18/20, hearing 15/15, pulse rate 80, condition of arteries good, height 66½ inches and nearly everything else normal. The only thing wrong was his "sacroiliac" joint which produced an "inability to walk." Lieutenant Commander Duncan C. Walton, Medical Corps, U.S. Navy was questioned as to what Hiram's injuries were and how he was afflicted with them: "From what cause does Colonel Bearss' disability proceed?"

> A. From an injury to the back, first received in February 1916 while on a military ride. He partly recovered from his injury, but it was aggravated by a fall into a shell hole in France in June 1918. As a result of these injuries, he now suffers from a relaxation of the sacroiliac joint, an injury to the transverse process of the fifth lumbar vertebra and a periostitis of the lumbar vertebra.
> Q. Is the disability permanent?
> A. Yes.[26]

Walton also replied in the affirmative when asked if Colonel Bearss' disability was such as to incapacitate him for active service." Hiram had no questions. He stated that he did not desire to rebut the evidence presented. This indicates he was, at this point, more than willing to accept a medical discharge. Otherwise, the balance of the questions were mainly directed to the two naval officers. Those were the queries and everyone seemed satisfied with the answers. Insofar as that board was concerned, Hiram was truly incapacitated.

On 24 October the Bureau of Medicine and Surgery recommended to the judge advocate that the findings of the Marine Retirement Board be accepted and that Hiram be discharged. The major general commandant concurred on 29 October and Josephus Daniels, the secretary of the navy, agreed on 2 November. They could move rapidly when they wanted to clear the decks. On 22 November Hiram was discharged from the U.S. Marine Corps. After 22 years and at only 44 years of age, he seemed to be all washed up. Although this did not turn out to be true, he was very unhappy. Even little Louise was unhappy. She is reported to have said, "I'd rather my daddy would be a corporal in the United States Marine Corps than President of the United States." Most likely her daddy would have agreed.

It was now evident that Colonel Blake, the U.S. Army doctor in Paris, had been right after all. If Hiram had taken his advice and gone back to the

Major General Lee received a direct appointment as a second lieutenant of Marines in August 1898. He served in the Philippines, China, Nicaragua, Haiti, Santo Domingo, and France. There he became CO of the 6th Marines when Catlin was wounded. Following the war, he was CO of the 2d Brigade in Santo Domingo, then the CG of Paris Island. On 13 May 1935, he died while on duty at Quantico.

States, his medical problems might have been properly addressed and he might have continued serving for some time after 1919. The affair at Philadelphia might also never have happened had he not been in extreme pain and under "medication." Speculation about what might have been is rather poor history but the fact that he spent an additional 18 years living a very active life gives some cause for thought. Hiram, in his presumed collaboration with Mr. Smith, appears to have given that man the impression that he spent the balance of his Marine career still at Philadelphia, which we know to be incorrect.[27] According to official documents he was transferred to Quantico and only came back to Philly during his disability retirement hearings.

10

Retirement Years

What to do now, at age 44 and with serious medical problems? The horrors to which Bearss had been subjected since his return from Europe had worn him out. He was finally in a position to spend some time in relaxation but he didn't know how. Just sitting in an easy chair in his apartment was completely alien to him. Besides, the three of them, Adelaide Louise, little Louise and he, would have to move from Philadelphia. He couldn't bear being near his old command, which had been torn from him, but he was at a loss as to where to live and what to do. And with only a retired officer's salary it wasn't going to be easy. Hiram was somewhat bitter at the treatment he'd received and even went so far as to tell his wife, "Louise, I'll never put it on again [his uniform] unless a national emergency or war enables me once more again to serve, and I will never again wear any medals."[1] He kept that last pledge except for one final exceptional occasion.

A family consultation resulted in a decision to live in New York City. Muhlfeld, his brother-in-law, would be in a position to help them get reestablished, socially and politically. In the meantime, Hiram was still a very sick man. Not only was his back still a major problem, his feet, which had earned him his famous nickname, had finally given out. They were no longer able to provide him with his favorite exercise; he could barely walk. But, with the determination of which he still had a copious share, he finally managed to improve on all accounts. His doctors prescribed activity as the cure-all for his aches and pains. And it worked, proving once again that you can't keep a good man down.

Hiram began to have interest in political affairs, especially in Indiana. After all, his family on both sides had always been intensely engaged in state and national politics. Why should our hero be any different? He had formed a friendship with Indiana senator James E. Watson, and it was he who sent for Hiram when his discharge came through. The coming year, 1920, was an election year and Hiram was just in time to get heavily involved. Upon arrival in Indianapolis Hiram went to Republican State Headquarters for an assignment. He was given carte blanche to "rig up something." In addition he was placed in charge of a subheadquarters to do whatever came to mind. His mind still being very fertile, he soon came up with a plan of action that would please many voters across the state.

Hiram somehow secured the services of a motor vehicle that had been constructed and painted to resemble a steam locomotive, and with a coal car attached. It belched forth smoke, had a bell that rang and even had a cowcatcher that appeared genuine. He named it the "Bearss Special" in honor of himself. And boy, did he have fun with that contraption.

All over the state they traveled, he and his gang, to small hamlets, large towns, even crossroads or vacant fields, where advance planning had arranged for a turnout of the local gentry. He took with him a band to entertain the crowd but the thing they came to hear was Hiram himself, the state's greatest war hero. Hiram was an accomplished speaker. He'd had years of experience speaking to soldiers and Marines, and sometimes reluctant natives. From the rear platform Hiram pontificated. The great question of the period was, "Should the U.S. join the League of Nations?" Hiram thundered that "the boys had not fought for the purpose of joining a league of any nations." Most Republicans, and many Democrats, were against it. So was Hiram and, it seems, the majority of Indianans. Therefore, his talks were always well received. One very valuable result of this traveling was that he finally was able to see most of his beloved state, although it greatly taxed his strength.

After the election, which his crowd won, it was back to Brooklyn Naval Hospital where he spent considerable time resting up. His doctors strongly recommended that he get away someplace out of the public eye. Someone suggested Texas, big and open, where he could get lost. Its climate was also considered to be a positive factor. Hiram, never one to set on his laurels nor anything else for very long, gathered together some money from various sources and in the latter part of 1920 engaged in drilling for oil. It was a complete failure and he returned to New York broke, or close to it.

Politics and Fighting the Klan

By 1922 Hiram had had enough of New York and its bright lights and determined to return back home again to Indiana. His intent was to buy a farm and work the soil, but instead he and Adelaide Louise had a 500-

acre farm turned over to them by his old dad, Frank. How productive his soil work became isn't clear; he instead decided to raise ponies, certainly falling back upon a boyhood pleasure. While back home he again entered the political scene but this time he worked for the Republican presidential candidate of his choice, Major General Leonard Wood. Wood was, like all the other Republican wannabees, trounced by the Harding faction — but not before Hiram refused to make the Indiana delegation's support for Harding unanimous. His was the lone vote for Wood, and he refused to back down under pressure.

It was during this period that Hiram again made a big splash in international news. He became a celebrity for taking action against an organization that he loathed but that, unfortunately, was popular in Indiana during those times. Although it had never completely died out in the south, the Ku Klux Klan saw a revival in a few northern states following the war. Indiana was one of those.[2] The Klan's battle-cry was still against blacks, Jews and Roman Catholics, but by the 1920s it was loudest against the latter group, mainly because they had a sizable and growing population that was getting involved in many facets of life including national politics. Anyone could join, if they had ten bucks to turn over to the organizers. For that amount one obtained a new sheet, white, of course, and all the benefits that accrued with membership. It was not entirely Republican nor Democrat. Both parties had their swine, and many were members.

On 16 December 1922 they held a great parade in Peru. Down the main drag they came with their white sheets flowing and carrying Old Glory at the forefront, further degrading our flag by handling it. Hiram happened to be at Ridgeview and drove down to town to look at the parading rabble. He reacted as he always reacted when he found something distasteful — this time by backing his open touring car directly into their parade.

> Headline: BACKED CAR INTO KLANSMEN
> subtitled: Col. Bearss, "Hiking Hiram," defied Indiana paraders with wrench.
>
> Peru, Ind., Dec 18 — This city still was in a furor today following the excitement occasioned when Colonel Hiram I. Bearss, known as "Hiking Hiram, the Fighting Marine," backed his automobile into a parade of the Ku Klux Klan here Saturday night.
>
> His car was immediately surrounded by the Klansmen, the door opened and, according to some reports, the World War I veteran was assaulted as he sat at the wheel.
>
> Obtaining a wrench, the Marine commander, who gained fame at St. Mihiel, got to the running board of his automobile, and, according to reports, shouted: "Come on you Kluxers, one and all; I'll take on the lot of you."[3]

The article continued by describing his services in various wars, but they didn't accurately describe what he said and did on this occasion. After the scum surrounded him, some demanded that he be forced to salute and kiss their flag. Hiram grabbed a wrench, climbed on the hood of his car and yelled, "I salute the flag when it is properly carried by proper people. I have followed that flag in places where you bastards would be afraid to look at on the map. Come on you sonsofbitches, all at once or one at a time. It matters little to me." Cooler heads prevailed, the parade was broken up and the crowd was dispersed. So it seems like Hiram had the last word after all, at least temporarily.[4]

In 1924, at the urging of some friends, Hiram decided to try running for Congress. He had been asked instead to run for governor, which he refused to do. Shortly after the Klan elected the governor, he was indicted for bribery and spent years in the slammer. Hiram's was an anti-Klan platform and in Indiana during this period, that in itself was one of the bravest stances a man could take. Round the district he went, denouncing the Klan at every stop. He was so appealing and so courageous, while receiving many threats against his person, that many of his foes rallied to his support. Even with the "machine" against him, his enemies, using severe fraud and manipulation of votes, managed to beat him by only 200 votes of the 50,000 cast. His friends demanded a recount but Hiram said no. He could see the handwriting on the wall and decided that it wasn't worth the effort. He recognized that he wasn't going to win against the Klan-backed machine. So, he and Louise went back to New York where he had another temporary respite in the naval hospital for observation.

Commander, Federal Reserve Guard

While so confined Hiram was selected by the Federal Reserve Bank in New York to organize and install a military-style security system. This was before the construction of the gold depository at Fort Knox, Kentucky. At this time the New York federal bank vault was the repository of the largest stock of gold in the world. Until 1924 a special guard for that system hadn't even been considered. But gangsters were rampant in the nation and they all seemed to have machine guns. This was right down Bearss' alley. We have seen how he loved doing something that no one else had previously had the opportunity to mess up. So, he set about the task and accomplished the job in short order.

A public announcement concerning the formation of a guard was proclaimed far and wide. Hiram's name was prominently mentioned as the founding director. The response was overwhelming. Many thousands of men replied, far beyond the numbers that could be hired. The announcement called for men who had served at least eight years in the military and had attained at least the rank of sergeant. They who were to be considered had to have a proven record of excellence and no adverse marks against them. Hiram himself established the rules of selection and it is said that he made up his mind that only former Marines would be seriously considered. The latter cannot be proven, and if true must have been difficult to enforce when other, equally capable men came forward.[5]

He set the maximum guard as 200 men and established barracks for them within the bank. Each man had a physical exam, much more stringent than he had received in the regular military service. All those accepted were issued a uniform designed for appearance and practical usage. Hiram held regular inspections of the men, in formation. They were issued regular .45 caliber automatics and a few Thompson submachine guns. In addition, the entrance to the gold depository was covered by a constantly manned Browning .30 caliber machine gun. Those guns were kept in the best possible condition, being cleaned and oiled on a daily basis.

During this period, which lasted approximately ten years, someone at U.S. Marine Headquarters complained that their best noncommissioned officers were frequently not reenlisting. They were instead opting for much higher paying jobs, fewer restrictions and no courts-martial with Hiram Bearss. But those that didn't already know him found that his discipline could be more severe than that of the Corps itself. Mr. Smith tells us that once he had an occasion, when visiting New York, to call upon Colonel Bearss, by appointment of course. He describes his visit:

> The author called upon the colonel [and] he was conducted step by step as though he was a foreign emissary in an enemy land. In turning one corner he walked face-to-face into the mouth of a mounted, and, he well knew, loaded machine gun, set for firing with the clips adjusted, manned by what appeared to be a Leatherneck in position for action, with aides and reserves ready at his side. Before he reached the colonel's inner sanctorum he was everything but blindfolded. Needless to say, Colonel Bearss received him with military decorum. There was no fun making. Duty was written indelibly in the atmosphere. The Federal Reserve Bank was never robbed.[6]

During this decade it was not all fun and games for Hiram. He spent some time each year in a hospital tending to his old wounds. While he was thus amongst the missing, his second in command, a former sergeant major of Marines, was in charge. The sergeant followed Hiram's philosophy of command and nothing ever went wrong when he was in control.

10. Retirement Years

During one hospital visit, Hiram's life was practically all but surrendered by those in attendance upon him. Both naval and civilian physicians predicted that his death was "imminent." His family was sent for and given the sad tidings. It is said that two navy chaplains, one a Protestant, the other a Catholic, and both old acquaintances, prepared to give him the necessaries for the life hereafter. Hiram was sitting up in bed looking like what the cat had refused to drag in. Everyone, family and all, waited breathlessly when the two chaplains came in. Hiram hadn't asked for them and they approached his bed gingerly. "Get the hell outta here," he is reported to have yelled, proving that his lung power was still in operation. Each of the chaplains criticized the other, saying, "I told you we shouldn't have gone into his room unless he'd called us," as they withdrew.

Hiram later described what then happened to him: "They took my insides out and fanned them like a deck of cards." His appendix was removed during this emergency operation. Within two weeks his wounds had healed so thoroughly and he had so completely recovered that he was back on his feet and raring to go, although with a decided limp. His feet were still in bad shape. The long hikes over many years had broken down his arches, making him almost unable to hobble let alone walk. But with the help of a so-called quack Hiram regained the use of his feet and was again able to walk without aid. A Canadian doctor named Locke, a graduate of a Scottish university, was then making a substantial living curing people's foot problems. Hiram tried him and although Locke had been condemned by the medical community, somehow Hiram's feet were saved. For many years he continued to spend every summer in Canada for Locke's treatment. He and the doctor, who only charged one dollar a visit, were soon on friendly intimate terms which continued at least until Hiram was satisfied that he was cured.

Though he spent his winters in both Indiana and in New York City Hiram was well known nearly everywhere and continued to have a multitude of friends. Hiram was a friendly guy who made lasting friendships with a disparate group of people and seemed to know many people no matter where he went. But his life was not always rosy. One very dark evening, while living at Ridgeview, he ventured forth down to Peru. Down the hill and under the railroad underpass he went. As he left the shadows, a young man approached him with a revolver in hand. "Hands up!" he shouted. Without missing a step, Hiram grabbed the gun and twisted it from the lad's hands and pocketed it. Hiram seized his arm in a vise-like grip, then forced the young fellow to accompany him through the town toward the bridge over the Wabash. Upon arrival Hiram tossed the gun into the fast flowing river below, then turned and marched the fellow back to the Bearss Hotel.[7] In they went and over to a corner where they both sat down to have a quiet discussion. Hiram told the boy not to carry weapons; he might get hurt, and there was always the slight danger that he might hurt someone else. The two spoke for some time while Hiram learned what problems the young fellow had. Determining that there was some good in the fellow, he gave him a small amount of money and put him aboard an electric interurban trolley bound for the lad's hometown.[8] This was typical Hiram — tough as hell with those that required it and soft on those who didn't. When he called those shots, they were usually right on.

In the early 1930s Marine Headquarters sent out a circular letter to all retired Marine officers inquiring whether, in case of war, they would or could return to active or limited service. Hiram responded immediately. Across his reply, which was sent Special Delivery, was written, "Active Duty — Front line, H.I. Bearss." Fortunately nothing ever came of it and his latter years were rather sedentary by comparison to his earlier years. As the years rolled by, he was drawn more and more to Ridgeview. His mother had died but his father, now nearly in his nineties and hale and hearty, lived vigorously. Hiram was still his little boy and still badly in need of parental guidance. At this time it appears that Hiram and Adelaide Louise were partially living separate lives — she in New York City and he in Ridgeview.

In 1934 he received a communication directing him to meet President Franklin Delano Roosevelt at the White House. There he and David D. Porter, with flash bulbs going off, were both finally presented with their Medals of Honor, earned on 17 November 1901 at the Sohotón cliffs, Samar, Philippine Islands. This was just after Roosevelt had returned from a "fishing trip" to the Hawaiian Islands aboard a U.S. Navy ship of war. Roosevelt had been photographed fishing from the fantail of the battleship. It happened during the worst of times for the economy. FDR was a generally popular president but the press was just beginning to lambast him for his personal excesses. Hiram the Republican had recently been involved in an auto accident and was on crutches. When Roosevelt asked why, he replied, "I got this tripping over that silver thread with which you caught that two hundred and fifty thousand dollar whale on your Pacific cruise." The president threw up his hands with a laugh and said, "I should have known better, I should have known better." Two years later, in 1936, Hiram was finally promoted to brigadier general, retired, a rank he had deserved 18 years before.

Illness again afflicted him and, according to the medicos, he was once again at death's door. He was directed to the local hospital but, of course, he refused. He would go nowhere but the great naval hospital at Bethesda,

Maryland, where an old shipmate was in command. So Hiram was carried to a train and with his brother Braxton in attendance started on his voyage. At the hospital he was directed to remain completely still. He was to have no visitors, including his relatives. In case of "extremis" they would be notified. They placed a "Do Not Disturb" sign on his door, and in strict navy compliance, no one did.

Two weeks later his brother-in-law, Oscar G. Muhlfeld, was given permission to enter Hiram's room but when he did, the room was vacant. Muhlfeld was told, "He just checked himself out this morning." Hiram had gotten out of bed, dressed and started on a voyage to Canada. So much for this death rattle. He didn't return to Indiana for several months and it appears that no one knew where he was during that period.[9] There is no doubt that when he retired in 1919 he was physically in bad shape. But Hiram was a man of indomitable will. Nothing, but nothing, could deter this man when he decided what he was going to do.

Hiram was always proud of his association with the U.S. Marine Corps and made that fact obvious whenever he could. He still spent some time in New York City and on one day he saw a parade of Marines striding down Fifth Avenue, with flags flying and brass blaring. Hiram did what any old warhorse would do in like circumstances; he joined in and marched in step alongside the others. Some of them recognized Hiram and soon the word was passed sotto voce to all the others. When they finally halted, he, with tears in his eyes, greeted the "boys" with handshakes and gentler words than he had ever used to Marines in the past.

At another time he became acquainted with a very young Marine reserve officer. The young fellow told Hiram that he had a problem to solve and asked Hiram to look over his solution. His, by the way, met the solutions already established by the Marine Corps Schools. Hiram took one look and advised the young man to do something entirely different. He instead recommended what he would do in like circumstances. The youngster said he wasn't sure if that would be accepted, but Hiram told him to try it anyway. He did and it was accepted. In fact it became standard operating procedure and the young fellow was commended.

In 1935 Hiram tried an entirely different course in order to get to a war. The Italians had invaded Ethiopia and Hiram asked several agencies if they would be interested in him as a war correspondent. The response was extremely positive, but his doctors refused to approve that activity for a sick man. He would have disregarded the physicians except that his aged father vigorously argued against his going. In the early 1930s, Hiram even went so far to ask why a battalion of Marines wasn't sent to Germany "to clean up that bum Hitler." As we know, nothing came of that.

Politics and Death

In 1938 Hiram was named without opposition as his party's nominee for the state senate. It looked like an easy victory; after all, he was a Hoosier, and a well-known one at that. He was a Republican and that seat was almost guaranteed to be held by a politician of that party during that period. The Klan had taken a nosedive and wasn't in a position to affect any elections in his part of the state. So, Hiram set about running for office in an almost no-lose situation. Up and down the state he wheeled. Speeches against this and for that, mostly anti-Democratic and of course, anti-Roosevelt. In 1938 the Democratic party was not doing all that well in the opinion of the voters and it looked as though FDR and his party wouldn't pull through another time. Hiram put his heart and soul into the race and it did look, for a while, as though he would become a full-fledged politician.

But something serious interfered. Hiram had attended an American Legion convention in Indianapolis, and then traveled to Chicago to pick up Miss Lillian Mae West, of Welland, Ontario, Canada, a 30-year-old graduate student at the University of Chicago. They were driving through to Williamsburg, Virginia. According to accounts, Miss West was driving the Ford V8 coupe along rain-soaked highways near Columbia City, Indiana, on 27 August 1938, when the car swerved on the slippery road and crashed. Hiram died, never regaining consciousness, while Miss West suffered a broken collar bone. The *Indianapolis Star* of 27 August 1938 described the accident as involving three vehicles. According to it, she sideswiped one car driven by Claud P. Shulfeldt of Springfield, Ohio, and then careened into a truck and trailer driven by Joseph A. Ambrose of Zanesville, Ohio.

Headlines in the *Peru Daily Tribune* for 27 August 1938 nearly bellowed, "Brig. Gen. Hiram I. Bearss Killed in Crash." According to their story it occurred at 12:30 a.m. and he was "thrown 15 feet, where he was found unconscious." The article further described his wounds as being primarily "a deep gash in the back of head and another bad gash on his right shoulder blade. He was pronounced dead at a hospital 20 minutes later where an ambulance had taken him." It continued, "Officers reported that he was still alive, but his pulse was very low, when he was placed in the ambulance at the scene of the crash." The article further mentioned that Miss West was "resting comfortably."

His family members were listed: wife Louise in New York City; his father Frank still alive at 92; brother Braxton H. Bearss and sister, Miss Lucy Bearss, "at home" in Peru. It also listed his daughter, Mrs. Frederick

Thwing of Kansas City, Missouri, and another sister, Mrs. O.G. Muhlfeld of Englewood, New Jersey.[10]

Hiram's body was buried at Ridgeview in the family graveyard. Messages of condolence came from all corners of the nation. One was from old comrade Thomas Holcomb, then commandant of the Marine Corps. Among other accolades, veterans remembered in newsprint with delight in one incident he had been "standing atop a trench in a hail of bullets yelling to a private who reared up 'Get down, you damn fool. Do you want to get killed?'" Two of his former sergeants, both wearing their uniforms, had come from a great distance and stood at attention by his flag- and flower-draped bier during the brief ceremonies. A former Marine private spoke of him by paraphrasing the famous Hymn:

> "From the Halls of Montezuma
> To the Shores of Tripoli
> *He* fought *his* country's battles
> On the land as on the sea
> First to fight for Right and Freedom
> And to keep her honor clean
> *He* was proud to claim the title
> of United States Marine."

Adelaide Louise was there from New York, as was their daughter Louise from Kansas City. According to tradition, when his wife learned of his death she, with a sudden start and evidently feeling his presence, half muttered to herself, "Hiram — Hiram — Hiram marches on!"

On 25 July 1943 the U.S. Navy Destroyer *Bearss* (DD–654) was launched by the Gulf Shipbuilding Corp. of Chickasaw, Alabama. It was sponsored by Mrs. Louise Bearss, widow of Brig. Gen. Hiram I. Bearss, and was commissioned on 12 April 1944 with Commander John A. Webster, USN. Its role during the war was, because of its launch date, limited to service in Hawaiian waters and later with Task Forces 92 and later 94, in anti-shipping sweeps in the Kurile Islands, as well as patrolling the Sea of Okhotsk until the end of the war. She returned to the U.S., arriving at Charleston, South Carolina, on 22 December 1945, and was placed in reserve commission on 12 July 1946. The *Bearss* was recommissioned 7 September 1951 and joined Destroyer Division 322, Squadron 32, Atlantic Fleet, cruising the Caribbean. She made a round-the-world cruise from April through October 1954. Her one battle star was for WWII action.

11

Conclusions

Hiram Iddings Bearss was a very complex individual whose audacity helped make him a superb fighting man. Badly lacking in discipline from his infancy until his appointment as a Marine lieutenant, he showed marked improvement in later years. But, even then, he did some rather stupid things that a grown, disciplined man would never have considered. His insulting behavior to at least one senior officer of Marines was outrageous. Sometimes his demeanor toward naval officers went beyond the realm of decency or decorum. The same could be said about his treatment of "stay-at-homes." He was rude, crude and ofttimes socially unacceptable. Hiram must have been the bane of Headquarters, USMC. Yet his compatriots, those field Marines he was closely acquainted with, all seem to have held Hiram in the highest esteem.

His scholarly attainment was narrow. Consequently, his potential for advancement beyond the rank of colonel was strictly limited. The Academy graduates had been academically trained and, for the most part, were well known to those who were in positions of authority. He wasn't from the "old school." This was a very serious problem that wasn't satisfactorily resolved until the appointment of Thomas Holcomb in 1936 as the seventeenth commandant. After that, things changed for the better. Quality, usually, became the requirement for promotion, rather than being an Academy graduate.

Hiram was a friend to almost all and never lacked for them during his service time, although the ranks of friends thinned out in 1919. Hiram was usually friendly and congenial, but beneath the surface he had a seething rage that would poke its ugly head up on occasion. When it did he sometimes made severe mistakes. His own childhood experiences, when he was almost entirely undisciplined, did not prepare him well for being in charge and as a result he was often a martinet. Hiram was a good man to take a bunch of nearly useless individuals and make them into a superb fighting machine. He proved it, especially in France, with the often faulty commands he was assigned to. What he performed with 3/9 before Verdun showed his outstanding ability as a leader of fighting men.

When he was in liquor he could do some very stupid things, and in later years he was often drunk or at least tipsy. It was then a common habit amongst many military people, especially in the postwar period after the imposition of Prohibition. The AEF came back from Europe with a taste for the "creature" and even though the WCTU proclaimed against it, it wouldn't just go away. Those that liked their booze didn't lose that taste when they disembarked at New York piers. Hence the success of the scum of the Roaring Twenties.

Some might say that Hiram was his own worst enemy. But that I believe is an exaggeration — there was many others only too happy to fill that bill. He had, as we have seen, a proclivity toward offending U.S. Navy officers— even when he was only a captain or major of Marines. However, many of his best friends were sailors, especially when he needed friends.

Enlisted Marines have always liked the charismatic characters who have led them in tough spots. The tougher they were, the more they were admired. Examples are plentiful. Butler, Dan Daly, John Quick, Lewis Puller, and Bearss are a few. Hiram was a stern disciplinarian; there was no fooling around when you served with him. On duty, he was all business. Off duty, he could, on occasion, be a proverbial "bum." As some friends have said, he was fun to have around. And he was even better to have around in a fight. But he got written up several times for drunkenness and frequently swearing at the wrong time before the wrong people. His pranks and stunts— like the waking of the commandant in Panama and directing all other officers to that poor man's tent that night — deserve contempt, even though it is amusing to read about them. Crossing a railway bridge on horseback, so that the poor horse had to pick its way across the ties, suggests a demented child rather than a Marine officer on duty. Fortunately for Hiram, Commandant Heywood had "been there and done that" himself and he wasn't chastened.

It appears that during the spring of 1919, persons unknown at Headquarters, USMC, wanted Hiram out of the way. There is no way that I can prove that but perhaps I have made a decent case for my assumption. I believe that Hiram was earmarked for destruction for just being Hiram. We have seen how for many years he shook up nearly every command he held, both Marine and army. Usually it was all for the good. But the incident at Philadelphia was what capped all the former trouble he had generated. This was the opportunity certain individuals needed to eliminate a burr under the saddle.

If this seems as though I am questioning members of the Adjutant and Inspectors Department you are right. My concerns are that perhaps direction from above ensured that all the i's were dotted and all the t's crossed. Perhaps Lauchheimer never forgave nor forgot Hiram's unforgivable insult. Perhaps Hiram had, in some way, insulted the commandant, George Barnett. He had, after all, vocally supported Waller's candidacy above Barnett's, but so had many other Marines including Butler. But then you see what happened to Smedley—he had to force his way over to France. Hiram went through similar travails in order to get to the fighting front. In one instance his wife went over the commandant's head to invoke a senator's known admiration of Hiram. That in itself was a no-no.

Obviously, there were many reasons for Hiram's difficulties, countless of which he brought upon himself. One, perhaps even the most important, was his illness and physical incapacity. He wanted promotion to general, which he saw as his right, and there was only one slot. It was not intended for Hiram. His attempts to bypass the usual path certainly didn't help his cause.

After reading McLemore's report in detail, I found that he had heard evidence that I couldn't find in the transcript of the hearing. McLemore served 28 years in the Corps.[1] In addition to the above, a separate report of an investigation by Col. Charles Lauchheimer strongly indicates that Hiram's management of funds while with the 2d Brigade at Gitmo was appalling. No malfeasance was mentioned, just bad handling of the post exchange and company funds. The words Lauchheimer used were:

> The irregularities in the post exchange and company funds ... show the lax methods adopted in the management of those funds while in charge of Captain Bearss, and the difficulty experienced in making a satisfactory audit of those accounts at this time.[2]

Hiram was asked to make a written reply. His response clearly stated what he had experienced during his tenure and it appears, unless he was lying, that there may have been some hanky-panky with the records—they having been moved by brigade headquarters—and that an audit done when he was leaving had left no doubt that his management was able, while he was there. Was this audit report by Lauchheimer accurate or were forces at work from some previous time? There is no question, according to several of his comrades, that Hiram was notoriously inept when it came to his own finances. Yet we know that he was judicious in handling funds belonging to the Corps. In one recorded instance he actually greatly improved the financial position of the enlisted men's funds at Guantánamo.

11. Conclusions

Hiram was ripe for promotion to brigadier general when he returned from France. He had served in violent combat in France during the war, commanding battalions, regiments and a brigade, both Marine and U.S. Army. His reputation was such that Pershing recommended him twice: once to be promoted to colonel and later to brigadier general. For Pershing to so honor a Marine officer means that Hiram was very good, or that he had many army friends rooting for him. The latter is far fetched and doesn't seem practical. So it must be the former. Yet Shelton, Bundy, Edwards and Harbord liked him — and all so stated in writing. There were several, including his division commander, Edwards of the 26th, who recommended that he be made a brigadier general in the National Army.[3] I believe that Hiram's reputation with the army is what did him in. There was only one Marine brigadier general vacancy to fill — that which had been the possession of the lately deceased Brig. Gen. Charles A. Doyen — and at least two deserving recipients. One man, Logan Feland, had commanded the 5th Marines in action and later the 4th Brigade. Feland was an excellent officer and worthy of any accolades and promotions he earned. Bearss had only briefly commanded the 5th Marines when he was moved aside for Wendell Neville. For some reason, Hiram wasn't made assistant to Neville. Perhaps Neville didn't want him looking over his shoulder and telling him how he did it. Feland was desirous of that position, even though he was still on the AEF staff at Chaumont. He was several numbers in grade lower than Hiram and although both had distinguished "colonial" records, Hiram had held more commands than Feland during that prewar period. For some reason, Hiram was shifted over to the 3d Battalion, 9th Infantry, which was admittedly in bad shape and which he turned around in very short order, and made into a topnotch fighting unit. When the time came, 3/9 earned accolades from nearly everyone, except the Germans.

Hiram was a severe disciplinarian who came to the Marine Barracks in Philadelphia and found, to his dismay, a complete disaster. He was tired and ill and possibly looking for an easy berth at this time in his life. Had things been reasonably acceptable, he might have been, not lax, but willing to take a slightly easier tack with the officers and men stationed there. According to reliable reports, the barracks, officers and men were dirty or unkempt. It is a matter of record that for some time before Hiram arrived there had been very little discipline imposed — and they weren't very happy when he came along and tried to change things. Few of the officers had served in France — Corbin and Crabbe are two exceptions and neither did all that well in their singular combat at Soissons. Yet neither had the temerity to accuse Hiram of any of the charges preferred against him. Only two stay-at-homes did, and even one of them was restrained to a degree.

What Hughes thought of the overall condition of the base and of some of the officers who were restricted is fairly straightforward, according to his testimony. He also raised hell about the condition of the mess halls and especially the food being served. Hiram was only indirectly connected with this phase but the overall situation was part of his other problems in trying to put this Marine station to rights. Hughes' complaints were forwarded to the commandant and an investigation was begun.[4]

One interesting thing did happen which bears note. Rear Admiral Charles F. Hughes, USN, was Hiram's superior and hence wrote his "Fitness Report for the period ending on 31 March 1919." In it he gave Hiram marks that were all over the map. Most of them were "good" or less, while Bearss had numerous Fitness Reports that he never went below "excellent" in any category, meaning 3.5 or above. Yet Admiral Hughes rated him as follows:

> Aptitude for Service:
> (a) In General Excellent 3.6
> (b) Liking for and interest in his profession Excellent 3.4

For general temperament he was candid:

> Excel able [?], imitable, forceful, bold.

Hughes ended with the following remarks:

> I have always had great respect for the professional ability of Colonel Bearss. I did not have much time to devote to his command but he did not readily subordinate himself to conditions at this Navy Yard. I realize that the change from an active command in the field to routine duties in a Navy Yard was radical and would be pleased to believe that poor health was the reason why he did not more readily adapt himself to the change.[5]

In other words, Hughes felt the base was OK, but Bearss was at fault. The report was dated received at Headquarters, USMC, on 17 June 1919, two and one-half months after the reporting period. Was this caused by the uproar in the April hearings? The reason I question Admiral Hughes is because some of his ratings are contradictory. He mentions "poor health" but in the previous category that asks about Bearss' health he states, "Excellent as far as my personal knowledge." In "Proficiency in Rank" he rates Hiram "3.6 Excellent" yet just below that he says, "Initiative 3.6, intelligence 2.5, judgment 2.5, and thoroughness 3.0." Under bearing and conduct he gives Hiram "good 2.5" but the next line, "Military appearance and manner," is "Excellent 3.5." He says "Manner of giving commands, Excellent 3.6," and "Neatness of person and dress Excellent 3.5," but his next entry, "Correctness and condition of uniform and manner of wearing it," was labeled "good 2.8."

Hiram seems to have made Admiral Hughes look bad in trying to clean up the mess at the Marine Barracks, and Hughes appears to have responded in kind with a faulty fitness report. Professionalism had no part in the preparation of that report.

Hiram Bearss was one of a very few men whom the U.S. Marine Corps would have had to invent if he hadn't existed. They would badly need every character of his kind to insure continuance of the Corps. Men admire real fighting men — especially the devil-may-care types, who do all those things the rest of us only dream of doing.

Was Hiram a drunk? Not really, but he certainly used his share of liquor. Was he a womanizer? I believe he was but can find little in the way of proving that, nor do I believe it necessary to do so. He was a man with most of the deficiencies of the breed, but with some advantages of character that most of the rest of us lack. He was one hell of a Marine!

Appendix A
Officers Assigned to the Samar Battalion

Major Littleton W.T. Waller, commanding
Captain Hiram I. Bearss, D company commander
Captain Robert H. Dunlap, C company commander
Captain Arthur J. Matthews, H company commander
Captain David D. Porter, E company commander
First Lieutenant James T. Bootes, D platoon leader
First Lieutenant John H.A. Day, Adjutant
First Lieutenant Charles C. Carpenter, D platoon leader
First Lieutenant Alexander S. Williams, C platoon leader
First Lieutenant Harry R. Lay, H platoon leader
Second Lieutenant John P.V. Gridley, C platoon leader
Second Lieutenant Frank Halford, E platoon leader
Second Lieutenant Austin C. Rogers, H platoon leader
Surgeon George A. Lung, USN, attached C
Assistant Surgeon John M. Brister, USN, attached H

Appendix B
Enlisted Marines Assigned to Company D

First Sergeant John S. Lipscomb
Sergeants John McCaffery and Bryan McSwiney
Corporals Joseph J. Murphy and Robert L. Leckie
Trumpeter Joshua Jones

    Privates George H. Ames, Roy W. Beal, Charles W. Black, Walter S. Black, Cornelius H. Brown, John Breen, Donald Cain, John N. Case, John V. Culleton, Oscar L. Davis, George Davis, Joseph Durgin, Eugene DeMozzi, Frederick Earnest, Frank Everly, Eugene Farrell, Reubon B. Franklin, Michael FitzGerald, Henry Forry, John G. Gautz, Charles G. Grotz, Franklin Green, James W. Heckler, Charles Hunt, Michael Hosty, William Harkins, Alfred Jenkins, James Jennings, Oliver L. Kerkendall, William Kilmer, Edward Kloman, Charles J. King, Arthur LaHar, Fred P. Lamb, Aubrey Lomas, Anton Lutz, Eugene C. Martin, Clarence E. Mathias, John McAvay, Francis McCarthy, Modock McKenzie, Walter McKay, Isaac Miller, Beverly J. Moore, Albert N. Neville, John J. Noon, Jacob LeR. Pawling, Thomas F. Pendergast, Vernon Propes, Michael Quinlan, William Heinhold, Jeremiah Reidy, George W. Roberts, William Ross, William Slattery, Jack H. Stanton, William M. Stevens, Samuel K. Stower, John J. Sullivan, Edgar H. Tingley, George L. Trippel, Benjamin F. Tywell, Edward L. Wagner, Elmer F. Whitesell.

Appendix C
Major L.W.T. Waller's Report on the Sohotón Cliffs Operation, 17 November 1901

The men in this march overcame incredible difficulties and dangers. The positions they destroyed must have taken several years to prepare. Reports from old prisoners said they have been three years working on the defenses. No white troops have ever penetrated to these positions, and they were held as a final rallying point. The cliffs were of soft stone of volcanic origin, in the nature of pumice. It cut the men's shoes to pieces. Many of the men were barefooted [after], and all had bad feet. The march was heroic, and too much praise cannot be given the men. We in the boats were not ten minutes away in point of distance, but unable to reach the flanking column at the point of the attack. The troops captured and destroyed 40 bamboo guns, rice, food, and curatels.

the men who distinguished themselves especially Capts. D.D. Porter and H.I. Bearss for either a medal of honor or a brevet. These officers carried out their instructions in the face of hardships, dangers, and incredible obstacles. Not only was personal courage of a high order displayed, but intelligence, discrimination, and zeal. Each footstep in the advance up the cliffs carried its own dangers... .

Of Captain Bearss' detachment, the following men are especially recommended: Sergeant McCaffery, and Corporal J.J. Murphy, for scaling cliffs to the right, an extremely courageous and hazardous undertaking. Corp. Robert Lakaye [sic], for swimming the river unarmed in the presence of the enemy, to secure bancas.

Gunnery Sergeant John H. Quick and Acting Corp. Harry Glenn, Company H, are especially recommended, the first for conspicuous conduct, Glenn for risking his life to pull out the fuse of a bamboo gun.[1]

Appendix D
Comments on Bill H.R. 12916

During World War I, Hiram Bearss was recommended by several U.S. Army officers, including John J. Pershing, for a higher rank in the National Army. This puzzling circumstance is explained by bill H.R. 12916, submitted and passed by both the House and Senate. It was late in the war, beginning on 4 October 1918, but the idea must have been known to Pershing and others. It reads in part:

> That commissioned officers of the Marine Corps, detached for duty with the Army under the provisions of section sixteen hundred and twenty-one, Revised Statutes, shall be eligible, in the same manner as officers of the Regular Army, for temporary promotion to higher grades in any of the forces provided by the Act entitled "An Act to authorize the President to increase temporarily the Military Establishment of the United States."

This was passed retroactive to 18 May 1917 but not signed by the president until 18 January 1919. Barnett, as late as 7 February 1919, referring to this bill, and with endorsements signed by him and Newton Baker, recommended that Hiram be promoted to brigadier general. He also included Col. Harry Lee and Col. Logan Feland in this blanket endorsement. Julius Turrill, Hugh Matthews and Thomas Holcomb were to be promoted to colonel in the National Army while Holland Smith, Ralph Keyser, and Littleton W.T. Waller, Jr., were up for lieutenant colonelcies. The only person of this group who seems to have been promoted was Logan Feland, to brigadier general, USMC.

Appendix E

Decorations of Hiram Iddings Bearss

Hiram I. Bearss was awarded numerous decorations during his career. In those earlier times few soldiers, sailors or Marines were the recipients of anything more than campaign medals. And it was only during World War I that a man could expect more than a Victory medal with clasps.

Spanish Campaign Medal
Philippine Campaign Medal

Expeditionary Medal with numeral three for:

    Panama 1903–04
    Cuba 1912

Mexican Service Medal
Dominican Campaign Medal
Dominican Republic 1916–17
Victory Medal with clasps:
    Aisne
    Aisne-Marne
    St. Mihiel

Meuse-Argonne with battle clasps and defensive clasps
Distinguished Service Medal (Army and Navy)
Distinguished Service Cross (Army)
Medal of Honor (Navy)
    French Awards
    Croix de Guerre (Palm)

Croix de Guerre (Palm)
Croix de Guerre (Silver)

with three diplomas awarded for above.

Fourragere
Legion d'honneur (officer)
Belgian Award — Croix de Guerre
Italian Award — Croce De Guerre

Citations for Some of the Above

Distinguished Service Medal (Army and Navy)

"For exceptionally meritorious and distinguished services. He commanded with distinction the 102d Infantry achieving notable success in the active operations in which that regiment was engaged. By his untiring energy and dauntless courage in overcoming the numerous difficulties confronting him he gave proof of military leadership of high order."

Distinguished Service Cross (Army)

"His indomitable courage and leadership led to the complete success of the attack by two battalions of his regiment on Marcheville and Riaville. During the attack these two towns changed hands four times finally remaining in our possession until the troops were ordered to withdraw. Under terrific artillery and machine gun fire he was the first to enter Marcheville, where he directed operations. Later, upon finding his party completely surrounded, he personally assisted in fighting the enemy off with pistol and hand grenades."

Medal of Honor (Navy)

"For extraordinary heroism and eminent and conspicuous conduct in battle at the junction of the Cadacan and Sohotón Rivers, Samar, Philippines Islands, 17 November 1901. Col. Bearss (then Capt.), second in command of the columns upon their uniting ashore in the Sohotón River region, made a surprise attack on the fortified cliffs and completely routed the enemy, killing thirty and capturing and destroying the powder magazine, 40 lantacas (guns), rice, food and curates. Due to his courage, intelligence, discrimination and zeal, he successfully led his men up the cliffs by means of bamboo ladders to a height of 200 feet. The cliffs were of soft stone of volcanic origin, in the nature of pumice, and were honeycombed with caves. Tons of rocks were suspended in platforms held in position by vine cables (known as bejuco) in readiness to be precipitated upon people below. After driving the insurgents from their position which was almost impregnable, being covered with numerous trails lined with poisoned spears, pits, etc., he led his men across the river, scaled the cliffs on the opposite side, and destroyed the camps there. Col. Bearss and the men under his command overcame incredible difficulties and dangers in destroying positions which, according to reports from old prisoners, had taken 3 years to perfect, were held as a final rallying point, and were never before penetrated by white troops. Col. Bearss also rendered distinguished public service in the presence of the enemy at Quinapundan River, Samar, Philippine Islands, on 19 January 1902."

Notes

Chapter 1

1. Most of the material pertaining to the Bearss family is obtained from the Smith biographical unpaginated manuscript or the *Peru Daily Tribune*, various dates.
2. One Marine fitness report listed him as being five feet, six inches in height with corresponding weight.
3. Mike always seems to have listed DePauw as the school he graduated from, but Norwich University lays claim to him (most probably because he was awarded the Medal of Honor).
4. From the October school paper, *Reveille*.
5. January 14 issue of *Reveille*.

Chapter 2

1. Smith.
2. It is now fairly well established that an internal failure caused the explosion, not a Spanish mine.
3. The Spanish regulars with smokeless powder and Mauser rifles were dangerous to American troops in Cuba. The United States won, or rather, Spain lost. It happened that they were more disorganized even than the United States.
4. Apparently, this description of what was going on in his mind at that time was what Bearss told Smith in later years.
5. Another Norwich alum who also did not graduate from that school.
6. The foregoing is derived from numerous sources. Especially see *Marine Corps Headquarters Bulletin*, February 1940, p. 10.
7. At that time Reid was a long-serving Marine. He had accepted his commission on 2 July, 1864, and was, at this time, adjutant and inspector. His nephew, same name, entered the Corps at the same time as Bearss and Smedley Butler and had a distinguished career, earning a Medal of Honor at Vera Cruz in April 1914.
8. Butler "altered" his age to 18 in order to be accepted. His father, a congressman, thanked Smedley for not pushing it further. "Don't add another year to thy age, my son. Thy mother and I weren't married until 1879." Thomas, p. 9.
9. It does not appear that he ever used "Mike" again although his relatives and friends from Peru did.
10. Richard S. Collum. *The History of the United States Marines Corps* (Philadelphia, 1890).
11. The School of Application, which later became the Basic School, opened on 1 May, 1891 and in April 1898, closed its doors until 1903. New officers of the Corps went without basic training until the latter date.
12. Muse had, until recently, remained a captain after more than 34 years. He

joined the USMC in 1864 and would retire as a colonel on 14 August 1900.

13. Waller would retire as a major general after a superb record as a fighting man. Lejeune had an even more illustrious career. He not only commanded the U.S. Army's 2d Division in France in 1918 but went on to become one of the greatest commandants the Corps ever had.

14. Heinl, pp. 117–18. Myers went on to become the hero of the Peking defense in 1900, among many other honors, and retired a major general on 1 February 1935.

15. Cole also had a distinguished career which included leading the 5th Marine Brigade to France in 1918, and while there, serving in command of a U.S. Army Depot division.

16. The consequences of severe alcoholism were a major problem in all services in those times. See Ballendorf and Bartlett, *Pete Ellis,* for a well-researched example of how service in the tropics afflicted one Marine officer.

17. Denby would later enlist as a Marine private and go through boot camp at (then) Paris Island. He would also serve as President Harding's secretary of the navy and suffer as part of the Teapot Dome crowd.

18. Gridley's Marine son, 2d Lt. John P.V. Gridley, served with Bearss several times over several years.

19. Lemly served in China during the Boxer Relief Expedition in 1900, retiring as a colonel. Gulick was also a colonel, and replaced Logan Feland in command of the 2d Marine Brigade in Nicaragua in 1927.

20. See, among many, Linn, *The Philippine War,* and Miller, "Benevolent Assimilation."

Chapter 3

1. Hiram was one of 30 2d Lts. recalled to active service and all were promoted to 1st Lt. Many were sent to the Philippines, and some later to China during the Boxer Rebellion.

2. Dewey would have some minor problems with a German fleet, then near by, and an anxious Japan, both of which wished to assume the burden if the U.S. relinquished the islands. See Miller, pp. 2, 50.

3. The official name was Remington-Lee, the latter being the inventor, James Paris Lee. It was used for many years by the British. It had a nice .45 caliber bullet, which must have impressed the Filipinos.

4. Pope was a veteran of the U.S. Civil War, having been commissioned a second lieutenant on 23 November 1861. Pope would receive a brevet captaincy for his part in the attack upon Fort Sumter on 8 September 1863 and later the Brevet Medal. He retired as a brig. gen. in February 1905 after 43 years of service. Spicer was born in the West Indies and accepted appointment from Massachusetts as a 2d Lt. on 13 March 1872. He retired on 5 March 1904 as a lt. col.

5. In 1903 Elliott would become the tenth commandant of the Marine Corps.

6. "Handsome Jack" Myers should be too familiar to require further details, but if required see the author's *Treading Softly: U.S. Marines in China, 1819–1949* (Westport: Praeger, 2001).

7. That ship was launched in 1887. When the dreadnaught *New York* was launched, this cruiser's name was changed to *Saratoga*. When a battleship was being constructed in the post-WWI period, and because of the Washington Treaty it was converted to an aircraft carrier *Saratoga*, the name once again changed: that time to the USS *Rochester*, which served as the flagship of the Special Service Squadron in the Caribbean for nearly 20 years.

8. All Bearss' changes of station and promotions have been verified and taken from his personnel records and Marine officer registers of various years.

9. Waller accepted an appointment as

a 2d lt. of U.S. Marines on 16 June 1880, and in short order gained a reputation as an efficient and popular (with his troops) fighting man. Waller served well in China, the Philippines, Panama, Cuba, and stateside. He strained hard to become commandant but fate opposed him. He retired a major general and died of pneumonia at Atlantic City, New Jersey, on 13 July 1926.

10. Mare Island would serve as the West Coast Marine boot camp during the First World War. It was widely utilized between the wars and also during WWII.

11. Frederick May Wise, *A Marine Tells it to You* (New York: J.H. Sears & Company, Inc., 1929), p. 5. Wise accepted his commission on 1 July 1899 and would have many adventures before retiring as a brigadier general in the 1920s. He served as CO of 2/5 at Belleau Wood and would transfer to command the 59th Infantry, 4th Division, USA, and later the 8th Infantry Brigade. All comments attributed to Wise are from this work.

12. Ibid., p. 6.

13. Ibid., p. 6. Bearss was actually a first lieutenant.

14. Needless to state, the navy and Marines didn't always honor their opposites nor treat them as equals. Much has already been said along these lines so no more need be added here. But how unfortunate for both services.

15. There are several versions of this stop at Hawaii. According to the Commandant's Report for 1900 the ship remained in harbor for a period of about two weeks. Another claims the ship left Honolulu the next day after arrival. We have stayed with the Commandant's Report for 1900. It is "official" and makes more sense.

16. Kelton held a brevet of major from 11 June 1898 and retired a colonel in 1909. Ingate died on the island 24 December 1899. Russell became commandant in the 1930s. He incidentally was returned home from his Guam assignment, ill from a fever. Carpenter lost an eye to infection but later retired a major in 1911. Carmody's fate is discussed shortly.

17. The governor was Comdr. Seton Schroeder, USN, also spoken of as "Satan" Schroeder by some of the Marine enlisted men who served under him at Guam.

18. John H. Clifford, *History of the Pioneer Marine Battalion at Guam, L.I., 1899 and the Campaign in Samar, P.I., 1901* (Foster, R.I.: The Brass Hat, 1981), p. 11.

19. Wise, p. 14.

20. In November 1900 they would be transported to the Philippines and most would participate in a really terrible affair known to history as the Ordeal of Samar.

21. Commandant's Report, 1899.

22. Wise, p. 12, only included the names of three officers. He must have forgotten poor Jonas.

Chapter 4

1. The U.S. fleet and the German fleet, standing in Manila Bay, were close to an eruption. Both were far from their closest base but Dewey had friends in the neighborhood. The Kaiser's brother, Prince Heinrich of Prussia, was a rear admiral with the German fleet.

2. The word was also spelled "Goo-Goo" but neither version was meant to be complimentary. The next derivation down was most likely "Gook." For details, see H.L. Mencken's *The American Language, Supplement One* (N.Y.: Alfred Knopf, 1945).

3. Elliott had made an excellent reputation for himself during the initial occupation of Guantanamo in 1898 and earlier during the assault on Panama in 1885. He was a reject from the U.S. Military Academy who just happened to join the Marines. It was a lucky day for the Corps.

4. Thomas, *Old Gimlet Eye*, p. 31.

5. These men were George Thorpe, Robert M. Gilson, and David D. Porter,

all 1st lts.' at that time. After the China expedition, Porter would join Waller's battalion and serve courageously on Samar. Porter and Thorpe were both later awarded the Brevet Medal, while Robert M. Gilson retired in 1903.

6. Heinl, *Soldiers of the Sea*, p. 122. Draper entered the Corps from Kansas as a 2d lt. on 1 July 1889. He was promoted to captain on 3 March 1899. His service included mainly navy yards in the U.S. until he was shipped to the Philippines in 1899. He went with Waller to China in 1901 and died in Hong Kong, China, on 20 September that year.

7. Radford earned an enviable reputation when he later took over control of the Marine Corps Quartermaster factory in Philadelphia. He brought about a great reduction in wasteful spending on uniforms, both enlisted men's and officers'.

8. Alcoholism was rife in the Corps and most probably in the army and navy also. It seemed to be especially a problem in the Marines assigned to the Philippines. Young 2d lt. Earl Ellis is described as having acquired the "habit" while stationed there in 1902. See Ballendorf and Bartlett.

9. For further details, see the author's *Few Scars of Violence, Few Wounds to Heal: The U.S. Marines in China, 1819–1949* (Pike, N.H.: The Brass Hat, 2000).

10. Recently I was asked by two retired U.S. Army colonels what I was working on at present. I told them a biography of a Marine named Bearss. They both nearly shouted "Hiking Hiram!" When I asked how come they had heard of him and his nickname, both replied that he was a legend in the U.S. Army for services during WWI.

11. He was also the subject of an affectionate song developed by the rank and file which went, "Hike 'em Hiram, with their shirttails hanging out." Regardless, "Hiking Hiram" was the more common and better known of the two.

12. "Skipper" was old-time Marine lingo for a company commander.

13. Robert Dunlap would become one of the greats of the Corps. He was appointed from Maine and accepted his commission on 8 April 1899. He would later concentrate on artillery and commanded the 17th Field Artillery, 2d Division, USA, in France. He later would be seriously considered for the role of commandant and later sent to the School of War in France. He died in the early 1930s while saving a French woman in an avalanche.

14. Letter from Lane to the district commander, dated 18 July 1901, with endorsement from Heywood dated 5 September 1901 for the Bearss file.

15. Goodrell was an old-timer from Ohio who joined in 1865. He had already served three years in the 15th Iowa Volunteers within the Army of the Tennessee. He held the usual appointments as would any Marine officer in the interim period, as well as the slow promotions. He retired as a brigadier general on 31 January 1906.

16. That relationship would again be kindled in 1917 in France when two regiments of Marines joined the 9th and the 23d Infantry in forming the infantry of the 2d Division.

17. Named for Col. Emerson H. Liscum, USA, who was killed in action in China on 13 July 1900. This brave officer had just removed the colors of the 9th Infantry from the dead fingers of the color bearer and was stoutly holding them himself when he bought the package.

18. See Schott, *The Ordeal of Samar*, pp. 27–55, for a good description of the events at Balangiga.

19. Smith had made quite a reputation in his service since the Civil War, suffering two courts-martial and numerous brushes with his seemingly uncontrollable temper. See Linn, *The Philippine War*, pp. 312–15.

20. Only the president of the U.S. had the authority to assign Marines to duty with the U.S. Army. See the appendices for a listing of the officers of this Samar battalion. Additionally, find the names of the enlisted Marines who were part of

Hiram Bearss' Company D. Most of the details of the troops assigned are in the 1901 Commandant's Report to the Secretary of the Navy.

21. This would come in very handy later when the U.S. Army, headed up by Gen. Chaffee, tried to court-martial Waller.

22. Schott, p. 71.

23. Smith issued a general order relative to clearing the area. A portion of it is included in the section about the Waller court-martial.

24. This was sometimes identified as the Sohotón River but is listed on modern maps as the Basey River.

25. Most of this description of the "fortress" comes from the various reports issued by the Commandant; Waller; S.C. Miller, p. 221; Schott, pp. 90–91.

26. They would both retire colonels, be late recipients of the Medal of Honor, and attain "tombstone" promotion to brigadier general long after retirement. Except for occasional lapses in judgment, they were two of the best fighting Marines of their time.

27. It seems that Porter made this decision all by himself and made changes to Waller's plans. This was the first of two times that he would make changes to Waller's orders. The next time men's lives would be lost because of it. See the following section, the "March Across Samar."

28. Smith.

29. Waller recommended Glenn for a Medal of Honor, as he did Cpl. Robert LaKaye. Neither of these were awarded. Waller also commended Surgeon Brister, Sgts. Quick, Grogan and Pvt. Campbell plus several of the Marine officers including Carpenter, Lay, and Austin C. Rogers.

30. It can be found in the appendices. Both Porter and Bearss were recommended by Waller for the Medal of Honor, or that each should be brevetted. The recommendation would not be enacted until 1934 when a recently elected president would have the opportunity to place the medal around the neck of each, 33 years after the event.

31. Smith's reply to Waller's endorsement of Bearss for award,, dated 19 November 1901.

32. Ibid., Rodgers' reply, undated except for "1901."

33. Chafee's acceptance of Waller's recommendation, dated 1 December 1901. It might be necessary to add that Gen Chaffee had no love for the Marines and would do his best to "hang" Waller soon after this.

34. For some reason, Linn, who seems to have had a real "problem" with Waller, suggests that it was Waller who proposed the exploration across Samar: "On 19 November he (Waller) notified Smith of *his intention* (to cross Samar) ... the rationale is still a mystery. Waller's reason — that Smith had suggested exploring a telegraph route — is clearly implausible: as a direct telephone line ran from Waller's headquarters at Basey to Smith's headquarters at Tacloban, there was no pressing need for a telegraph line" (p. 316). The problem is, Smith wanted to communicate with his U.S. Army posts on the east coast of Samar. The suggested line was to go across Samar for Smith's benefit, not Waller's. Obviously Linn is very confused. Emphasis added.

35. Locating a map of Samar isn't easy. Those available have few if any details of areas over which the Marines marched and fought, even those prepared for the War and Navy Departments during WWII.

36. These were well utilized by bush Filipinos when they were upset, which was most of the time.

37. Linn contends that no copy of Smith's "howling wilderness" order was ever found. Of course not. Waller seemed to believe (foolishly it seems) that he was serving with gentlemen. At a time in the not too distant future, Waller would require proof to avoid a conviction. This memo, while not signed, was more important than Waller realized at that time.

38. This chapter will not cover the complete details of that march but only where it affects Bearss. Schott's book is an excellent place to start for the complete story.

39. It appears as though that name has been now changed to "Llorente." On maps prepared prior to WWII, the Lanang River flows eastward down toward a town of that same name on the coast. A more recent map renames the river and the town Llorente.

40. According to Schott, "Halford, was so downcast at being left out that Waller relented and allowed him to go too." Lucky guy.

41. The following material has been derived and adapted from many sources, including Schott, Miller, Linn, Heinl, Smith, and the Commandant's Report. But the very best, though not lengthy, is that written by an enlisted Marine who was a participant in all that happened to Waller's Battalion of Marines in the Philippines: see John Clifford, especially pp. 35–40.

42. This could not have been the Suribao. If it had been, the column would have been so far north that they would never have made the crossing of the island, and would only have been able to get back to the east coast. There is some difficulty in determining where this information came from. It is from two different sources and it seems that both are wrong. Or at least, if Waller believed them, he was dead wrong. Of course, given the changing and error-ridden maps of Samar, it might have been another river, not now shown on maps.

43. It isn't clear from existing records where they were at that time but common sense would put them farther west and not on the Suribao River. Possibly they were as much as halfway across the island.

44. It isn't clear what Waller meant by "twenty-nine days" since they started on 28 December and arrived at Basey on 6 January, a total of nine days. Perhaps, and most likely, the message came through incorrectly as twenty-nine instead of nine.

45. This statement does not take into account his later scandalous conduct and dismissal from the Marine Corps in 1915, nor his commission as a colonel in the Belgian army during WWI, in which he is reported to have served honorably. The details of what transpired following the long march are derived from much the same sources, including especially Clifford, Schott, Smith, *Correspondence Relating to the War with Spain*, and Metcalf, pp. 275–79.

46. Bootes had already had some problems at Sohotón, such as losing a raft that sank with him and 15 privates and their rifles on that river. But he did make colonel in 1919 and commanded the Marine Barracks at the Brooklyn navy yard, so he had some saving graces.

47. Schott, p. 126.

48. In a paper titled "*We will go heavily armed*": *The Marines' small war on Samar, 1901–1902*, delivered before the Ninth Naval History Symposium, 20 October 1989, by Brian McAllister Linn, Waller and his Marines are the villains, not heroes, of this entire affair. Linn especially blamed Waller himself.

49. During this conference Waller learned that there had been several insurrections along the south and east coasts. One army company sent to Quinapundan had not reported in. That was one reason Smith wanted some men sent in there but since this town was well within the area of U.S. Army responsibility, it isn't clear why he wanted to send Marines. What happened to that missing company also isn't clear.

50. Smith.

51. Smith.

52. The Navy Department, *Medal of Honor 1861–1949*, Washington, D.C.: N.d. (c. 1950). See appendix E for the full citation.

53. Taking the islands from Spain was one thing, holding them was another. Holding them caused innumerable deaths and 40 years later a much greater expense

and great defeat. Meanwhile, most of the Filipinos wanted to be entirely free of all foreign interference, including Americans'.

54. This is not to excuse Day but to set the scene as to why he seemed so highly agitated and anxious to eliminate the native population of Samar.

55. Schott, p. 136.
56. Ibid., p. 134.
57. Ibid., p. 140.
58. Ibid., p. 145.

59. The oft recited tale that when a man who had made the march entered a room someone would stand and state, "Stand, gentlemen he was on Samar," wasn't worth that price. Waller must be held responsible for continuing the walk after a few days of travail clearly indicated it was a bad situation. Professor Linn concurs but doesn't allow Waller much room. He accuses Waller of being addicted to the bottle, among other crimes; however, no liquor was available on that long walk. Waller's ego and pride in his Marines was the real problem.

60. Schott, p. 146.

61. Forney was an old-timer from Pennsylvania who joined the USMC in 1861. He was brevetted captain for his exploits in 1863, 1864, and 1867 at Formosa. He died in 1921, several months before the Brevet Medal was actually issued, though one had been prepared for him.

62. Chaffee had it in for the Marines and was dedicated to throwing a famous one to the lions. Waller was famous, and worse: he was capable and generally successful where the army hadn't been. Of course Chaffee never admitted to having those feelings toward the Marines or Waller. No mention of any part of the affair is in the Chaffee biography by Maj. Gen. William H. Carter.

63. Had Bearss been at Basey, he too would have urged the executions. But he wasn't, and that saved him from the further ordeal of being charged as an accessory. He would, however, be a secure witness for the defense.

64. Stuart Creighton Miller in *The War of 1898* and Benjamin R. Beede, editor, *U.S. Interventions 1898–1934, an Encyclopedia* (NY: Garland Publishing, 1994), p. 575. This is a little farfetched because it would be another eight years that either would be close to that kind of an appointment. It is a fact, though, that Biddle was all for Waller's conviction and voted that way; the only Marine officer on the court who did.

65. The defense counsel's name was Major Edwin F. Glenn; he was the same officer who brought the infamous water torture to Samar for the Marines to see. The army would eventually get him for criminal acts.

66. The quoted testimony is from Schott, pp. 223–24 and Smith.

67. According to other reports, Waller died of pneumonia in Atlantic City, New Jersey, in 1927.

Chapter 5

1. The two men were engaged in exchanging insulting letters.

2. Because of the recent victorious war with Spain the Corps had nearly 100 percent growth. The additional naval bases required a larger navy and a Marine base defense force to protect them.

3. Commandant's Report of 1 October 1901, p. 1,253.

4. See Commandant's Report 23 September 1903, p. 1,237, for a description of the difficulties inherent in obtaining medical doctors from the USN. He had "been compelled to employee civilian physicians."

5. Clifford, *Progress and Purpose*, p. 10.

6. Thomas, *Old Gimlet Eye*, pp. 94–101, for an excellent description of what happened to him a few months later. Possibly Bearss' experience was similar.

7. Smith.

8. There were then only two nations that might have had an interest in the Atlantic and a fleet large and powerful

enough to contest the U.S.—Great Britain and Germany. In the Pacific there was only one, even then—Japan.

9. Some nasty people have intimated that Teddy was pulling a fast one on the Columbians. He was just trying to protect the Panamanians and the future of a potential canal. That was the same reason we "aided" the Nicaraguans so often.

10. When Hiram fooled around, he really went the distance. The general was Charles Heywood, major general commandant, U.S. Marine Corps. It wasn't unusual for the commandant to accompany his Marines when they were engaged in duty that required a large landing party, such as this.

11. Smith. Like all stories, it depends upon who made it up.

12. Evans was a regular who resigned and then returned for duty in WWI. "Daddy Pat," as he was later known to his young son, would become adjutant of the 6th Marines, France, 1918. He was also at Philadelphia in 1919.

13. Smith.

14. Mahoney accepted his commission as a 2d Lt. on 1 July 1883, after graduation from the Naval Academy. He served at Guantánamo during the Spanish-American War, at Vera Cruz in 1914, was CO of the 3d Provisional Brigade in Cuba, 1917, and CO of the Marine brigade at Galveston, Texas, during WWI. Though promoted to brigadier general on 1 July 1918, he was reduced to colonel on 8 March 1919. Mahoney retired after 40 years' service.

15. Smith.

16. The young man is reported to have eventually become a Marine officer but I can find no record to confirm that. The reference to "senior service" has to do, of course, with the stance taken by the USN for so many years, that the Corps was a subordinate service, with few, if any rights. They treated members of that Corps like-wise.

17. This is reported in Smith, but I could not locate a entry in his medical records that showed that he requested medical help for the concussion. That is not unusual, because although he seemed to be accident and illness prone throughout his career, he seldom "officially" asked for medical help, and sometimes avoided it.

18. This story is related by Smith. Hiram later met her husband. He'd heard the story and laughed, admitting that the British navy had not yet gotten "chain less anchors" nor was he expecting to see them very soon.

19. Thomas, pp. 115–16.

20. Ibid.

21. Butler and his wife had already been subjected to the same indignity. In Venzon's collection of letters of Butler, his letters explain that though funds were available ($50K as of the Appropriation Bill of 27 April 1904) Major Doyen had resisted using the funds and then established that each of the officer's quarters could be divided into two units instead of the one provided for. Hence Bearss' anger.

22. Broatch accepted a commission on 1 July 1899 as a 1st Lt. and had been one of the men to serve at Guam during the mutiny period. He was born in the Dakota Territory but appointed from Nebraska. It appears that he resigned his commission in 1908.

23. It is easy to see how these two men, both paragons of the Corps and each a genuine fighting man of the first chop, would be in competition one with the other during most of their careers. Each joined at nearly the same time and, at times, both were shunted aside for lesser men. Both were physically small men in comparison to most of the other Marines of their time. But the reputation of each transcends most of their contemporaries.

24. Capt. Wendell C. Neville, known as "Buck," was also known, even then, to have the loudest voice in all of Christendom. He eventually became major general commandant, following Lejeune, but died in office.

25. According to Butler, in a letter to

his mother dated 6 February 1906, he and Cole didn't get along very well: "Cole and I don't speak socially." Venzon, p. 52.

26. Presumably, this was in retaliation for bettering Butler's time; the latter reported to Pendleton and Bearss to Cole.

27. See previous mention of his tour in the Philippines in 1899–1900 and also the part concerning Hiram's command of the 102d Infantry during the Great War.

28. Hiram's fitness reports, except one, never gave him less than "excellent" (3.5 to 4.0) in any category. He was always at the top of his form.

29. Doyen, as colonel, later commanded the 5th Marines as they went to France. As a brigadier general he then commanded the newly forming 4th Marine Brigade and for a period was the first commander of the 2d Division. This gave him the honor of being the first Marine to ever have commanded a division. Unfortunately, he was replaced in May 1918 as CO of the 4th Brigade because he failed an AEF physical. He died of the flu shortly after arriving in the United States.

30. Davis, a native of D.C., entered the Corps on 8 April 1899. He served the usual path of most officers, was on recruiting duty during WWI and as a colonel served with the 3d Brigade in China in 1927–28. However he disappears from sight after that and must be presumed deceased after that date.

31. A listing of his official and unofficial illness and injuries is so varied that one would need a medical dictionary to interpret them. They ranged from migraine headaches to a variety of gastrointestinal attacks, with hemorrhoids, abscesses, gout (left great toe), and chronic diarrhea among others.

32. Ben H. Fuller was a relatively quiet Marine whose service was rather sedate. He graduated from the Naval Academy and accepted a commission as a 2d Lt. in the USMC on 1 July 1891. He stayed the course and eventually was appointed commandant following Neville's death in office. He generated no excitement in his career.

33. Lauchheimer, then a major general, died in office in 1920. He was not a combat Marine but has been considered to be the "father of Marine Corps marksmanship."

34. Although I believe that is a correct statement, later events might prove otherwise.

35. Poor Ostermann was still subject to confirmation as a Marine officer, and if the complaint had been allowed to go forward without interference, it might have stopped his entire career cold. Instead, in 1943 he retired as a major general.

36. Penrose insisted that his future was tied up with the Biddle's and that Taft, an ex-governor of the Philippines, should remember that Waller had been court-martialed in the Philippines. That killed Waller's chances. Biddle was a decent sort but was given the nickname "Sitting Bull" for obvious reasons.

37. The appointment of academy graduate Lejeune in July 1920 satisfied both groups but it wasn't until Holcomb was appointed in 1936 that a non–academy graduate became commandant. In fact, Holcomb was not even a college graduate and is considered to be one of the best commandants of the Marine Corps.

38. Rear Admiral David D. Porter, USN, 1863, in a letter to the Marine commandant.

39. Hiram was a victim of *Nausea marina*, as it was officially termed. Or, as you probably have figured, *mal de mere*, or in plain English, seasickness. Several times he had even gone so far as to turn in for treatment.

40. Smith would one day be the second naval aviator in the Marine Corps. In 1912 he went with the first Marine aviator, Capt. Alfred A. Cunningham, to flight school at Annapolis.

Chapter 6

1. The word and the situation was later included in one Bearss newspaper obituary.

2. Most of his Marine comrades claimed that Hiram was always personally broke. He certainly had that reputation. But he was also acclaimed as being willing to share his last "kopek" with any friend at any time.

3. Apparently he wasn't always so successful. In a report dated 15 April 1913, Col. Charles Lauchheimer, Hiram's pal, sent in a devastating report concerning a later fund management while he was with the 2d Provisional Brigade at Guantanamo.

4. Wise, p. 113.

5. Ibid., p. 112.

6. The Advanced Base School had originally been established at New London, Connecticut, as early as 1909, but had moved to Philadelphia in June 1912.

7. See Ballendorf and Bartlett for a detailed description of when and where the concept was established.

8. Colonel Moses was another long-service Marine, having been commissioned on 1 July 1883, after graduating from the Naval Academy. He served until 1914 when he disappears from the registers. Consequently we must assume that he perished at about that same time.

9. Barnett would become commandant in 1914 and remain so throughout the period of WWI. Karmany had a long and distinguished career, which began in July 1883 and ended when he retired on 10 February 1923 as a full colonel. Pendleton, another Academy graduate, accepted his commission as a 2d Lt. on 30 June 1884 and would become best known for his time in Santo Domingo and his command of the 4th Marines while there and at San Diego. He retired as a major general on 2 June 1924.

10. Wilson had problems with Mexico in 1914 and again in 1916, Haiti in 1915, Santo Domingo in 1916, Cuba in 1917 and of course Europe in 1917. His foreign policy kept the Marines very busy.

11. Long entered active duty on 1 July 1891 after graduation from the Naval Academy. He attained the rank of brig. gen. during the Great War.

12. Philip S. Brown was from Maine, accepted commission on 13 April 1899 to the USS *Brooklyn*, USN; was part of the Advance Base Force; was made major in 1912; disappears from the records in 1916 so he probably died. Logan Feland joined the Corps on 3 March 1903 and made steady advancement. He would command the 5th Marines in France and eventually retire as a major general, being seriously a contender for the role of commandant.

13. It was probably named after the new assistant secretary of the navy, Franklin D. Roosevelt. The Marine Corps was within his area of responsibility. In 1903 a Camp Roosevelt was the home of a permanent garrison of Marines on Culebra, but then, obviously, named for President Theodore Roosevelt.

14. Mayo and Hiram became good friends, as will be seen, in the days following the Great War.

15. Most of what follows can be found in Quirk, pp. 1–77 and Beede, pp. 561–63.

16. The story of what transpired between the *Ypiranga* and the U.S. fleet blocking its passage is worth being partially described. *Ypiranga* was boarded and her papers examined. It seems that the guns were originally from New York, by way of Hamburg, Germany, to confuse the gringos. Fletcher was eventually ordered to allow the ship to go wherever the captain wished and after a few days she set sail for Puerto Mexico, a port about 125 miles further south, and there unloaded Huerta's machine guns. Wilson and his State Department, led by William Jennings Bryan, were still unable to get a policy together.

17. Neville's group was not sent because of the whaleboat incident but was part of the then-current policy of having Marines available, if needed, for advance

base work. They just happened to be on station at that time.

18. Most of the details are extracted from the essential Miller and Johnstone, *Chronology of the United States Marine Corps.*

19. Catlin commanded the 3d Regiment of Marines ashore. This was composed of Marines gathered together from the various offshore ships' detachments.

20. Funston had been a volunteer from Kansas who had made a reputation during the Philippine Insurrection by capturing Aguinaldo in his lair. He died in February 1917. MacArthur later made a claim that previously, Funston had already been selected to command any U.S. forces to be sent to Europe.

21. Lejeune. *Reminiscences of a Marine*, pp. 213–14.

22. In his 1935 confirmation hearings this matter was brought out and seriously threatened Russell's future. Some unnamed officer came to Russell's defense by stating that he and Russell had "encountered at least a squadron of Mexican cavalry, but they subsequently disappeared." There were numerous witnesses who told the opposite story. Russell was, however, appointed commandant.

23. Not long before this time, the U.S. Naval Service had authorized the award of a Medal of Honor for officers, something that until recently only the U.S. Army had allowed. Even the naval commander, Admiral Fletcher and his nephew and aide of the same name, received that highest of awards. The only Marine officer who seemed to be thoroughly ashamed (and initially refused the award) was Smedley D. Butler. He was told by his superior (Neville?) that he had "better take it and shut up or face charges of disobedience."

24. His help managed to save the Corps many times during the troubles of the teens and twenties. Some historians fault his son Smedley for using his father's influence. Without Pa Butler and his son, who kept him posted, there might not be a Marine Corps today.

25. It was while at Leavenworth that Hiram fell from a horse and received a break in his vertebrae that would haunt his health and eventually help to drive him from the Corps. This description of Hiram's Leavenworth experience comes through Smith and we can assume from Hiram.

Chapter 7

1. Calder, *The Impact of Intervention*, pp. 1–12; also Fuller and Cosmos, *Marines in the Dominican Republic 1916–1924*, pp. 6–8. Both cover the background and period very well.

2. Kane, the son of a USN captain, was a graduate of the Naval Academy who accepted his commission as a 2d Lt. on 1 July 1890. He was part of the fighting element of the Corps and served in many places during the following 34 years, retiring as a colonel in 1924.

3. For details, see Miller and Johnstone, pp. 116–17.

4. Joseph Pendleton was a first-class Marine in every sense of the word. His career began 1 July 1884, two years after graduation from the Naval Academy. He twice had command experience in the Philippines. In Nicaragua, Pendleton commanded the 4th Marines from 1912 intermittently until Nov. 1916 when he assumed command of the 2d Brigade in Santo Domingo. His varied career continued until, in 1924, he retired as a major general. He died in Feb. 1942.

5. A perfect example of the occasional efficient interaction between the U.S. Navy and Marines.

6. This and the following material is derived from Langley, *The Banana Wars*, pp. 147–48. See also Fuller, pp. 20–22.

7. Ibid.

8. On 1 January 1940 McDougall retired as major general after 30 years service. Among many other highlights of a

fighting Marine's career he had been a founding member of the Nicaraguan *Guardia Nacional* in 1927.

9. Condit and Turnbladh, *Hold High the Torch*, pp. 58–62.

10. It appears that Hiram became a confirmed cigar smoke while in this most important cigar center.

11. Naul, in addition to his Episcopal rank, had been the president of Santo Domingo in 1912–1913 and a more or less faithful friend of the United States.

12. It was learned that Calcona was waiting for Hiram to buy horses so that he and his men could then come to town and as usual take the money away from the locals.

13. This was what Butler would have run into if he didn't Have "pull"—meaning his father was chairman of the House Naval Appropriations Committee. Butler had many run-ins with chairborne troopers.

14. It is known that a few Marine deserters had gone over to the side of the enemy, in Haiti and in Santo Domingo and later in Nicaragua. Perhaps the *insurrectos* were being helped by that clique.

15. Sometime after Hiram had left the island Evangelista broke his word and went back to his old tricks. Another group of Marines went out after him, captured his men and shot him. Hiram later said he believed he was making a mistake and probably should have shot him at their meeting, but he had given his word that he wouldn't.

Chapter 8

1. For details about the 4th Marine Brigade, read Clark, *Devil Dogs: Fighting Marines of World War I*.

2. Some Marine was quoted as saying, "Don't let Smedley over there. He'll finish the war off too damn fast for the rest of us," or words to that effect. The same might have been said for Hiram, and it would have been true.

3. Feland proved his worth, especially as Neville's assistant regimental commander of the 5th Marine Regiment at Belleau Wood. If any officer of the 5th could be recognized as truly being its leader, it was Feland. He was a graduate of the Massachusetts Institute of Technology.

4. Members were Col. Charles A. Doyen, Lt. Col. George Van Orden, and Capt. Seth Williams. Doyen was selected to head up the 5th Regiment of Marines, soon going to France, then later the 4th Marine Brigade. Van Orden obtained command of the 11th Marines, 5th Brigade. Seth Williams wound up a major general of Marines. All in all, they each did quite well.

5. Clark, *Devil Dogs*.

6. LeRoy Hunt, a Californian, would make a great name for himself in France and during WWII.

7. See Mary Sayward Cole, *A Bridge of Remembrance* (Cambridge, Mass.: N.D., c. 1998), for an excellent biography by his daughter-in-law of that fine fighting man. He was later KIA at Belleau Wood. He threw a "potatomasher" back at a German position but it exploded and blew off his arm. He died soon afterwards.

8. Le Bouf might very well have been correct in his claim that he was the grandson of the famous field marshal who turned in a not too creditable performance during the Franco-Prussian War, but he was from Fall River, Massachusetts, not France.

9. The French Mission was a group of officers assigned to "assist" the U.S. officers in getting settled in France. Mostly they were encumbrances.

10. See Clark, *Devil Dogs*, for details.

11. Smith.

12. Ibid.

13. Actually, Bearss relieved Fritz Wise, who had been acting regimental commander on a temporary basis.

14. Smith.

15. For the most part, American soldiers did not serve in trenches, except

those serving with British units up north and in the beginning at places near Verdun in the early spring of 1918. Otherwise they traveled light, and cross-country. Often times they took heavy casualties but always because the execution was flawed, not the concept.

16. This is based upon a very interesting law then being debated in Congress. See the appendices for further details.

17. He was shunted aside when Logan Feland arrived. Feland had formally been second in command of the 5th, as of 1 July 1917. He had requested temporary assignment to a French regiment to observe the fighting around Verdun and spent that period with the 55th Regiment of the French army.

18. This was a fairly new tactic and the Germans were extremely successful with it. Because of this, the situation on the Western Front became extremely serious for the Allies and Americans. Hiram had noted what had been going on and was trying to forestall a disaster for his battalion.

19. *Ninth U.S. Infantry in the World War*, pp. 4–5; Spaulding, *The Second Division American Expeditionary Force*, pp. 23–24. Certainly the engineers of the 1st Division had been caught by an attack but they hadn't actually been in the line and the objective of the raiding party whereas 3/9 was.

20. Smith.

21. *War Diaries*, 2d Division, volume 7, unpaginated.

22. Copy of the original in Smith.

23. Smith wrote to Bundy concerning his allocation of Bearss to the 9th Infantry. Bundy's response on 15 July 1935 was extremely laudatory. Copy of Bundy letter in Smith.

24. Copy of letter in Smith, "By direction of General Pershing to Lieut. Col. Hiram I. Bearss, 5th Regiment, Marines (Through Military Channels)," dated 2 May 1918. The gist is how bad discipline was and how wonderfully Bearss changed that and handled the 3d Bn, 9th Infantry, especially on the night of 13/14 April 1918.

Harbord personally added the postscript to Bearss.

25. See Clark, *Devil Dogs*.

26. I can not find a Colonel Grant listed with the 2d Division. This came from Smith.

27. Although Hiram "graded" Feland by nine numbers, it appears that they wanted Feland and not Hiram.

28. The 6th Marines would possibly have been better led during the war if Bearss had commanded them instead of Lee. He and Feland would have made a great combination.

29. Copy of the letter included in Smith.

30. This and the previous quote from Smith. Information probably provided by Bearss.

31. A formal complaint was made against the previous occupants of those trenches. It was the considered opinion of many in the "YD" that the trenches were filthy and after much effort were made habitable when completely cleaned. For this reason, since the 1st Division was considered to be Pershing's "own," he may have resented the division and its general long afterward.

32. The soldiers tended to call him "Hike 'em Hiram." That doesn't preclude other, less pleasant, nicknames he might also have acquired.

33. Although the Chauchat has gotten bad press it was a fairly good piece when using the appropriate caliber French ammunition. Besides, it was the only automatic hand held weapon then available for use by the AEF.

34. Undated letter from Nelson to Smith. Internal evidence makes it appear to be from the late 1930s.

35. This story has also been told adding that the fellow with the grenade was an officer. Why then would he have been in the ranks and why did he not use his pistol instead of a grenade, which an officer wouldn't normally have in his possession? Possibly, as an officer, his come-down was all the more important to the story.

Notes — Chapter 8

36. Smith.
37. Strickland, *Connecticut Fights*, p. 230.
38. The entire story is related, among other sources, in Strickland, pp. 220–33, including congratulatory documents from Pershing, Edwards, Shelton, FM Haig, Marshal Foch, Father Leclerc of Rupt-en-Woevre, among many others.
39. The plan was simple. The AEF would continue going forward after the salient was reduced and by so doing would cut off the several main German rail lines running north and south plus take the very important source of captured German wealth. See Hallas, *Squandered Victory*, for a detailed explanation. Since it didn't happen, no one knows if the plan would have succeeded. But if it had the war would probably have ended sooner and largely due to the AEF, which was not what the Allies wished.
40. The plans were altered to force the Germans to relieve their forces on the British front, thereby relieving the British from German pressure and allowing them to effect a large-scale attack with minimum interference. They later claimed to have won the war on that day.
41. See Strickland, p. 242, note 78.
42. This was undoubtedly to ensure that the enemy didn't release forces to head north in order to counter the beginning of the major American attack upon the Argonne on 26 September 1918.
43. Sibley, *With the Yankee Division in France*, p. 288. A surprising entry, since Sibley seemed reluctant to make mention of the Connecticut 102d, possibly because he was a reporter from Boston. His book completely ignores the advance of the regiment to Vigneulles and mentions only peripheral situations of what the Massachusetts regiments were doing at that time. He never once mentions that Bearss was a Marine officer.
44. Hanson was in the 103d Infantry.
45. Bates had only been with the 103d since 10 September, two days before the drive began, but he earned a DSC for his work on this day. Hiram had to have been the officer who recommended him since he served with Bearss all that day.
46. Supposedly, an entry in his service record for 27 September notes that Hiram was captured by the enemy. But if so, for that same date it should also read, "escaped from the enemy."
47. Coverage of this action and Bearss' part in it is from Strickland, pp. 242–56.
48. Apparently no serious study of this personal animosity towards the 26th Division and Edwards has ever been written.
49. Strickland, p. 255.
50. Ibid., p. 256. In January 1919 the division received notice that Marshal Pétain had decorated the battalion's (1/102) colors with the Croix de Guerre, Order of the Army on the 14th.
51. Ibid., p. 265, note 91.
52. A German unit composed of older men, certainly not of "shock" quality.
53. It was true and it wasn't Hiram at his thinking best. Later he would pay for this lapse of judgment.
54. Lewis was a fighting man of the first chop. He earned two DSCs; one at Marcheville in September and an oak leaf cluster at Beaumont on 10 November.
55. Of course he wasn't directly to blame for what happened. It seems that on 4 November a group of Germans surrendered to the 104th. One of the prisoners had a bottle of schnapps and offered the guards a drink. Being Americans, naturally they accepted.
56. Brig. Gen. Charles H. Cole was the brother of Maj. Edward B. Cole, USMC, KiA at Belleau Woods in June 1918. He was a political appointment who, from every evidence, did not like other Marines.
57. According to Lt. Col. Robert Ramsey, USA (ret.), who did some serious digging and came up with the following as the reason for Edward's relief: Fraternization was rampant throughout the division and Chaumont did the only thing they could think of to squelch it—fire Edwards.
58. Sibley, p. 309.

59. Strickland, p. 266.
60. Ibid., p. 269.
61. Ibid., p. 270.
62. Ibid., p. 272.
63. Ibid., p. 281. Ahearn's company, "C," was also known as the Sarsfields after a famous Irish general of the late 1680s and '90s.
64. Ibid., p. 283.
65. Sibley, pp. 269–270. Sibley came down hard on him as though Edwards all of a sudden had made the decision to relieve his senior commanders. It was made at AEF headquarters so as to engineer a "thorough housecleaning." Interestingly, Bearss, the Marine, was apparently never considered for this ultimate degradation.
66. Later Cole claimed it was the 102d Infantry that had fraternized with the Germans. This was not a correct statement but would have a great impact on Bearss after the war. See details in chapter 11.
67. See chapter 11 for details.

Chapter 9

1. It was policy suggested by Gen. Peyton March, the army chief of staff, and approved by the secretary of war, Newton D. Baker. It enraged Pershing and other entitled senior army officers in the AEF.
2. Mayo was a Vermonter and a graduate of the Naval Academy at Annapolis in 1876. He was, if you remember, the officer who demanded that the Mexicans salute the American flag at Vera Cruz in 1914. He later commanded all American warships in the Atlantic and European waters during the war, becoming commander of the combined U.S. fleet in January 1919. Mayo retired in December 1920.
3. According to newspaper accounts it was the *Pennsylvania* but several other sources, including official USMC documents say it was the USS *Texas*.
4. In those times in order to be elected governor or hold any Indiana state office, one had to be a member of the Ku Klux Klan, an organization that had a grip on Indiana then and for some years to come. In fact, Hiram would gain national prominence for giving the Klan "what for" in the early 1920s.
5. At about this same moment in time the girl was being reconfirmed in the Episcopal faith.
6. *The Evening Telegram,* New York City, 28 December 1918.
7. *The Boston Post,* 17 March 1919.
8. Bearss stated for the record that it was on 21 January 1919.
9. Meade was a nephew of the Civil War general, Sutherland had been serving at Paris (Parris) Island, and both Hughes and Owens would be retired for "incapacity" in July 1919. Hughes is extremely well known to many because of his services in the 4th Brigade. "Pat" Evans served with Hiram in Panama. Otherwise, see Clark, *Devil Dogs.*
10. Norris doesn't appear to have been interrogated during this hearing.
11. Transcript of trial, 9 April 1919.
12. Ibid.
13. Ibid.
14. Ibid.
15. It is my belief that McLemore, acting for himself or for others, was out to "hang" Hiram. See chapter 11 for more evidence of this.
16. According to Asa Smith's manuscript this had to do with Hiram not wearing medals on stage in public. Roosevelt's subsequent letter to Bearss should lay that fallacy to rest.
17. Smith.
18. Copy of letter to Barnett in Smith.
19. This matter was a source of great concern to Pershing and his staff in Europe. The details do not pertain to our story but the matter was vexing to those who had been on the "cutting edge" in France.
20. The friend may have been David D. Porter, although it could also have been Harry Lay, with whom he also served both in the Philippines and in

France. Each at that time was serving at Headquarters.

21. As an example, there is a letter in the Bearss file from George Barnett, major general commandant, apologizing to Hiram for leaving his name out of a listing of those that landed and served at Vera Cruz in 1914.

22. It appears as though Hiram's foolish attempt to "negotiate" with a German lieutenant while clothed in an enlisted man's uniform was behind this recantation. Edwards most likely heard from someone, perhaps Brig. Gen. Cole, who had already piled it on Hiram for his indiscretion — or perhaps it was Durfee, who had been the brief replacement. Regardless, Clarence Edwards doesn't come out smelling very well.

23. Bearss' personal file.

24. Another victim of the Academy group at or around Headquarters. Butler was another, as was Dunlap.

25. Bearss' medical record.

26. Record of the proceedings of a Marine Retirement Board, 16 October 1919.

27. The author has no concrete knowledge that the two men ever met nor any details of the presumed collaboration. That assumption is based entirely upon the many unusual details Smith came up with, most having at least a sparkle of truth. It seems that only Bearss could have told him those details and, naturally, his story would always work to his advantage.

Chapter 10

1. Smith.

2. David C. Stephenson was the grand wizard. He murdered a young woman and was sent to prison for 30 years. Our Asa Smith was the prosecuting attorney and loved every minute that he was so engaged. A movie about this case was made a few years ago, and it plays on cable TV from time to time.

3. *The New York Times*, 19 December 1922, p. 8, column 2.

4. Smith. This incident is still well remembered by Hoosiers. I spoke with a woman publisher in Indianapolis who told me that she had never heard of Hiram Bearss — that is, until I mentioned the KKK incident and she immediately realized that when she was a young girl it had been a big event amongst the better sort of people in Indiana.

5. A newspaper account giving details about his death mentioned that "he was given charge of a detachment of *250 marines* guarding the New York Federal Reserve Bank" (emphasis added).

6. Smith.

7. This hotel was constructed by Frank Bearss and was at that time still owned by the family. According to an informant, a retired Marine colonel who was a native of the town, the hotel was still there when he was young. The wiseguy youths of the town called it the "Bareass Hotel." According to another local informant, the hotel was renamed the Broadway Hotel and presently is named the Peru Motor Lodge.

8. The interurban "Toonerville" trolleys were a common mode of transportation during the post-WWI era. For a modest fare one could travel for many miles and frequently between several towns and cities. They were extensively used in the growing Midwest of that period.

9. A guess is that he was visiting his "niece" Miss West, whom we shall meet shortly.

10. There was no mention of exactly how his "niece" Miss West from Ontario, Canada, was related to him. "G.O." Muhlfeld was either George Oscar or, in some sources, Oscar George, Muhlfeld.

Chapter 11

1. McLemore was brevetted while with Company E, under the command of

Colonel Huntington during the occupation of Guantánamo in 1898. In 1919 he was working directly for Maj. Gen. Lauchheimer, whom Hiram had insulted many years before. Following that insult Hiram was written up twice by Lauchheimer or a member of his inspection staff for not being able to maintain proper financial records. It doesn't pay to make enemies.
  2. Copy in Smith.
  3. That situation amazed me until I discovered that a law was passed by congress in which U.S. Marine officers serving with the U.S. Army could be promoted with army rank, on a temporary basis. Although I have copies of letters from Barnett which prove that he considered it for Hiram, I do not believe the law was ever implemented by the army or Marine Corps.
  4. See Hughes' statement to Haggerty during the hearing.
  5. Fitness report, for March 1919.

Bibliography

U.S. Government Publications and Documents

American Battle Monuments Commission. *American Armies and Battlefields in Europe.* Washington, D.C.: 1938.

Annual Reports of the Major General Commandant of the United States Marine Corps for the years 1898 to 1921. Washington, D.C.: U.S. Government Printing Office.

Annual Reports of the Secretary of the Navy, 1900 to 1938. Washington, D.C.: U.S. Government Printing Office.

Clifford, Kenneth J. *Progress and Purpose: A Developmental History of the United States Marine Corps 1900–1970.* Washington, D.C.: History and Museums Division, Headquarters, United States Marine Corps, 1973.

Condit, Kenneth W., and Edwin T. Turnbladh. *Hold High the Torch: A History of the 4th Marines.* Washington, D.C.: Historical Branch, G3 Division, Headquarters Marine Corps, 1960.

Correspondence Relating to the War with Spain, and Conditions Growing out of the Same, Including the Insurrection in the Philippine Islands and the China Relief Expedition, ... from April 15, 1898, to July 30, 1902. 2 volumes. Washington, D.C.: Government Printing Office, 1902.

Decorations United States Army, 1862–1926. Washington, D.C.: War Department, Office of the Adjutant General, 1927.

Fuller, Stephen M., and Graham A. Cosmas. *Marines in the Dominican Republic 1916–1924.* Washington, D.C.: History and Museums Division, Headquarters, U.S. Marine Corps, 1974.

Gordon, Martin K., compiler. *Joseph Henry Pendleton, 1860–1942: Register of His Personal Papers.* Washington, D.C.: History and Museums Division, Headquarters, U.S. Marine Corps, *1975.*

Miller, William M., and John H. Johnstone. *A Chronology of the United States Marine Corps 1775–1934.* Washington, D.C.: Historical Division, Headquarters, U.S. Marine Corps, 1970.

Navy Department. *Register[s] of the Commissioned and Warrant Officers of the Navy of the United States and of the Marine Corps January 1, 1899–January 1, 1922.* Washington, D.C.: U.S. Government Printing Office.

U.S. Army. *U.S. Army, Records of the Second Division (Regular).* 10 volumes. Washington, D.C.: The Army War College, 1927.

_____. Fifth Army Corps. *General Orders, No. 19.* American E.F., September 18, 1918. (Commendation for actions of the 102d Infantry and its leader at St. Mihiel.)

_____. Headquarters, Second Division, AEF *Recommendation — Lieut. Colonel H.I. Bearss*. France, April 27, 1918. (Commendation for the "excellent services" of Bearss.)

U.S. Marine Corps. *Major Littleton L.T. Waller Report on the Shohotón Campaign*.

_____. Major General Commandant. *Commendation for Services at Vera Cruz, Mexico, in April, 1914*. Records of Major Hiram I. Bearss, 122ZE.

_____. *Military History of Major Hiram I. Bearss, U.S. Marine Corps. (For promotion)*. 23 July 1900 to 13 May 1916. Headquarters, Washington, D.C.: May 13, 1916.

_____. Bearss, Hiram I. *Fitness Reports*. Various years.

_____. Bearss, Hiram I. *Transcript of Colonel … Court-Martial, Philadelphia Navy Yard*, 1919.

_____. Bearss, Hiram I. *Record of the Proceedings of a Marine Retirement Board, 16 October 1919*.

U.S. Navy. *Medical Record: Colonel Hiram Iddings Bearss, U.S. Marine Corps, from 1900–1919*. Department of the Navy, Bureau of Medicine and Surgery.

_____. *Medal of Honor 1861–1949*, Washington, D.C.: N.d. (c. 1950).

Personal Papers and Unpublished Biographies

Smith, Asa. Untitled biography of Hiram I. Bearss. About 700 pp.

Selected Publications

Ballendorf, Dirk A., and Merrill L. Bartlett. *Pete Ellis, an Amphibious Warfare Prophet, 1880–1923*. Anapolis: Naval Institute Press, 1997.

Beede, Benjamin R., ed. *The War of 1898 and U.S. Interventions 1898–1934: An Encyclopedia*. New York and London: Garland Publishing, 1994.

Calder, Bruce J. *The Impact of Intervention: The Dominican Republic During the U.S. Occupation of 1916–1924*. Austin: University of Texas Press, 1984.

Clark, George B. *Devil Dogs: Fighting Marines of World War I*. Novato: Presidio Press, 1999.

Cronon, E. David. *The Cabinet Diaries of Josephus Daniels, 1913–1921*. Lincoln: University of Nebraska Press, 1963.

Faust, Karl Irving. *Campaigning in the Philippines*. San Francisco, Hicks-Judd Company, 1899.

Hallas, James H. *Squandered Victory: The American First Army at St. Mihiel*. Westport, Connecticut and London: Praeger, 1995.

Heinl, Robert D., Jr. *Soldiers of the Sea*. Annapolis: U.S. Naval Institute Press, 1962.

Langley, Lester D. *The Banana Wars: An Inner History of American Empire 1900–1934*. Lexington: University Press of Kentucky, 1983.

Lejeune, John A. *Reminiscences of a Marine*. Philadelphia: Dorrance and Company, 1930.

Linn, Brian. *The Philippine War 1899–1902*. Lawrence: University Press of Kansas, 2000.

_____. "'We will go heavily armed': The Marines' Small War on Samar, 1901–1902." In *New Interpretations in Naval History: Selected Papers from the Ninth Naval History Symposium Held at the United States Naval Academy, 18–20 October 1989*. Roberts, William R., and Jack Sweetman, eds. Annapolis: Naval Institute Press, 1991.

Metcalf, Clyde H. *A History of the United States Marine Corps*. New York: G.P. Putnam's Sons, 1939.

Miller, Stuart Creighton. *"Benevolent Assimilation": The American Conquest of the Philippines, 1899–1903.* New Haven and London: Yale University Press, 1982.
Millett, Allan R. *Semper Fidelis: The History of the United States Marine Corps.* New York: Macmillan, 1980.
Musicant, Ivan. *The Banana Wars: A History of United States Military Intervention in Latin America from the Spanish-American War to the Invasion of Panama.* New York: Macmillan, 1990.
The Ninth U.S. Infantry in the World War. N.p. (Neuwied am Main), n.d. (c. 1919).
Quirk, Robert E. *An Affair of Honor: Woodrow Wilson and the Occupation of Veracruz.* Lexington: University of Kentucky Press, 1962.
Regimental Headquarters, Second Engineers. *Official History of the Second Engineers in the World War 1916–1919.* N.p., n.d. (c. 1919).
Schmidt, Hans. *Maverick Marine: General Smedley D. Butler and the Contradictions of American Military History.* Lexington: University Press of Kentucky, 1987.
Schott, Joseph L. *The Ordeal of Samar.* Indianapolis and New York: The Bobbs-Merrill Company, 1964.
Schuon, Karl. *U.S. Marine Corps Biographical Dictionary.* New York: Franklin Watts, 1963.
Sibley, Frank P. *With the Yankee Division in France.* Boston: Little, Brown, 1919.
Spaulding, Oliver L. *The Second Division American Expeditionary Force in France 1917–1919.* New York: Hillman Press, 1937.
Strickland, Daniel W. *Connecticut Fights: The Story of the 102d Regiment.* New Haven: Private printing, 1930.
Sweetman, Jack. *The Landing at Veracruz: 1914.* Annapolis: United States Naval Institute, 1968.
Thomas, Lowell. *Old Gimlet Eye — The Adventures of Smedley D. Butler.* New York: Farrar and Rinehart, 1933.
Venzon, Anne Cipriano, ed. *General Smedley Darlington Butler: The Letters of a Leatherneck, 1898–1931.* New York, Westport, London: Praeger, 1992.
_____. *The United States in the First World War: An Encyclopedia.* New York: Garland, 1995.
Wise, Frederick M., and Meigs O. Frost. *A Marine Tells It to You.* New York: J.H. Sears 1929.

Newspaper Articles

Boston Post. Boston, Massachusetts, 17 March 1919.
Evening Telegram. New York City, 28 December 1918.
Indianapolis Star. Indianapolis: Indiana, 27 August 1938. Front page and obituary.
New York Times. New York City, 19 December 1922.
Norwich University Record. Norwich, Vermont, various dates, 1898–1923.
Peru Daily Tribune. Peru, Indiana, 27 August 1938. Front page and obituary.
Peru Daily Tribune: Bicentennial Edition. 2 July 1976. Various pages, mainly about the Bearss family.

Index

Adams, Capt John Quincey, USMC 140–41
Ahearn, Cpl Timothy, USA 197
American Expeditionary Forces (AEF): at Base Hospital No. 5 157; at Base Hospital No. 20 213; at Chaumont 229; 1st Division at Soissons 172, at St. Mihiel 180, 182, 253n31; 2d Division at Belleau Wood, 166–69, at Soissons 172; 3d Brigade *9th Infantry* 4, 161–65, *23d Infantry* 168, 172; 4th Brigade 4, 157, 158, 166–70, 178, 211; 5th Marines 4, 158, 165, 168, 169, 172 (*67th Co* 169, *3d Battalion* 153, 158–60, 169, *Base Detachment* 151–56); 6th Marines 4, 158, 168, 169, 172–73, 206, 211, 253n28 (*74th Co* 4); 6th Machine Gun Battalion 158, 168; 2d Artillery Brigade 168; 3d Division *7th Infantry* 161, 168, 169, *30th Infantry* 172, *38th Infantry* 172; 26th Division 4, 175–99, 253n31, 255n66; 51st Brigade 4, 180, 195–99, 210, *102d Infantry* 3, 4, 176–95, 199, 210, 254n37, n38, n43, n46, n47, (*1/102* 186, 188, 197, 254n50, *2/102* 186, *3/102* 186, 196, 197, *Company H* 196); 52d Brigade 195 *103d Infantry* 189 (*1/103* 188), *104th Infantry* 198, *102d Machine Gun Battalion* 188
Anderson, BG Thomas M., USA 22
Arayat, USS 54, 56, 75
Army, U.S. units *see* American Expeditionary Forces; Philippines; Vera Cruz
Arnold, Maj Alfred C., USA 166
Azua 145, 148

Baker, Sect of War Newton D. 236, 255n1
Balangiga 43, 44, 46, 53, 54, 69, 74
Baltimore, USS 24
Bannon, Capt Philip M., USMC 27, 37
Barnett, MGC George, USMC 113, 122, 150–52, 205, 210, 228, 250n9, 256n21
Bartlett, Maj Harry G., USMC 161
baseball 9, 10, 12, 96
Basey 47, 48, 52, 56, 62, 63, 67, 70, 72, 73, 77
Bates, 1stLt Charles E. H., USA 189, 254n45
Bearss, Hiram: "capture" 191–92, 254 n46; in Caribbean 4; charges and hearing 204; citations 238–39; commendations 164, 193, 196; in Cuba 108–09; death 224–25; decorations 237–38; Distinguished Service Cross 3, 193; education 8, 10–12, 241n3, n4, n5; family 7, 241n (*see also* Bearss family); with Federal Reserve Bank Guard unit 219–20, 256n5; in France 154–200 (*Paris* 165, 167, 170–73, 200, *Belleau Wood* 167–70, *St. Mihiel* 3, 175, 176, 178, *Marcheville* 3, 189–92); fund management 109, 123, 250n3; at Guantánamo 106–12, 113, 123, 228; health and hospitalizations 4, 92, 96, 100, 113, 121–22, 165–66, 170–75; Medal of Honor, 3, 222; medical record 213–15, 220–21, 222, 228, 249n31, n39; in Mexico 117–21; in Panama 86–88, 101–02; performance reports 123, 230–31, 257n5; in Philippines 4, 32–80, 94–100; in politics,

263

219, 224; rank: *2d lt* 16, *1st lt* 22, *capt* 39, *major* 122–23, *lt col* 139, *brigadier general* 210–11, 222; recruiting duty 81–82; in retirement 216, 217–18, 256n25, n26; in Santo Domingo 124–49; with U.S. Army 9th Infantry 165, 166, 168, 172, 210, 244n16; with U.S. Army 102d Infantry and 51st Brigade 162–65, 173–74, 177, 179, 191–92

Bearss family: brother, Braxton aka Bragg 8, 10, 11, 12, 99, 224; daughter, Louise 98, 99, 106–12, 122, 149, 202–03, 215, 216 (*as Mrs Frederick Thwing* 224–25); father, Franklin aka Frank 7, 12, 14, 212, 217, 224; mother, Desdemona Iddings 7; sister, Desdemona 8; sister, Lucy 99, 224; sister, Emma Muhlfeld aka Mrs Oscar George 8, 99, 225; wife, Adelaide Louise Madden 25, 80, 90–100, 106–12, 122, 151–52, 202–03, 205, 210–11, 212, 216, 217, 224–25

Bearss, USS 225
Belleau Wood, battle of 166–70
Berkeley, 1st Lt Randolph C., USMC 37
Bicknell, RA George A., USN 102
Biddle, Nicholas 87–8
Biddle, MGC William P., USMC 79, 80, 99–100, 103, 247n64, 249n36
Bisbee, BG William H., USA 78, 80
Bissell, Maj Harry B., USA 196
Bisset, Capt Henry O., USMC 37
Blake, Surg Joseph, USA 174–75, 215
Blondat, General, French army 193
Bois de Belieu 196
Bois de Warville 187
Bookmiller, Capt Edwin C., USA 47, 55
Bootes, 1st Lt James T., USMC 56, 66, 68, 74, 75, 233, 246n46
Bordeaux 156
Braisted, USN (MD, rank not known) 213
Breckinridge, 1st Lt James C., USMC 27
Brewster, MG André W., USA 164, 177
Brister, Asst Surg John M., USN 55, 223
Broatch, Capt James W., USMC 32, 95, 248n22, 248–49n25, 249n26
Brown, Capt Philip S., USMC 115, 250n12

Brown, Col Preston, USA 169
Bundy, MG Omar, USA 160–61, 162, 164, 166–67, 169, 170, 204, 229, 253n23
Burton, 2d Lt Norman G., USMC 27
Bussaires 169
Butler, MG Smedley D. USMC 1, 3, 16, 36, 37, 80, 83, 85, 86, 95, 96–7, 112, 122, 150, 227, 228, 241n8, 248n21, 252n13, n2
Butler, Cong Thomas S. 122, 251n24, 252n13
Buttrick, 2d Lt James T. USMC 42

Calcona, Juan 137–39, 252n12
Camp Stotsenburg 96–7
Campbell, Pvt Walter, USMC 51
Cancelmo, J. James, USN 206
Caperton, RA William B., USN 124, 125
Carmody, 2d Lt Robert E., USMC 31, 243n16
Carpenter, 1st Lt Charles C., USMC 70, 71, 88, 223
Carpenter, 1st Lt Henry W., USMC 31, 243n16
Carroll, Cpl John H. USMC 76
Carty, Pvt James B., USA 179
Catlin, BG Albertus W. USMC 118, 168, 251n19
Cavite 22, 23, 32, 36, 37, 42, 44, 78, 94, 97, 98, 100
Celtic, USS 125, 126
Chaffee, MG Adna, USA 52, 73, 77, 78, 245n21, n33, 247n62
Charleston, USS 19
Chateau Thierry, battle of 167, 172
China 38, 43
Clifford, Pvt John, USMC 31, 243n18
Clifford, 1st Lt William H., Jr., USMC 27
Cline, Capt George, USN 112
Coffin, Lt Comdr Frederick W., USN 30
Coghlan, RA Joseph B., USN 83, 84, 89
Cole, BG Charles H., USA 195, 198, 254n56, 255n66, 256n22
Cole, Maj Edwin B., USMC 153, 242n15, 254n56
Cole, BG Eli K., USMC 19, 96, 97, 98, 100, 213, 248–49n25, n26

Collins, Sgt Alfred B., USMC 159
Colombia 86, 87
Connell, Capt Thomas W., USA 43, 44
Connolly, 1st Lt Gregory P., USA 196–97
Corbin, Capt William O., USMC 206, 229
Crabbee, Capt William L., USMC 206, 229
Cradock, RN, Adm Sir Christopher 121
Cuba 14, 19,73
Culebra Island 83, 85, 89, 112, 114; Camp Roosevelt 115
Cummings, Sgt Frank J., USA 177, 181–82, 188, 191, 200
Curtis, Capt Donald, USMC 206
Cyclops, USS 121

Daly, Sgt Maj Daniel., USMC 1, 227
Daniels, Sect of the Navy Josephus 115, 140, 211
Davis, Capt Austin R., USMC 37, 42,
Davis, Capt Henry C., USMC 98, 249n30
Day, 1st Lt John H. A., USMC 53, 55, 80, 233, 246n45, 247n54
Denby, Edwin 20, 242n17
Dewey, Adm George 22, 27, 72, 242n2
Dickens, Maj Randolph, USMC 37
Dillard, Capt Alexander W., USA 187, 188, 196, 197
Dixie, USS 86, 88, 89
Dolphin, USS 116
Doran, 2d Lt James E., USMC 206
Doyen, BG Charles A., USMC 98, 157, 160, 164, 211, 229, 248n21, 252n4
Draper, Capt Herbert L., USMC 27, 37, 38, 40–1, 244n6
Dunlap, BG Robert H., USMC 40–1, 56, 60, 63, 66, 67, 70, 73, 75, 115, 142, 233, 244n13
Durfee, BG Lucius L., USA 199, 256n22
Durrell, Lt Edward H., USN 84

Edwards, MG Clarence, USA 175; initial attitude toward HB 176; Pershing's attitude toward 192; relieved of command 195, 196, 198–99, 202, 211–12, 229, 254n57, 255n65, 256n22
Elliott, MGC George F., USMC 23, 36, 37, 87, 104, 242n5, 243n3

Elliott, 1st Lt Stephen, USMC 27, 37, 86
Emory, Capt William, USN 90
Evangelista, Vincentico 144–49, 252n15
Evans, Lt Col Frank E., USMC 87, 205, 248n12, 255n9

Feland, MG Logan, USMC 27, 38, 115, 150, 168, 229, 236, 242n19, 252n3, 253n17, n27
Fletcher, Adm Frank F., USN 116, 121, 251n23
Football 10, 12
Forney, Col James, USMC 78, 247n61
Fort Leavenworth 122, 251n25
Fortson, Capt Eugene, USMC 124, 128
France *see* American Expeditionary Forces (AEF)
French army 154, passim, 252n9; 1st French Colonial Division 172; 2d Cavalry Division 180; 26th Division 178
Frolic, USS 46
Fuller, MGC Ben, USMC 36, 37, 101, 121, 249n32
Funston, BG Frederick, USA 120, 251n20

Georgia, USS 111
German army 162, passim, 198; 3d Division 187; 10th Division 187; 77th Division 187; 88th Division 187; Saxon Landwher 194–95; Sturmtrupp 162–63
German Allies: Austro-Hungarians: 51st Regiment 188; 64th Regiment 188
Gilson, 1st Lt Robert M., USMC 37, 243n5
Glenn, Maj Edwin, Judge Advocate, USA 68, 69, 247n65
Glenn, Cpl Harry, USMC 50, 235
Goicoecha, Slustiano (aka Chachá) 140–43
Goldsmith, Pvt Julius, USMC 130
Goodrell, Lt Col Mancil C., USMC 43, 89, 244n15
Grant, BG Fred, USA 24
Greene, Maj Edward S. "Verdie," USMC 153
Greene, BG Francis V., USA 23

266   Index

Gridley, 1st Lt John V. P., USMC 53, 66, 67, 69, 70, 72, 74, 75, 233, 242n18
Grogan, Sgt John, USMC 51
Guam 19, 30
GuGu (GooGoo) 36, 38, 41, 47, 75, 243n2
Gulick, BG Louis Mason, USMC 20, 27, 32, 242n19

Haddonchatel 179
Haggerty, Cornelius, Esq. 206, 257n4
Haines, Capt Henry C., USMC 24, 37,
Halford, 2d Lt Frank, USMC 55, 60, 70, 233, 246n40
Hancock, USS 90, 114, 117
Hanson, Major, USA 189, 254n44
Harbord, MG James, USA 165, 169, 170, 211, 229, 253n24
Harrington, 1st Lt Samuel L., USMC 145
Harrison, Benjamin 82
Harrison, Russell 82
Hatch, Maj Charles B., USMC 126
Hatfield, Pvt, USMC 39
Henderson, USS 153
Heywood, Col Commandant Charles, USMC 16, 42, 227, 248n10
Hill, Col Charles S., USMC 38, 213
Hobbs, Col H. P., USA 198
Holcomb, Asst Srg Richmond C. USN 27
Holcomb, LGC Thomas, USMC 225, 236, 249n37
Honolulu 29, 30
Horses 8, 9
Hotel Crillion & Bar 165, 200; Bearss' abuse of young captain 171–72
Huerta, Gen Victoriano 116, 117
Hughes, Adm Charles F., USN 230–31
Hughes, Lt Col John A., USMC 205–08, 255n9
Hunt, MG LeRoy, USMC 152, 252n6
Huntington, Lt Col Robert, USMC 106, 256–57n1

Idaho, USS 101
Indiana (Ridgeview & Peru) 2, 4, 13, 14, 81–82, 92, 100, 122, 157, 168, 203, 216, 221–22; politics 216–17, 224, 256n4

Ingate, Capt Clarence L. A., USMC 31
Isbell, Col Ernest L., USA 176

Jolly, Capt Wade L., USMC 27
Jonas, 1st Lt Edwin A., USMC 32
Jones, Trumpeter Joshua, USMC 234

Kane, Col Theodore, USMC 124, 134, 140, 213, 214
Karmany, Col Lincoln, USMC 113, 250n9
Kelton, Maj Allan C., USMC 31, 243n16
Kent, QM Clerk Wilfred L., USMC 205
Keyser, BG Ralph, USMC 236
Kilcourse, 2d Lt Thomas J., USMC 205
Kilpatrick, AT 80
King, Maj Charles A.E., USMC 206
Kingsbury, Maj Henry P., USA 78, 80
Klos, 2d Lt Stanley, USMC 205
Knapp, RA Harry S., USN 143
Kresge, Pvt Omer, USMC 75, 76
Ku Klux Klan 4, 5, 218–19, 224, 255n4, 256n4

La Grande Tranchee 178, 179; Bearss' march down 180–82
Lanang 54, 56, 60, 64, 65, 66, 74
Lane, BG Rufus H., USMC 42, 97
Lauchheimer, BG Charles H., USMC 101, 228, 249n33, 250n3, 257n1
Lawton, AT 77
Lay, Maj Harry R., USMC 233, 255n20
Le Bouf, 1st Lt Albert A., USMC 156–57, 252n8
Leckie, Cpl Robert L., USMC 234
Lee, BG Harry, USMC 168, 213, 214, 236, 253n28
Lejeune, MGC John A., USMC 18, 86, 117, 119, 120, 121, 151, 242n13, 249n37
Lemly, Col William B., USMC 20, 37, 242n19
Lewis, Lt Col Evan E., USA 195, 200, 254n54
Leyte 32, 34, 43, 44, 73
Lillibridge 2d Lt Hoxsie W., USMC 205
Lipscomb, Sgt John S., USMC 71, 234
Liscum, AT 43, 244n17
Little, MG Louis McC., USMC 27,

Index 267

Long, BG Charles G., USMC 37, 114, 117, 205, 211, 250n11
Loog Mountains 53
Loog River 61, 62
Louisiana, USS 103, 104, 124
Low, 1st Lt William W., USMC 32
Lukban, Vincente 43
Lung, Asst Surg George A., USN 63, 64, 66, 70, 74, 233
Luzon 32, 34–43
Lyles, 2d Lt DeWitt C., USA 55, 60, 61

Magill, Col Louis J., USMC 213
Mahoney, Col James E., USMC 89, 121, 248n14
Manila 22, 23, 28,
Marcheville 188–93, 199
Mare Island 28, 81, 92, 243n10
Marine Barracks (Norfolk) 26
Marine Corps units: Advance Base Force 112, 115, 250n6, *1st Advance Brigade Base Force* 117, *2d Provisional Brigade* 113, 149, 228; First Marine Regiment 113, 114, 117, 119, 149 (*Company F* 114); Second Marine Regiment 117, 119, *2d Provisional Regiment* 112, 149 (*Company C* 112); Third Marine Regiment 119; **in France** *see* American Expeditionary Forces; **in the Philippines:** 1st Brigade 46, 92, *1st Regiment* 43, *First Battalion* 23 (*Company C* 46, 50, *Company D* 46, 71, 234, *Company E* 50), *Second Battalion* 23 (*Company H* 46), *Third Battalion* 27, 31, *2d Regiment* 43, 100; **in Santo Domingo:** 2d Regiment (*4th Company* 124, 126, 128, 130, *5th Company* 124, *6th Company* 124, *9th Company* 126, *24th Company* 124, 126); 3d Provisional Regiment 140, 149; 4th Regiment 125, 130, 131–32, 135
Marshall, Ens Albert W., USN 24
Marshall, Gen George C., USA 178
Matthews, Capt Arthur J., USMC 55, 70, 233
Matthews, Maj Hugh, USMC 143, 236
Mayo, RA Henry T., USN 116, 200–01, 250n14, 255n2
McCaffery, Sgt John, USMC 65, 234, 235

McCanless, Pvt William J., USMC 69, 76
McClaskey, 2d Lt John W., USMC 42
McCoy, Sgt, USMC 39
McCreary, Capt Wirt, USMC 27
McDougall, BG Douglas, USMC 130, 132, 133, 251n8
McGee, Pvt James, USMC 75, 76
McLemore, Col Albert S., USMC 204–08, 212, 228, 256–57n1
McSwiney, Sgt Bryan, USMC 71, 234
Meade, Maj James J., USMC 205, 255n9
Meade, Col Robert L., USMC 37, 81, 83, 89
Meade, USS 113
Medal of Honor 121, 222, 245n26, n29, n30, n31, 246n52, 251n23
Memphis, USS 124
Mercy, USS 29
Merriam, Cmdr Greenlief A., USN 88
Merrill, Capt William, USMC 206
Metz 185, 187, 193
Meuse-Argonne campaign 185
Mexico 111, 113, 114, 116, 117; El Tejar 120; Tampico 116, 117; Vera Cruz 116–21
Meyer, Sect of Navy Vaughan L. 103
Michigan, USS 20
Miller, Col Ellis B., USMC 145
Mississippi, USS 117, 119
Morrison, 1st Lt Victor, USMC 143
Moses, Col Franklin J., USMC 112, 250n8
Muhlfeld, Oscar G. 203, 208–10, 216, 223; *see also* Bearss family
Murphy, Sgt James, USMC 60, 64, 67, 75
Murphy, Cpl Joseph J., USMC 234, 235
Muse, Maj William S., USMC 18, 241n12
Myers, MG John Twiggs, USMC 19, 24, 242n14, n6

Naval Brigade at Vera Cruz 118–19
Naval Hospital: Bethesda 222–23; Brooklyn 217; Philadelphia 92, 121, 122
Navarette 131
Navy Yards and Marine Barracks: Brooklyn 81, 83, 89; New York 23,

112; Norfolk (and as Portsmouth) 18, 102, 103, 112; Philadelphia 83, 91, 92, 112, 113, 114, 149, 153, 203–10
Nelson, Pvt A.G., USA 179, 253n34
Neville, MGC Wendell C., USMC 117, 119, 158, 161, 248n24, 250n17
New Jersey, USS 124, 126
New Orleans 115–16
New York, USS 24, 46, 78, 242n7
New York City 149, 202, 216, 220, 221, 223
Norris, Maj John F. S., USMC 206
Norwich University 10–12

Oberlin, Capt A. Frederick, USA 181–83, 187, 200
Olongapo 32, 38, 39–43, 70, 94–95, 99, 100
Oregon, USS 37
O'Shaughnessy, Nelson J. 117
Ostermann, 2d Lt Edward A., USMC 102, 249n35
Owens, Maj Arthur B., USMC 205, 255n9

Panay, USS gunboat 70
Panther, USS 83, 86
Parker, Cmdr James P., USN 84
Parker, Col John H., USA 176
Parker, 1st Lt William H., USMC 27
Pendergast, Pvt Thomas, USMC 51, 89
Pendleton, Joseph H., USMC 95, 97, 113, 125, passim, 132, 145, 250n9, 251n4
Pennsylvania, USS 201–202, 255n3
Penrose, Sen Boies 103, 249n36
Pershing, Gen John J., USA 4, 36, 152, 157, 160, 165, 177, 185, 199, 200, 202, 236, 255n19
Philippines 21, 32–80; U.S. Army units in: Sixth Brigade 74, 77; *7th Infantry* 54, 55–56 (Company K 54); *9th Infantry* 43, 69 (Company C 43, 47, 53, 54); *17th Infantry* 44, 46
Pickering, Capt James N., USA 54, 56, 65
Pierce, Capt Francis E., USMC 206
Pond, RA Charles, USN 135
Pope, Col Percival P., USMC 23, 242n4
Porter, BG David D., USMC 1, 3, 37, 46, 49–69, 75, 80, 222, 233, 235, 243–44n5, 255n20
Prairie, USS 19, 112, 117
Puerta Plata 124, 126, 130, 132

Quantico 149, 151–53, 210, 212
Quantico Stock Company 151
Quick, Sgt Maj John, USMC 1, 50, 55, 60, 64, 65, 75–76, 227, 235
Quinapundan 54, 55, 69, 72, 74, 79

Radford, BG Cyrus, USMC 37, 244n7
Rechen, Pvt Josef, Jr., USA 195
Red Cross or YMCA, HB relations with 160, 167
Reid, Col George C., USMC 16
Reid, Lt Col George C., USMC 98, 119
Rhode Island, USS 124, 126
Riaville 188–92
Riordan, Pvt John, USMC 31
Roben, 2d Lt Douglas B., USMC 130
Rodgers, RA Frederick, USN 46, 52, 80
Rodman, Surgeon Samuel S., USN 113
Rogers, 2d Lt Austin C., USMC 71, 233
Roosevelt, Pres. Franklin D. 3, 222; as Asst Secretary of the Navy 170, 208–10, 250n13, 255n16
Roosevelt, Pres. Theodore 85–6, 103, 151, 248n9, 250n13
Root, Sect of War Elihu 74
Russell, MGC John H., USMC 121, 251n22

Sacramento, USS 124
St. Hilaire 186, 187, 188, 191,
St. Nazaire 154–57
Salano, Juan 42
Salem, USS 124
Salladay, Maj Jay McC., USMC 140
Samar 32, 34, 43, 44–78, 89, 246n38, n39, n41; "Long March across Samar" 54–66
San Juan 145, 146, 147
San Juanico 34, 72
San Pedro de Marcoris 140–42
Santiago 126, 131, 132, 139
Santo Domingo 112–13, 144
Santo Domingo city 113, 144
Schroeder, Comdr Seaton, USN 31, 243n17

Index

Shelton, BG George H., USA 185, 198–99, 204, 229
Sherman, USS 92, 99
Sixth Brigade, U.S. Army *see* Philippines
Slattery, Pvt William, USMC 51, 89
Slim & Smoke (native Filipinos) 55, 65
Smith, Mr. Asa J. 4–5, passim, 215
Smith, Maj Bernard L., USMC 105, 115, 249n40
Smith, Gen Holland McT., USMC 236
Smith, BG Jacob H., USA 44, 46, 52, passim, 80, 244n19, 246n49
Snyder, Capt Clate C., USMC 206
Sohotón cliffs 3, 47, 48–53, 66, 89, 222
Sohotón River 47, 62
Solace, USS 28–29, 31–32
Soriano, Joaquin 42
South Carolina, USS 149
Spain 14, 73
Spear, Asst Surg Raymond, USN 25
Spicer, Maj William F., USMC 23,
Steele, Congressman George 15, 16, 18; Mrs. Steele 15
Stephenson, David C. (KKK) 4, 256n2
Stewart, Corpsman Fred, USN 42
Stone, 1st Lt Howard W., USMC 132
Stuart, Capt Daniel D. V., USN 102
Sutherland, Maj Albert R., USMC 205, 255n9

Taft, Pres Howard 111, 112
Taussig, Capt Edward D., USN 102
Texas, USS 255n3
Thomas, Gen Gerald C., USMC 4
Thompson, 2d Lt John H., USMC
Thorpe, BG George, USMC 37, 38, 243–44n5
Torcy 169
Torture: water-hose treatment 68
Tracy, Sgt James J., USA 188
Trask, Capt Arthur J., USMC 206, 208
Treadwell, Capt Thomas C., USMC 91
Troyon Sector 186–199
Turrill, Col Julius Turrill, USMC 236
Twining, Gen Merrill B., USMC 4

Utah, USS 112

Van Orden, BG George, USMC 252n4
Vera Cruz, U.S. Army, units in 120–21
Victor (Filipino rebel) 61, 69, 76, 79
Vigneulles 179–84, 202

Wadonville 186, 188
Wald, 2d Lt Charles, USMC 206
Waller, MG Littleton W. T., USMC 18, 29, 30, 37, 42, 44, 102–03, 110, 120, 125, 151, 214, 228, 236, 242n13, 242–43n9, 244n5, 247n67; courts-martial 78–80, 245n21, n22, n23; on Samar 46–78, 233, 244n27, 245n34, n35, n37, 247n59
Walton, Lt Cmdr Duncan C., USN 214
Wax, Sgt Maj Julius Y., USA 195
Webster, Cmdr John A., USN 225
West, Lillian Mae 224, 256n9, n10
Westley, Sgt, USMC 138
Williams, Col Alexander S., USMC 55, 64, 65, 75, 77, 233
Williams, BG Dion, USMC 37
Williams, 2d Lt Kenneth P., USA 55, 56, 65, 66
Williams, Asst Surg Richard B., USN 70–71
Williams, MG Seth, USMC 252n4
Wilson, Pres Thomas Woodrow 116, 136, 149, 150
Winterhalter, Capt Albert G., USN 104–05
Wise, BG Frederick M., USMC 1, 28–9, 30, 32, 42, 111, 115, 118, 124, 132, 160, 243n11, 252n13
Wood, MG Leonard, USA 218
Wood, Capt Thomas B., USMC 205
Wood, Capt Thomas N., USMC 24,
Wynne, Capt Robert F., USMC 37

Yipranga, SS (German ship) 117, 250n16
Yokohama 31
Yosemite, USS 31

Zafiro, USS 46

www.ingramcontent.com/pod-product-compliance
Ingram Content Group UK Ltd.
Pitfield, Milton Keynes, MK11 3LW, UK
UKHW041931140426
5217IPUK00014B/420